Requirements Engineering and Rapid Development

An Object-Oriented Approach

Requirements
Engineering
and
Rapid
Development

An Object-Oriented Approach

Ian Graham
Chase Manhatten Bank

 **ADDISON-WESLEY**

Harlow, England • Reading, Massachusetts • Menlo Park, California • New York
• Don Mills, Ontario • Amsterdam • Bonn • Sydney • Singapore • Tokyo •
Madrid • San Juan • Milan • Mexico City • Seoul • Taipei

© Addison Wesley Longman Limited 1998

Addison Wesley Longman Limited
Edinburgh Gate
Harlow
Essex CM20 2JE, England

and Associated Companies throughout the World.

The rights of Ian Graham to be identified as author of this Work have been asserted by him in accordance with the Copyright, Designs and Patents Act 1988.

The publisher wishes to thank the following for permission to reproduce material in this book: Peter Llewelyn Jones, Director, Bezant Ltd, for material resulting from research carried out by Bezant Ltd and described in his forthcoming book *Rapid Development for Distributed Object Architectures,* to be published by Addison-Wesley (1999), on event and task performance properties, task associations sets and task sequence diagrams, agent classes and class daemons, event traces, active context models, model animation, operation scripts, executable rulesets, animation scripts, discrete time and discrete event simulation, event trace cross-referencing and active state diagrams.

Cover designed by Designers and Partners, Oxford
Printed in Great Britain by Biddles Ltd, Guildford and King's Lynn.
Typeset by the author.

First printed 1998

ISBN 0-201-36047-0

British Library Cataloguing-in-Publication Data

A catalogue record for this book is available from the British Library

Library of Congress Cataloguing-in-Publication Data

Graham, Ian, 1948–
    Requirements engineering and rapid development : a rigorous,
    object-oriented approach / Ian Graham
        p.   cm.
    Includes bibliographic references and index.
    ISBN 0-201-36047-0
        1. Object-oriented methods (Computer science) 2. Computer
software--Development. 3. Systems engineering.   I. Title.
QA76.9.O35G75   1998
005.1'17--dc21   98-36223
                                                          CIP

This book is for my mother Peggy and our friend Martin

PREFACE

Although much has been written about requirements engineering, rapid application development and object modelling, there is little material that tells the developer or manager how to put it all together. The safety-critical and formal methods communities have addressed the question of rigour but have shown little awareness of the value and rôle of object technology (OT). While there are many books on rapid application development (RAD) only a tiny number pays attention to OT, and those that do restrict their coverage to the use of OT to describe computer systems, rather than requirements and the general business context or soft systems aspects. The DSDM[1] method for rapid application development deliberately leaves the question of object-orientation out of consideration, on the arguable ground that object-orientation is merely a 'technique'. Object-oriented analysis and design methods also usually ignore the question of how to capture requirements, and those that do not generally base themselves on Jacobson's 'use case' techniques, which – whatever their positive qualities – are gloriously *ad hoc* and lack any kind of theoretical basis. This means that any notion of rigour must be achieved by making extensions to the basic techniques.

I believe that it can no longer be argued that object-oriented development is a new or special approach; it underpins nearly all modern software development. This means that there is a profound need to move object-oriented approaches towards greater rigour and generality. Equally strongly, I feel that rapid, or incremental, delivery is a key need for modern businesses and that object technology is a prime enabler of rapid development. Ever since Bertrand Meyer introduced ideas about rigour and correctness into object-oriented development in the 1980s, methodologists have argued about the 'seamlessness' of the approach. One of the key discoveries presented in this work is that this idea can be applied to

---

[1] DSDM is a proposed standard process for rapid application development (Stapleton, 1997). We describe it in Chapter 2.

requirements engineering to obtain a very high level of rigour. This is achieved by linking a sequence of object models to ensure traceability and by insisting on a very 'pure' idea of what constitutes an object-oriented description. That is why this book has to start from first principles and challenge many of the assumptions and practices common in mainstream object-oriented methods. It challenges, for just one example, the idea that current CASE tools that focus on drawing and storing 2-dimensional diagrams have anything but the most limited value. This, of course, is not a good way to make friends with the vendors of such software or their unfortunate customers. However, I hope that my words will be taken in the spirit of friendly criticism in which they are intended, most especially by my fellow methodologists, nearly all of whom have influenced my work and taught me much.

THE BOOK'S MESSAGE
Despite the need to situate this work in the context of the work of other methodologists and other literature, the message of this text is very simple. I believe that software development should be done both well and quickly. Systems that take years to develop are usually quite out of kilter with their users' requirements by the time they are delivered. Even big systems can be delivered incrementally to overcome this problem. I believe that rapid development is best accomplished by using requirements workshops that involve and engage users and developers. The success of these workshops depends heavily on the talents of a good facilitator. Chapter 3 offers extensive guidance on running workshops. The collaboration between the business and developers should not end after the first workshop; joint user/developer teams must be built and given the power to complete the project. Workshops and joint development teams can build a shared understanding of the requirements and potential solutions using the object modelling techniques presented herein. This means that object modelling is central to the approach. It should also be remembered that every system development project is also an opportunity for business process re-engineering. For this reason we build object models of the business as well as object models of potential software solutions to its problems.

This book offers a definite, standard structure for requirements gathering, modelling and analysis, the core of which is presented in Chapter 5. The knowledge acquisition process proceeds by establishing the project's mission and then elaborating a set of definite business objectives, which are assigned measures and priorities. We then develop an object model of the agents that interact with the business, both from outside and within, and the network of commitments between them. These conversations imply the performance of tasks, and these too are modelled as objects. Finally, the task descriptions can be analyzed to discover the business objects that must be represented. All these models are linked together so that we can validate the business object model against the business objectives, and look at the impact of any changes to it on the latter. This technique means that it is possible and important to build a first-cut business object model in the requirements workshop itself. The approach also promotes early testing of the analysis products, rather than waiting until the code is delivered to test the model it implements against user requirements. We test the models and the seamless links between them using walkthrough and rôle playing in workshops and, later, by animating the specification models using a high level scripting language. In principle, any suitable tools can be used for this, but in this book we use *SOMATiK*, which is purpose built for this job, for the illustration of the method. Early testing and the rapid production of a workshop report means that it becomes possible to get user sign-off in the workshops, contributing to the sense of shared understanding and commitment that I believe is necessary to ensure project success.

The main text of this book is an exegesis on these themes and a practical guide to the approach. However, the ideas can be summarised in the following few words.

- Do it fast.
- Do it correctly.
- Use facilitated workshops.
- Build joint user/developer teams.
- Objects are crucial for representing knowledge.
- Development is an opportunity for business process re-engineering.
- Analyze requirements according to a standard structure: mission, objectives, agents, tasks, business objects.
- Develop the business object model in the workshops.
- Test as you go: use walkthroughs and model animation.
- Obtain sign-offs as soon as possible.

Despite the practical nature of the approach, we do not eschew theoretical issues completely. After all, there is nothing so practical as a good theory. For the reader who requires a more prescriptive exposition the forthcoming book by Jones (1999) works through an extended case study that illustrates the SOMA philosophy with a case study abstracted from many actual projects and expands on the theory presented herein with more step-by-step guidance on the execution of the method. It also deals more completely with implementation issues than is appropriate within the provenance of a book on requirements engineering.

 When we do have occasion to digress from the exposition of this philosophy, we warn readers that a section can be skipped without interfering with their understanding of the substantive argument by placing a diversion symbol in the margin as shown to the left of this paragraph. Other digressionary material, supporting the main arguments will be found in appendices. This material is important but can be safely omitted at a first reading.

This book is a condensation and elaboration of the ideas and techniques that have been developed in the course of my practical work over the past ten years or so. It builds consciously on the seminal work of Booch, Jacobson, Meyer, Odell and Wirfs-Brock as well as on ideas from outside the domain of object technology. It also extends and updates the material in my books *Object-Oriented Methods* and *Migrating to Object Technology*. The method presented here is part of the

Semantic Object Modelling Approach (SOMA) defined in the latter work. SOMA was one of the methods that informed the OPEN[2] Consortium's synthesis of object-oriented methods and remains compliant with the OPEN philosophy. However, many of the techniques presented here have not been included in OPEN yet. This is partly due to my failure to explain them adequately to the other consortium members who are scattered throughout the world. I decided that SOMA should retain an identity separate from OPEN in order to facilitate innovation within the framework. This book therefore may be regarded either as an elaboration of SOMA or as an extension to the techniques available within OPEN.

Where appropriate, diagrams are presented using both OML and UML[3], although I have been forced to take some liberties with the former. Neither OML nor UML have symbols adequate to represent some SOMA concepts, such as agents or messages between them. Also, both contain many symbols that are irrelevant to the needs of a modeller of requirements or business objects. In this way SOMA is distinguished from OPEN by retaining its minimalist approach to notation. I use the bare minimum of symbols from OML while adding some necessary new ones. Another principle of SOMA is that software should draw as many diagrams as possible automatically. As we shall see, many of these diagrams are best presented in a multi-dimensional space and lose their clarity when printed in two dimensions. For that reason, many diagrams are presented using *SOMATiK*, which is free of references to either OML or UML because of its approach to automatic diagram generation.

THE BOOK'S STRUCTURE The book is divided into two parts. Part I exposes the SOMA approach to requirements engineering and rapid development in a language and tool independent fashion, although we use *SOMATiK* for illustrative purposes occasionally. Part II contains appendices covering certain technical material supporting the arguments of Part I.

Chapter 1 re-presents the fundamentals of object technology that, sadly, are so often ignored by object methodologists. It also offers a short Cook's tour of current object technology. Chapter 2 provides a condensed survey of current approaches to requirements engineering and rapid application development along with a discussion of the OPEN/SOMA development process and reuse management model. This too is very brief because the material has been recently presented in full in a book devoted to the topic (Graham *et al.*, 1997). The process is described, however, in sufficient detail to support the use of the requirements engineering techniques presented herein within the context of a disciplined approach to project management. Chapter 3 is a very detailed discussion of how to organize and approach requirements workshops within the overall process set out in Chapter 2

---

[2] OPEN is an international consortium of methodologists that has proposed a standard process model (Graham *et al.*, 1997a) and notation, OML, for object-oriented development (Firesmith *et al.*, 1997).

[3] UML is another proposed standard notation for object-oriented design (Rational, 1997).

and using the techniques presented in Chapter 5. The reader may therefore wish to review Chapter 2 after reading the subsequent chapters.

Chapter 4 is the most theoretical chapter and presents the details of what I conceive of as an object model. The motivation given is that of conventional software objects modelling, even though that is the last thing one builds using the SOMA approach. Such models are preceded by agent and task object models. It is necessary to present things in this order because one cannot build these latter models without a clear understanding of what constitutes an object model, and the most natural way to motivate this is to use the example of software objects. With this preparation, Chapter 5 presents the full set of requirements engineering techniques that I advocate.

Chapters 6 and 7 take up various topical issues in software engineering from the viewpoint of SOMA: agent-based systems, architecture, reuse and patterns.

The book is designed to be read sequentially. However, the careful reader may wish to read the appendices as they are discussed in the chapters that rely on their results. The reading map below indicates the dependencies between the book's chapters.

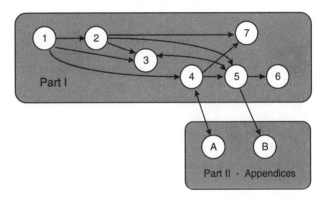

READERSHIP This book will be of direct, practical use to any developer or analyst charged with the elicitation of requirements for new computer systems and to anyone managing such a project. It will also interest researchers and students in the fields of requirements engineering, object technology and software engineering in general. The book contains *en passant* several discussions of programming languages and design issues that will be of interest to designers, architects and programmers too.

SOMATiK I have used a commercial product, *SOMATiK*, to illustrate the ideas presented in this text extensively. Further details on *SOMATiK* can be found in Jones (1999). Bezant can be contacted as follows.

Bezant Ltd, 6 St Mary's Street, Wallingford, Oxon OX10 0EL, England
Telephone: +44-(0)1491-826005
Email: bezant@compuserve.com
Website: www.bezant-ot.com

ACKNOW-LEDGEMENTS The huge contribution of Peter Jones of Bezant Limited to the genesis of this book must be acknowledged first. He and I have collaborated over a very long period, including producing a book in the mid-1980s (Graham and Jones, 1988). Jones had developed first the REVEAL system, a financial modelling package incorporating fuzzy rules, and then *Leonardo*, a widely used expert systems 'shell'. I, having originally developed the SOMA method, was inspired to do so partly by my critique of the lack of object-orientation in the architecture of *Leonardo* and other products of its generation. I wrote a prototype of *SOMATiK* in Visual Basic to prove the concept of automatic diagram generation from fully encapsulated class descriptions. Jones and his colleagues then developed a commercial version in C++, which evolved into the form used for illustration herein. During this whole period both our ideas have been modified, extended and tested: the tool shaping the method as much as the method has shaped the tool. Many of the ideas presented in this book are thus Peter's direct and major contribution. He helped greatly with the writing, in parts of Chapters 2 and 5 especially, although the end product reflects my views and is my responsibility alone. Julia Bischof of the University of New South Wales helped develop the ideas presented as Appendix A and Larry Constantine of Sydney's University of Technology influenced the presentation of Appendix B.

Other people who have helped by discussing, criticizing and developing some of the ideas used in this work include Mark Addison, Faramarz Farhoodi, Brian Henderson-Sellers, Michael Jackson, Neil Maiden, Alan O'Callaghan and a number of anonymous referees. Don Firesmith's work on OML and critique of UML influenced my presentation of these. I am also conscious of my debt to the object technology, task and requirements engineering communities at large and to my colleagues at Chase, notably Nick Lukic, John Welch, Benoit Xhenseval and the many people who attended my training courses there, from whom I have learnt much. Mark Lewis of Bezant not only reviewed the manuscript but contributed many new ideas. Recent discussions with Franco Civello, Alistair Cockburn, Dan Rawsthorne and Tony Simons have helped to reassure me that I was not entirely isolated in my critiques of use cases and UML. I am grateful to Al-Noor Ramji of Deutsche Kleinwort Benson for developing the concepts of differentiating and customer facing processes discussed in Chapter 5 and for convincing me, and many others, of their significance. Finally I would like to thank the staff at Addison Wesley Longman for their help and professionalism in bringing this project to fruition, most notably Margaret James, Fiona Kinnear, Sally Mortimore and Elaine Richardson.

Ian Graham, Balham
August 1998

CONTENTS

Preface　　　　　　　　　　　　　　　　　　　　　　　　　　　vii

PART I　Oʙᴊᴇᴄᴛ-ᴏʀɪᴇɴᴛᴇᴅ ʀᴇǫᴜɪʀᴇᴍᴇɴᴛꜱ ᴇɴɢɪɴᴇᴇʀɪɴɢ　　　　**1**

1　Basic principles of object technology　　　　　　　　　　　**3**
　　1.1　Historical and social background　　　　　　　　　　4
　　1.2　Encapsulation and polymorphism explained　　　　　　7
　　1.3　Language, broker and database technology　　　　　　13
　　　　　1.3.1　Object-oriented programming languages and environments　13
　　　　　1.3.2　Object-oriented databases　　　　　　　　　16
　　　　　1.3.3　Object wrappers　　　　　　　　　　　　17
　　　　　1.3.4　Object request brokers and middleware　　　　20
　　1.4　Applications　　　　　　　　　　　　　　　　22
　　1.5　Methods of object-oriented analysis and design　　　　22
　　　　　1.5.1　Responsibility-driven versus data-driven approaches　24
　　　　　1.5.2　Analysis, design and seamlessness　　　　　24
　　　　　1.5.3　Analysis and design soup!　　　　　　　　26
　　1.6　Bibliographical notes　　　　　　　　　　　　28

2　Approaches to requirements engineering and rapid development　**31**
　　2.1　Approaches to requirements engineering　　　　　　32
　　2.2　The need for incremental development　　　　　　　39
　　2.3　Principles of dynamic system development　　　　　40
　　2.4　How and why object technology helps　　　　　　　43
　　2.5　The development process　　　　　　　　　　　44
　　　　　2.5.1　Managing projects by contract　　　　　　45
　　　　　2.5.2　Reuse management　　　　　　　　　　50
　　　　　2.5.3　Project rôles and responsibilities　　　　　54
　　2.6　From project initiation to workshops　　　　　　　56
　　2.7　Bibliographical notes　　　　　　　　　　　　57

3 Organizing and running workshops   **59**
3.1   The benefits of a workshop based approach   59
3.2   Rôles within a workshop   61
3.3   Who should attend   61
3.4   Selecting the location   64
3.5   Logistical requirements   65
3.6   Workshop organizer's and facilitator's checklists   68
3.7   Facilitation skills   72
3.8   Who should scribe?   73
          3.8.1 Recording the event   73
3.9   Running the workshop   74
          3.9.1 Setting and enforcing the rules of engagement   75
3.10 Keeping up momentum   76
3.11 Concluding the workshop   77
3.12 Other knowledge elicitation techniques   78
          3.12.1 Interviewing techniques   78
          3.12.2 Repertory grids and laddering   79
          3.12.3 Textual analysis   81
3.13 Using *SOMATiK* to prepare a workshop report   81
3.14 Bibliographical notes   82

4 Object modelling   **83**
4.1   The nature of models   83
          4.1.1 The need for multiple models   87
4.2   Notation and semantics   88
          4.2.1 Describing individual objects   88
          4.2.2 Structural links between objects   95
          4.2.3 Building object models without drawing pictures   105
          4.2.4 Rulesets and class invariants   111
          4.2.5 State transition modelling   117
          4.2.6 Packaging strategy: wrappers   120
          4.2.7 Fuzzy objects   122
4.3   Bibliographical notes   125

5 Business process modelling   **127**
5.1   De-scoping large problems – the mission grid   128
5.2   Discovering business objectives and priorities   130
5.3   Agents and conversations   131
5.4   From conversations to tasks   138
5.5   From the Task Object Model to the Business Object Model   141
5.6   Seamlessness   149
5.7   Ensuring the completeness of scenarios   154
5.8   Model animation and simulation   156

5.8.1 Executable specifications   156
5.8.2 Running simulations from the Agent Object Model   159
5.8.3 Discrete event and time-based simulation   161
5.8.4 Combining script and time-based simulation   164
5.9   Task associations and sequence diagrams   165
5.9.1 Sequence diagrams   166
5.9.2 Conjunctive, disjunctive and nested association sets   171
5.10   Bibliographical notes   175

6 Modelling intelligent agents   **177**
6.1   The rôle of intelligent agents   177
6.1.1 Agents, objects and modern information technology   178
6.2   What is an agent?   179
6.2.1 Current trends and pitfalls   182
6.2.2 The architecture of agents   183
6.3   Modelling agent systems with objects   187
6.3.1 Modelling business processes with agents   190
6.4   The Agent Object Model   191
6.5   Bibliographical notes   195

7 Architecture, reuse and requirements patterns   **197**
7.1   The importance of architecture   197
7.2   Problem frames and requirements patterns   201
7.3   Component-based development   205
7.4   Business object libraries   207
7.5   Metrics and process improvement   210
7.5.1 MOSES   211
7.5.2 The MIT metrics   212
7.5.3 A critique of the MIT metrics   213
7.5.4 Connasence   214
7.5.5 Other approaches   215
7.5.6 The SOMA metrics   217
7.5.7 Process improvement   220
7.6   Getting started   221
7.7   Bibliographical notes   222

PART II   **APPENDICES**

A Associations, integrity and rules   **227**
A.1   Associations and encapsulation in object-oriented methods   228
A.1.1 Associations as types   228
A.1.2 Associations versus mappings   229
A.2   Integrity constraints   230

A.2.1 Inverses   231
A.2.2 Integrity and encapsulation   233
A.2.3 Rules for referential integrity   234
A.3 Associations in object databases   237
A.4 Summary   240

B Use cases and tasks   **243**
B.1 Problems with use cases   244
B.2 Task scripts as generic use cases   249
B.3 The syllogism pattern for use case generation   252
B.4 Summary and conclusions   253

References   **255**

Name index   **261**

Subject index   **263**

Trademark notice

Action Technologies Workbench™ is a trademark of Action Technologies Inc. CORBA™ is a trademark of the Object Management Group. Delphi ™ is a trademark of Borland Inc. Rose™, Objectory™ and UML™ are trademarks of Rational Inc. Eiffel™ is a trademark of Interactive Software Engineering Corporation. Excel™, Intellisense™, OLE™, Visual Basic™, MS Studio™ and Microsoft Office™ are trademarks of Microsoft Inc. Jasmine™ is a trademark of Computer Associates Inc. Java™ is a trademark of Sun Microsystems Inc. Lotus Notes™ is a trademark of Lotus Development Corp. NewWave™ is a trademark of Hewlett Packard Inc. O2™ is a trademark of O2 Technology. Objective-C™ is a trademark of Stepstone Corp. Objectory™, UML and Rose™ are trademarks of Rational Inc. ObjectStore™ is a trademark of Object Design Inc. ObjectStore™ is a trademark of Object Design International. OpenSTEP™ is a trademark of NeXT Inc. Oracle™ is a trademark of Oracle Corporation. OS/400™, CICS™ and Visual Age™ are trademarks of International Business Machines Inc. PDP-11™ and VAX™ are trademarks of Digital Equipment Corporation. POET™ is a trademark of POET GmbH. PowerBuilder™ and Sybase™ are trademarks of Sybase Inc. REVEAL™ is a trademark of ICL Ltd. Simula™ is a trademark of Simula AS. SOMATiK™ and Leonardo are trademarks of Bezant Ltd. Telescript™ is a trademark of General Magic Inc. Universal Server™ is a trademark of Informix Inc. Unix™ is a trademark of AT&T. Versant™ is a trademark of Versant Object Technologies.

Part I

Object-oriented requirements engineering

1

Basic principles of object technology

Conservatism discards Prescription, shrinks from Principle, disavows Progress; having rejected all respect for antiquity, it offers no redress for the present, and makes no preparation for the future.

Benjamin Disraeli (Coningsby)

The purpose of this book is to explain in detail a coherent set of techniques for eliciting and modelling requirements for computer systems in such a way that developers and their clients can be assured of the correctness of the systems that result, in relation to the requirements. These techniques form a substantial part of the Semantic Object Modelling Approach to system development (SOMA). The original form of SOMA was described by Graham (1995). In explaining these techniques we shall assume that they will be used within the context of rapid, evolutionary development, with prototypes playing an important rôle. The key messages of the book have already been spelt out in the Preface.

In order to proceed with this agenda we must understand the nature and principles of object modelling with absolute clarity and this chapter will provide the reader with this understanding. It will also outline the technology at a high level in terms of languages, databases, middleware and so on. No assumptions about the reader's background are made other than a general computer literacy, including some familiarity with object-oriented concepts.

In the next chapter I give an overview of other approaches to requirements engineering and rapid application development and introduce the OPEN/SOMA development process model. At the centre of the approach is the use of facilitated workshops, so Chapter 3 provides guidance on this important discipline. With these process considerations behind us we can return in Chapter 4 to the subject of object modelling. There we investigate the art and science of object modelling in sufficient detail for our purposes in the remainder of this text and provide a condensed description of the semantics of our modelling language. After that we can apply this language to business process modelling and software development itself.

▤ 1.1 Historical and social background

Modern software development organizations, whether they be internal IT departments, consultancies or software houses, have adopted object technology for a number of commercial reasons. The promises of higher programmer productivity, quality and interoperability resulting from reuse have been important drivers, although the holy grail of reuse has often proved elusive in practice. This book will try to explain the reasons for some of these failures. Faster speed to market, through the use of rapid development and because of reuse, has also contributed and, here, there have been notable successes at many companies. Greater traceability to business requirements is important in an environment where increased flexibility to changing requirements must be accommodated and this will be a key theme of this work. However, the most important benefit of object technology is, in my opinion, the lower maintenance burden that it should support.

Amid repeated claims that reuse is a major benefit of object technology we must remind ourselves that reuse is not unique to object-oriented approaches. For many years function libraries provided solid reuse in conventional COBOL and FORTRAN environments. However, it is known that conventional top-down decomposition leads to application specific modules that are unlikely to be reusable. Encapsulation and inheritance help to maximize reuse potential but they do not guarantee that the benefit will be achieved. Success requires changes to both the organization and the development process itself. It also requires a clear understanding of the basic principles and the determination to succeed; reuse is a deferred benefit and it is not free.

Since the 1970s studies have shown that software maintenance is by far and away the biggest cost faced by IT organizations, with many experts estimating maintenance cost as up to 95% of the data processing budget. Other surveys have broken down maintenance costs into their components and find that, for example, changing requirements accounts for approximately 43% of change requests. This is natural and, I think, unavoidable and it is the prime reason why I advocate rapid application development; systems can be evolved easily. The second most important factor identified is the cost arising from changes to data structures and this accounts for over 17% of all maintenance costs. If you believe these figures and many do, then that means that changes to data structures account for over 16% of IT spend. Shaving even 1% off this figure world-wide would amount to savings measured in thousand of millions of dollars.

As Taylor (1992) pointed out, the commercial drivers towards more flexible and robust computer systems are largely predicated on the increasing rates of change to the environment that businesses are subjected to. The pace of change in technology, society and competition continues unabated. The increasingly global nature of a company's operations exacerbates this; multiple currencies, regulations and languages must be dealt with routinely. Decentralization and distribution of businesses implies a greater need for distributed computer systems, as does the greater empowerment of front line staff in terms of decision taking. Increased competition encourages a focus on product quality and the desire to produce a product customized to the needs of individual customers – but while still retaining the economies of scale associated with mass production.

Work by Alan O'Callaghan and his students at De Montfort University and British Telecom (Graham and O'Callaghan, 1997) reinforces these conclusions, suggesting that accelerating competition enforces the need for flexibility, reduced time to market and the necessity of driving up the productivity of both users and developers. Object technology offers the only known approach to computing that can tackle flexibility and productivity simultaneously, as I have argued elsewhere (Graham, 1995). O'Callaghan divides the drivers into business and technical categories. The business drivers are that 'enabling' component architecture is needed to give competitive edge, that overheads must be reduced by building a shared understanding of requirements and systems among users and developers and that software infrastructure must be driven by business needs. Notice that the call here is not just for object technology but for better requirements engineering and rapid application development practices. The technical drivers are bottom up and include increasingly cheap computing power, maturing object-oriented tools, the emergence of architectural standards such as CORBA (Common Object Request Broker Architecture) and the appearance of Internet, Intranet and Java based applications. The barriers to the adoption of this technology were found to be as follows. There is widespread scepticism in the business community because much of object technology has matured invisibly within apparently non-OO applications; e.g. IIOP (Internet Inter-ORB Protocol) in Web browsers and the use of object-oriented databases to power busy Web sites. It was found that mainly 'risk absorbing' organizations had made large investments in OT; i.e. those with large R&D budgets, those operating in risk intensive sectors such as Finance or Telecommunications and those small enough to be highly flexible in their approach to business. On top of all this the major barrier has been the existence of huge, mission-critical legacy systems.

Object technology is based on a far from new set of ideas that have their origin in the mid-1960s with the development of the Simula language, which was aimed at solving problems in discrete event simulation. These ideas were taken up by Alan Kay during his doctoral work and later, in the 1970s, at Xerox PARC, where the Smalltalk language was designed as part of the Star workstation's operating environment. The Smalltalk project is responsible for the coinage 'object-oriented' and is the paradigm for all subsequent truly, object-oriented languages. Simultaneously, workers in artificial intelligence (AI) adopted the ideas of classes and inheritance from Simula and went on to extend Lisp in various ways that ultimately were standardized in CLOS (Common Lisp Object System). Apart from a few fairly obscure AI applications, up until the 1980s object-orientation was largely associated with the development of graphical user interfaces (GUIs) and few other applications became widely known. However, the programming language community became interested and several languages emerged under the influence of these ideas. The most notable were two extensions of C, C++ and Objective-C, and Eiffel, a language influenced by COBOL, Simula and Ada and incorporating many ideas about formal correctness of programs. Ada itself used the idea of classes but lacked inheritance until recently. Up to this period not a word had been mentioned about analysis or design for object-oriented systems. In the middle of the 1980s Grady Booch published a paper on how to design for Ada but gave it the prophetic title: *Object-Oriented Design*. Booch was able to extend his ideas to a genuinely object-oriented design method by 1991 in his book with the same title, revised in 1993 (Booch, 1994) [*sic*].

With the advent of the 1990s came both the increased pressures on business outlined above and the availability of cheaper and much more powerful computers. This led to a ripening of the field and to a range of applications beyond GUIs and AI. Distributed open computing and client/server became both possible and important and object technology was the basis of much development, especially with the appearance of so-called 3-tier client/server systems, although relational databases played and continue to play an important rôle. The new applications and better hardware meant that mainstream organizations adopted object-oriented programming and now wanted proper attention paid to object-oriented design and (next) analysis. Object-oriented databases also matured during this decade and are now beginning to be used commercially. The appearance and popularization of the World-Wide Web eventually provided the problem that this solution had been looking for. Since the Web was to present multiple media – text, graphics, sound, video – relational databases could no longer be relied upon to deliver the required performance. Also the natural style of programming to handle these media was object-oriented. The first widely known Web-aware language therefore was a fully object-oriented language: Java. Companies operating busy Web sites, such as Microsoft and IBM, were forced to use object-oriented databases, such as Versant and ObjectStore, to provide the replication, version control, speed and resilience they needed. Network computing, thin clients and agents, now cry out for an encompassing theoretical framework and software engineering method. Object technology offers the best hope yet. We will see throughout this work the development of this solution.

Concern also shifted from design to analysis from the start of the 1990s. The first book with the title *Object-Oriented Systems Analysis* was produced by Shlaer and Mellor in 1988. Like Booch's original paper it did not present a genuinely object-oriented method, but concentrated entirely on the exposition of extended entity-relationship models, based on an essentially relational view of the problem and ignoring the behavioural aspects of objects. Shlaer and Mellor published a second volume in 1992 that argued that behaviour should be modelled using conventional state-transition diagrams. In the meanwhile, Peter Coad had incorporated behavioural ideas into a simple but object-oriented method (Coad and Yourdon 1989, 1991). This was followed by an explosion of interest in and publication on object-oriented analysis and design, a subject that we shall return to over and over again in this book.

At the time of writing, taken as a whole, object-oriented programming can be regarded as a mature discipline worthy of regular use by commercial organizations. The technologies of object-oriented databases and object request brokers too can be viewed as relatively mature, as we shall see later in this chapter. However, if there is a worry about maturity then it is in the methods area that this is true. To understand why we must return to the very basic principles of object-orientation.

1.2 Encapsulation and polymorphism explained

In despite of other views, I maintain that object technology has only two basic principles from which all others derive: encapsulation and inheritance polymorphism. These are rather pompous technical terms but are really quite easy to understand. It is therefore surprising that many of the defects in current object-oriented methods and practices result directly from a failure to grasp and adhere to these fundamental principles.

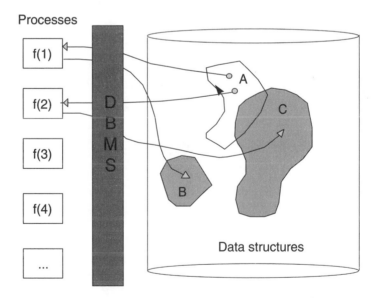

Figure 1.1 The architecture of a conventional computer system

As noted above, changes to data structures account for around 16% of IT spending. In order to understand the basics of OT let us try to understand why this is so for conventional computer systems and see how OT helps to reduce the burden if properly applied.

Being based on the so-called Von Neumann architecture of the underlying hardware, a conventional computer system can be regarded as a set of functions or processes together with a separate collection of data; whether stored in memory or on disk does not matter. This static architectural model is illustrated in Figure 1.1 which also indicates that, when the system runs, the dynamics may be regarded as some function, f(1), reading some data, A, transforming them and writing to B. Then some other function, f(2), reads some data, perhaps the same data, does whatever it does and writes data to C. Such overlapping data access gives rise to complex concurrency and integrity problems but these can be solved well by using a database management system. The question that I ask you to consider before reading on is: what must be done when part of the data structure has to change?

Considering this from the point of view of a maintenance programmer, the only conclusion that one can come to is that every single function must be checked to see if it may be destabilized by the change. Good documentation can help with this but is rarely available in practice. Part of the reason for this is that good documentation for this task would itself consist in an object-oriented description of the system and is unlikely to be divorced from an object-oriented implementation; or at least design. Furthermore, every function that is changed to reflect the new structure may have side effects in other parts of the system. Perhaps this accounts for the extraordinarily high costs of maintenance.

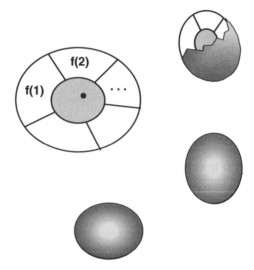

Figure 1.2a The architecture of an object-oriented system

Figure 1.2a illustrates a completely different architectural approach to systems. Here, all the data that a function needs to access are encapsulated with it in packages called *objects* and in such a way that the functions of no other object may access these data. Using a simile suggested by Steve Cook these objects may be regarded as eggs. The yolk is their data structure, the white consists of the functions that access these data and the shell represents the signature of the publicly visible operations. The shell interface hides the implementation of both the functions and the data structures. Now suppose again that a data structure is changed in the egg shelled for maintenance in Figure 1.2a. Now the maintenance programmer need only check the white of this particular egg for the impact of the change; maintenance is localized. If the implementation changes no other object can possibly be affected. This is **encapsulation**: data and processes are **combined** and **hidden** behind an interface.

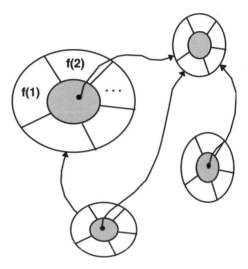

Figure 1.2b Message passing eliminates data duplication

The data structures and implementation details of an object are hidden from other objects in the system. The only way to access an object's state is to send a message that causes one of the methods to execute. Strictly speaking the attributes are shorthand for methods that get and put values. This makes classes equivalent to abstract data types in programming. Some of the methods of an object may also be hidden behind the interface: its *private* methods. The interface is best regarded as a public declaration of the *responsibilities* of the object. Attributes may be regarded as *responsibilities for knowing* and operations as *responsibilities for doing*. Another way of thinking about this is to say that the public interface defines the *questions we can ask* of an object and the *instructions we can give* to an object. Thinking about objects in this way is sometimes called 'anthropomorphizing' an object – treating it as an intelligent homunculus in the machine, able to hold a conversation with and reason about its own capabilities. This turns out to be a very good way to think about objects during requirements elicitation.

As it stands, there is a problem with this model. Suppose that every object contains a function that needs the same datum. In that case the potential for data-duplication is staggering and the approach would be quite impracticable. The solution is to permit the objects to send messages to each other. In this way object X may need data A but not encapsulate them. Provided that X stores in its yolk the identity of another object, Y, that does contain the required data, it may send a message requesting the data or even some transformed version of them. This is depicted in Figure 1.2b, where the small sperm-like dot represents the identity of a target object and the arrows show the outward direction of the message. This, in a nutshell, is 50% of the idea behind object technology. The other 50% involves allowing the objects to be classified and related to each other in other ways. Notice that with this approach the maintenance problem is localized and thus greatly simplified. When a data structure changes, the maintainer need only check the functions in the albumen that encapsulates it. There can be no effect elsewhere in the system unless the shell is cracked or deformed; that is, if the interface changes. Thus, while we may claim to have reduced the maintenance problem by orders of magnitude, we now have to work very hard to ensure that we produce correct, complete and stable interfaces for our objects. This implies that sound analysis and design are even more worthwhile and necessary than they were for conventional systems. This extra effort is worthwhile because object technology leads to some very significant benefits.

The curious thing is that this principle of encapsulation is regularly ignored by the creators of object-oriented analysis methods, as we shall see later. So, echoing the sentiments of Disraeli's character, we can only wonder at the extent of conservatism in most current object-oriented software engineering practice.

EXAMPLE:
A DATE
CLASS

At the time of writing, much is being heard of the 'year 2000 problem' or the 'Millennium Bug'[1], and this provides a convincing example of the strengths of object technology. In a nutshell, the question is that of how to interpret correctly a date described by a two-digit year field containing 99 instead of a four-digit year field containing 1999. The massive quantity of legacy code in use across the world is having to be examined line-by-line to uncover instances of date structures and date conversion and manipulation routines. To some extent this can be automated – but a lot of old programs from days when computer memory was at a premium may have highly convoluted code in them, where the programmer used a set of memory locations for more than one purpose, one purpose being a data buffer. There were even cases where the representation for the date 9/9/99 was used as a special override password. Discovering those examples on an automated basis is difficult. Estimates of the cost of this exercise vary widely, the only common feature being

---

[1] Of course, everyone knows that the Millennium doesn't start until January 1st, 2001 – except our governments it seems!

their denomination in thousands of millions of dollars. The task is well illustrated by Figure 1.1; all the data structures must be examined and potentially modified, and then all the contingent functions identified and brought into line.

How would matters fall out if all the code were object-oriented? Anthropomorphize a date object and consider the questions and instructions we might wish to give it. Actually, there are only three. The first is when we say to the date *class* 'Construct an *instance* of yourself representing this date …'. The second is when we say to the date class 'Present your value according to this format …' – which might be a picture of a string for display purposes, or a binary format such as Julian for the purposes of date arithmetic. Of each member of the *collection* of date instances, we have one question: 'Are you less than this date …' (TRUE or FALSE) and this simple question takes care of all the selection and sorting tasks. We could add other operations, such as 'return the number of days since …' but these three will suffice for illustration. All this gets nicely encapsulated in an object as in Figure 1.2. We can remain in ignorance about the internal storage layout of the date value. We are only aware of the operations available on the published interface of the class – *construct, format* and *test*. Now when the time comes to worry about the new, high- numbered years,we have the simple task of modifying and testing the code underlying the public methods. As long as we continue to honour the published interface, nothing else in our code inventory need be modified or even examined. And the next time we need to vary the algorithm, the same simple task applies. (Note in passing that this is a problem which will not be made to go away on January 1st 2000. One still has to decide upon the rules for interpreting a two digit year field as if it were a four digit field, and these rules will change over time. Mostly, people handle them by using a 'window' – an imaginary hundred year overlay sliding across the continuum of years. For example, the window might initially be slid to December 31st 2010, so the date string 1/1/10 would be interpreted as January 1st 2010, while the date string 1/1/11 would be interpreted as January 1st 1911. Sliding the window as time passes could require further changes to the code. Again, object orientation in the design of the code will mitigate the problem – and may even continue to do so for the year 10,000!

THE TERM 'OBJECT' Objects are the basic units of model construction, be it for conceptualization, design or programming. An object is anything with unique unchanging identity. Object instances can be organized into classes with common features. These features comprise attributes, and procedures called operations or methods. Strictly speaking, methods are the functions that implement operations and operations are the abstract specifications of methods. Objects should, as far as possible, be based on the real-world entities and concepts of the application or domain. Objects can be either classes or instances, although some authorities use the term object synonymously with instance. I object to this usage since there is scope for confusion when two words are used for the same thing and, as Berard (1993) has also observed, in some languages a class itself can be an instance of some higher level class or metaclass. Throughout this book I shall use the term object, as if it were slang, to mean either a class or an instance. The precise term will be used where the difference matters, otherwise the context will always make the meaning clear.

Objects, both classes and their instances, communicate by passing messages. This eliminates much data duplication and ensures that changes to data structures encapsulated within objects do not propagate their effects to other parts of the system. Messages are often implemented as function calls. An object can only send a message to another if it stores that object's identity or receives it in a message from another object. This may be regarded as a weakness of the object-oriented metaphor when it is necessary to broadcast messages to many objects, though we will see later that there are ways round the problem.

POLY-MORPHISM

Polymorphism is the ability to use the same expression to denote different operations. This occurs, to give a simple example common to all programming languages, where + is used to signify real or integer addition. Notice precisely what happens here: the token '+' is interpreted by the compiler depending on the associated arguments, and the compiler generates the appropriate floating point or integer machine code statements. This is referred to as 'early binding' or 'static typing' – everything is determined at compile time, nothing is decided at runtime. Polymorphism represents the ability of an abstraction to share features. Polymorphism is often implemented by dynamic binding which, as a droll commentator once observed, is the computing equivalent of picking up the cutlery after having selected the meal. Inheritance is a special kind of polymorphism (inclusion polymorphism) that characterizes object-oriented systems. Some authorities claim that polymorphism is the central idea in object-oriented systems, but there are non-object-oriented metaphors that take this point further, as exemplified in languages such as ML or Miranda.

Also, polymorphism can be used to extend the power of the inheritance metaphor. Instances (usually) inherit all and only the features of the classes they belong to, but it is also possible in an object-oriented system to allow classes to inherit features from more general superclasses. This permits two extensions to the model: inherited features can be overridden; and additional facilities can be added to the derived classes. Overriding inherited operations effectively defines object-oriented polymorphism, and it is important to understand where the benefit of this ability accrues. It lies in the maintainability, security and extensibility of the code inventory. Consider this fragment of pseudo-code, which iterates through some collection of objects, printing each one:

```
for all objects
    nextobject.Print()
```

If all the objects in the collection are of the same class, the same Print() routine will be invoked on each occasion. Polymorphism allows a range of subclasses to be derived from a superclass, each requiring a different print routine. In this case, at runtime the appropriate overridden Print() routine will be selected for each object.

Crucially, if we add new object types (i.e. new derived classes) to our model, this fragment of mainstream code needs no modification. Simply create the new subclass, with its appropriate Print routine, and link it into the image. Once again, encapsulation is ensuring that we only need to focus on the new class, not the rest of the code.

Inheritance implements the idea of classification and represents a special case of a structural inter-relationship between a group of objects.

The reason that inheritance is important can be derived from our boiled egg simile. We agreed that maintenance could be localized and thus reduced because changes to the implementation were hidden from other objects by the interface. Therefore to get this benefit we assumed that the interface never changed. However, we do not live in an ideal world. People – even developers – make mistakes. Requirements do change. So the interface is bound to change and we could be even worse off than with conventional development, because of the newness of the technology. The answer is to legislate against making changes to interfaces and insist that modification be made by introducing subclasses that extend or override the features of existing objects. Any deviation from this regime must be regarded as a major architectural rewrite of a system. This rule implies that our classes must be designed for extension and reinforces the need for sound object-oriented analysis even further.

These basic ideas of object modelling, encapsulation and inheritance will be further explained in Chapter 4. For now readers should carry this one idea at the forefront of their mind: processes and data should not be separated. Everything else will follow from that.

1.3 Language, broker and database technology

In this section we shall review the state of the art of object technology very briefly and mention most of the important tools available to the OO developer. These are principally object-oriented programming languages and environments, object request brokers and middleware and object-oriented databases.

1.3.1 Object-oriented programming languages and environments

Popular object-oriented languages include, at the time of writing, Smalltalk, C++, Eiffel, Java and Delphi. There are others related to particular problems or platforms but these are arguably the prevalent languages. Object COBOL, standardized in 1997, has yet to make a significant impact, though it may. Objective-C is an object-oriented extension of C that is similar to Smalltalk in many respects. One major difference is that Objective-C supports a variety of multiple inheritance through its use of so-called protocols. Multiple inheritance is the ability of a class to inherit features from more than one parent class. Objective-C forbids the multiple inheritance of implementation details but a class's interface may inherit from multiple protocols. The language is currently mainly associated with the OpenSTEP environment. C++ became popular, originally in the Unix world, because it is completely upwardly compatible with C. C++ was designed to add the *class* concept introduced in Simula to the widespread availability and runtime efficiency of C. This is both a strength and weakness. The weakness lies in the fact that C++ *enables* OO programming, but it does not *mandate* it. As a result, it is all too possible to develop a body of C++ that is a horrible mixture of design metaphors. This is particularly true for experienced C programmers converting to C++.

Smalltalk is a great deal easier to learn and use than C++ and is popular in organizations previously associated with mainframe development and which want to re-skill their COBOL developers. It is a true OO language and enforces the OO metaphor. IBM's Visual Age provides an excellent interactive development environment for Smalltalk and, more recently, Java. C++ is a small but very complicated language. Its use of pointers and upward compatibility with C mean that developers can make mistakes very easily. The typical errors are memory and resource leaks that make testing very difficult. However, C++ code can be very efficient and the language is more suitable for systems programming than Smalltalk. C++ defaults to early binding and is not really at home with the full idea of polymorphism, though it does support inheritance, both single and multiple. Eiffel is perhaps the best object-oriented language ever, although it is not as widely used as it deserves. Eiffel (Meyer, 1988) extends the vanilla-flavoured notion of objects by including pre- and post-conditions in the specification of operations and class invariants in the interface. This means that formal correctness of code is much emphasized and that Eiffel can be regarded as a program design language as well as a programming language. The Eiffel environment also offers a powerful extensibility feature: its 'melting ice' technology. This means that one can think of source code as a liquid that is 'frozen' when compiled. With most languages a module must be completely defrosted before it can be changed, refrozen and linked to other modules. With Eiffel you only need to melt the lines that need changing. These can then be tested as interpreted code running alongside all the still frozen elements of the system. Eiffel developers rely heavily on the use of multiple inheritance to deliver genuinely reuseable components (Meyer, 1994). Eiffel aims at efficiency and correctness. It is statically and strongly typed, so that classes are not objects. As I have said, there is a strong influence from and link to formal methods using assertions on methods (pre- and post-conditions) and class invariants. Eiffel runs on many platforms and is now a public domain language, though that was not always so. Eiffel emphasizes seamless development and reuse more than most other languages. Many experts view Eiffel as the best object-oriented language overall, but concede that it has not attained, nor may never attain, the appropriate market share against C++ and now Java.

Java is rapidly becoming the language of choice for Web developers but is also a respectable object-oriented programming language in its own right. Java is very similar to Objective-C and uses the same ideas of protocols (which it calls interfaces) to separate type inheritance from implementation inheritance and permit multiple inheritance. The syntax of Java is however very similar to that of C++ although dangerous pointers are forbidden. This means that Java is simultaneously safer, easier to learn and more powerful than C++ in the hands of the average developer. It is also, at least in its 'pure' form, machine independent; it compiles to a p-code that runs on a Java Virtual Machine that is available on nearly all platforms. This praiseworthy objective of machine independence is of course not new. It was claimed for COBOL and it was claimed for C. At the time of writing, it remains to be seen just how well it is achieved for Java. One of the most important factors in the appeal of Java is that it is a Web-enabled language, with features that make it easy to write 'applets': small programs that are downloaded with a web page and can handle tasks such as animation and data validation. The main problems with early releases of Java were the lack of good tools and the potential instability of its class libraries, but the situation is improving. Java's portability comes at the expense of speed. However, there are machine specific 'just in time' compilers available for which integer benchmarks performed by one of my colleagues produced executables only half as slow as the equivalent C++. This is to be compared with 100 times slower for Visual Basic and ignores the fact that disk bound or network bound problems would perform much closer to C++, although floating point and string problems will perform rather worse of course. Alternative to the full-blown general purpose object-oriented programming language is the visual programming environment. The first example of such a thing was Visual Basic and the finest example is Delphi. Delphi embeds a full-blown object-oriented language, Object Pascal, within a very rich environment for creating graphical user interfaces and database and OLE links. It is very fast when compiled, very productive and very easy to learn.

Is Visual Basic (VB) an object-oriented language? This is quite an important question for developers today, because VBA (Visual Basic for Applications) is now a pervasive language in the Microsoft universe, and Visual Basic itself is just another client of VBA, along with all the Microsoft Office applications. The language certainly allows you to create a thing called a class, but this is really just an extension to the idea of a user defined type. The 'classes' in VB5 support encapsulation, and polymorphism to a degree. But inheritance and proper classification are not supported. Sadly as well, VB5 has begun to acquire some of the bad habits of C++ in terms of pointers and all the woes they bring in their train, without supplying the language power which C++ delivers in exchange for its bad habits. So, few organizations will choose to develop mainstream applications in VB, using it instead to develop demonstrable prototypes, to front-end C++ applications, and to extend and profile applications developed in Access or Excel. Visual Basic and PowerBuilder are similar in some ways being based on object-based languages that could not support inheritance without recourse to coding in

C++. The architecture of the current generation of these tools still reflects this. The practical consequence is that many people have found that applications written in these environments do not scale up. This is partly due to the architecture and partly to poor performance. VB really finds its apotheosis as a very good prototyping tool and in its rôle within Microsoft Office. PowerBuilder was mainly used as a front end to two-tier client/server applications based on Sybase. It is interesting to note that a modelling approach such as that found in OMT or UML with a relational flavour is very suitable for applications written in this way, whereas fully distributed, object-oriented applications written in Java, Eiffel or Delphi can be compromised by the limitations of and philosophy behind UML, as we shall see in Chapter 4.

Object-oriented COBOL has been shipping for some time but was only standardized in 1997. Undoubtedly some mainframe sites will adopt it but many commentators regard it as having arrived on the scene too late. A large number of loyal IBM sites have already turned to Smalltalk and VisualAge to retrain their COBOL teams in.

There are several other object-oriented languages such as Ada95 in fairly wide commercial use but it is not my purpose here to develop a full survey, merely to outline the most popular choices in industry at large.

1.3.2 Object-oriented databases

Object-oriented databases have now emerged as a genuine alternative to both relational and pre-relational storage strategies. Relational systems superseded many network and hierarchical databases because they made schema evolution and *ad hoc* enquiries much simpler; it was possible to add a new field to the database without rewriting all the programs and enquiries that accessed the dataset. However, this flexibility came at the expense of performance and many applications of that generation still had to use the older technologies: typically IMS or IDMS. The new object-oriented databases can be 100 times faster than their relational equivalent for certain problems. This is because enquiries (and indeed updates) follow pointers to objects, just like a network database but now at a logical rather than physical level. This means that the speed approaches that of a network database – for the right application – but that an object-oriented database retains the flexibility of the relational approach as well.

As a side effect of the fact that object-oriented databases were developed later than their relational sisters, they support a few very useful features not usually found with these ladies. The most notable examples of this are support for long transactions and automatic version control. The latter supports the former so that a deadlock condition leads to two versions of the transaction rather than the destruction of work that may have taken several hours – or even months. These facilities have only a little to do with object technology; it was natural to provide them when developing on networks of Sun workstations, whereas the relational products were originally developed in the days when stand-alone PDP or VAX minicomputers were the machines of choice.

Another major reason for adopting an object-oriented database is that there is no 'impedance mismatch' between the structures that appear in the code (classes) and those that appear in the database (classes). A C++ program that accesses a relational database has to convert its classes into tables and *vice versa*. This gives rise to an 'impedance mismatch' between the language and the database.

Although the arguments for using an object-oriented database are strong, there are several reasons for keeping the RDBMS. The most persuasive of these is the huge investments that most companies have made in their existing database systems. Also the relational approach works well for most record-oriented DP applications and the largely standardized SQL access language provides well for *ad hoc* queries.

There are three types of object-oriented database product on the market. Persistent extensions to object-oriented languages, such as ObjectStore and POET, provide a way of dealing with persistence with no impedance mismatch but are usually relatively weak in terms of the facilities of a traditional database *management* system. Proper object-oriented database management systems, such as O2, Objectivity and Versant, are better equipped with database management system facilities. For example O2 supports a 4GL and Versant has event notification facilities. Presently, both types of product tend to be closely coupled to one object-oriented language (usually C++) with additional bindings to other languages added on.

The Object/Relational DBMSs, such as Oracle 8, UniSQL and Universal Server (Illustra), behave like OODBMSs but rest on an underlying relational implementation. This means that they can match features with the pure OODBMSs but can never match the performance. The only rational reason for choosing this kind of product is to smooth the upgrade path from an earlier relational database; and really only the most timorous management should disdain a full OODBMS for a new application, especially where the application will have to perform many small joins, as is typical for industrial CAD or derivatives trading for example. It is with this kind of problem that the true object-oriented databases excel.

1.3.3 Object wrappers

Object wrappers can be used to migrate to object-oriented programming and still protect investments in conventional code. The existence of large investments in programs written in conventional languages such as Assembler, COBOL, PL/1, FORTRAN and even APL has to be recognized. It must also be allowed that the biggest cost associated with these 'legacy' systems is maintenance. As we saw, maintenance is costly because, in a conventional system, any change to the data structure requires checking every function to see if it is affected. This does not occur with object-oriented systems due to the encapsulation of the data structures and the functions that use them by interfaces. However much we would like to replace these old systems completely, the economics of the matter forbids it on any large scale; there just are not enough development resources. What we must do is build on the existing investment and move gradually to the new world of object technology.

It is possible to create object wrappers around this bulk of existing code, which can then be replaced or allowed to wither away. Building object wrappers can help protect the investment in older systems during the move to object-oriented programming. An object wrapper enables a new, object-oriented part of a system to interact with a conventional chunk by message passing. The wrapper itself may often be written in the same language as the original system, COBOL or RPG for example. This may represent a very substantial investment, but once it is in place virtually all maintenance activity may cease; at least this is the theory.

Imagine that the existing COBOL system interacts with users through a traditional menu system, each screen offering about 10 options and with the leaf nodes of the menu tree being normal 'enter, tab and commit' data entry screens. This characterizes a very large number of present day systems. The wrapper must offer all the functions of the old system as if through the interface of an object, as illustrated by the 'Gradygram' in Figure 1.3 where the small rectangles on the boundary of the wrapper represent its visible operations, which in turn call the old system's functions and thereby access its data too[2].

Effectively, the wrapper is a large object whose methods are the menu options of the old system. The only difference between this new object and the old system is that it will respond to messages from other objects. So far, this gives little in the way of benefits. However, when we either discover a bug, receive a change request or wish to add a new business function the benefits begin; for we do not meddle with the old system at all but create a new set of objects to deliver the new features. As far as the existing users are concerned, they may see no difference when using the old functions; although their calls are being diverted via the wrapper. Wrappers may be small or large, but in the context of inter-operation they tend to be of quite coarse granularity. For command driven systems, the wrapper may be a set of operating system batch files or scripts. If the old system used a form or screen-based interface, the wrapper may consist of code that reads and writes data to the screen. This can be done using a virtual terminal. This is fairly easy to accomplish on machines such as the VAX though it is not always possible with systems such as OS/400 where some specialist software or an object request broker may be required. All new functions or replacements should be dealt with by creating new objects with their own encapsulated data structures and methods. If the services of the old system are needed, these are requested by message passing and the output is decoded by the wrapper and passed to the requester.

---

[2] The term *Gradygram* was coined to stand for the icons with operations indicated by small boxes on the boundary of a rectangle representing the object used by Grady Booch since his work on design for Ada in the mid-1980s. The Booch'93 method uses them for its module diagrams to this day and variants have appeared in several other methods.

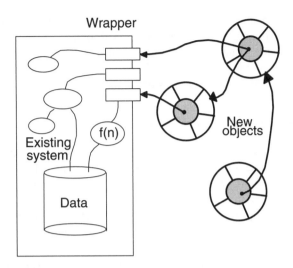

Figure 1.3 Object wrappers for legacy systems

So much for the propaganda! Implementing wrappers is not as easy as it sounds in several respects. Much of the literature on wrappers is aimed at deriving the necessity of either object-oriented databases or object request brokers. When these are not available, for whatever reason, developers have to face up to the implementation details directly. One such issue concerns granularity. Most of the theoretical arguments and a good deal of the practical experience of object-oriented programmers indicate that small or medium-sized objects are usually more reusable than large ones. Recall the usual set of guidelines for object design from your favourite text on the subject: interfaces should be small and simple; no more than about 17 operations per object; and so on. However, with the legacy system we are faced with a *fait accompli*; the system is as it is. There are irreducibly large grain 'objects' often present in the design of legacy systems. Object request brokers are specifically aimed at dealing with this kind of coarse grain reuse. The question is whether, without such a broker, we can still gain from the use of a hand-made wrapper. Some developers find that coarse grain objects arise naturally even with new requirements and deduce that object-oriented models are not always appropriate.

One of the biggest problems with the concept of object wrappers concerns data management. Using the wrapper is easy until you need to split the storage of data across the old database and some of the new objects. Detailed strategies for dealing with this problem are discussed by Graham (1995).

There can be several reasons for wrapping an existing system. Broadly though, these can be classified into three main types: migration, reuse and extension. Migration is the motive when an organization is concerned with the evolution of important legacy systems that are too large to rewrite at a stroke or with the migration of an existing system to a future object-oriented implementation. Reuse could include the reuse of highly optimized algorithms or specialized functions, combining relational databases with object-oriented databases or even building on existing 'packages'. Examples of extension include creating graphical front-ends for existing systems, building other new features onto existing 'packages', embedded expert systems or co-operating with existing systems across networks.

1.3.4 Object request brokers and middleware

The *ad hoc* approach to wrapper construction described above was the only one available until the appearance of object request brokers (ORBs) and object-oriented database (OODB) products. Now it is very common to use an ORB to implement a wrapper around a legacy system.

Object Request Brokers are products based on the Object Management Group's application architecture, illustrated in Figure 1.4. The basic idea is that an application that needs to use the services of some object, whether on the same machine or remote from it, should do so via a broker rather than by using some sort of remote procedure call that would require it to know the location of the server object. The ORB takes care of locating and activating registered remote servers, marshalling requests and responses, handling concurrency and detecting communication failures. The Object Management Group (OMG) also defined a standard for interfaces: its Interface Definition Language (IDL). IDL resembles C++ syntactically but may only be used to define interfaces; it is not a full programming language.

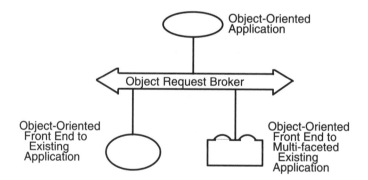

Figure 1.4 The Object Management Group architecture

CORBA Version 1 defined IDL as a protocol for inter-object communication. Version 2 defined a way for ORBs from different manufacturers to inter-operate. The advantage of this in terms of vendor independence is obvious. IIOP is the CORBA Internet Inter-ORB Protocol. It is a lightweight transport protocol that allows heterogeneous ORB products to communicate via TCP/IP; that is to say it consists of a set of message formats. The OMG's General Inter-ORB Protocol

(GIOP) defines a way to map IDL interfaces to messages. IIOP converts GIOP messages into TCP/IP, which means that that can be sent over networks or the Internet.

Java has its own, built-in, object request broker: RMI. Java RMI (Remote Method Invocation) is not compliant with CORBA. It allows Java applications to use the services of other Java applications as if they were local, regardless of location. To use a server written in another language the developer must create a proxy in Java on the same server and then use the JNI (Java Native Interface) to connect them. With RMI, Java acts as its own IDL. However, pure Java now also includes IIOP and a separate CORBA-compliant Java IDL.

Microsoft offers a partial alternative to CORBA in the guise of COM and DCOM (Distributed Common Object Model). These developed from OLE (Object Linking and Embedding) which allowed applications to be launched automatically when an item that they had created was accessed in a foreign document. COM assumes the immediate availability of local services but DCOM allows COM to communicate between machines using remote procedure calls. This is a far less elegant and general solution than CORBA but is much easier to implement and therefore popular with developers.

ORBs allow organizations to implement service-based architectures very easily. A good example is the implementation of a volatilities publishing system at a leading wholesale bank. Here traders provide the prices of derivatives for salesmen based on proprietary algorithms and upon the volatility of the underlying instrument prices. Unfortunately, most of the requests for prices from the sales desk do not lead to real, profitable trades. This meant that much valuable time was being wasted. The bank therefore created a system whereby the traders prepared the volatilities and algorithms using their Excel spreadsheets and a library of C++ functions callable from the spreadsheets. The results were then published to a server that could be accessed (via OLE) by other users of Excel or from Java enabled Web browsers across an object request broker. This bank offers many ORB-based services such as this to its internal clients. Another example is its calendar service that enables any user to find out when the various markets around the world are on holiday or closed. This service based architecture has eliminated much duplication of effort on the part of developers building such functionality into their systems.

The rôle of middleware in software architecture will become increasingly important in the coming period; object request brokers, transaction monitors and message delivery mechanisms all have a crucial rôle to play in the delivery of robust flexible systems. Unfortunately, we still operate in a culture where middleware is often jocularly defined as 'the software that no-one wants to pay for'.

1.4 Applications

Object technology can be used for almost any kind of application. It has already been used extensively for GUI construction, real-time systems, artificial intelligence, client/server systems and distributed computing, front-ends to legacy systems, multi-media systems and Web applications, CASE tools, repositories, CAD/CAM, geographic information systems and data warehousing. Currently many commercial organizations are using it to deliver robust mission-critical systems across the range of management information systems requirements, with the most prominent adopters being those in the telecommunications and finance sectors.

Meyer and Nerson (1993) review seven applications that used Eiffel. The studies cover applications in telecommunications, AI, class library development and 3D animation. It is a technical work that will be mainly of interest to Eiffel programmers. However, the general conclusions drawn by the chapter authors have consequences with great relevance outside that language. Harmon and Taylor (1993) and several subsequent publications have listed case studies of success with object technology in general. It is not the purpose of this book to reiterate them and I assume that the reader is reasonably convinced of the argument for object-orientation.

The sort of applications that the method presented here is suitable for is very wide, although I have no experience of applying it in real time domains. Certainly it will work in management information systems, data processing, business process re-engineering, operational research, simulation, financial engineering, record keeping, and many other common business areas.

To my knowledge, the method presented in this text has been used on well over 100 projects in a diverse range of industry and application types. Its target language neutrality has permitted it to be used for applications to be deployed using Smalltalk, C++, Java and Ada95, with persistent storage implemented in both OO databases and wrapped RDBMSs.

1.5 Methods of object-oriented analysis and design

The history of object technology recapitulates the history of computing. As we saw above, it took 20 years of object-oriented programming before object-oriented design and analysis appeared on the scene, just as it took nearly 20 years of the existence of computers and programming before any structured methods appeared.

The essential principles of object-oriented software engineering are those of:

- Encapsulated implementations

- Structured interfaces
- Small, simple, stable interfaces
- Minimal coupling

Recall also that analysis and design are even more important for OO systems because our interfaces **must** be stable if we are to lower maintenance costs. However the principle that really differentiates object-oriented development from its predecessor structured approaches is that data and processes combine to form coherent entities. They are **never** separated. Curiously, it is this principle that is most often forgotten by methodologists in their desire to keep their methods upward compatible with earlier approaches such as Information Engineering.

For those readers with a background in structured methods I should note that object modelling can be viewed as building on such methods, although there are some significant differences arising principally from the union of data with processes. Object models can be compared with dataflow models in a number of ways since data do flow between objects that are linked structurally. The first major difference is that data flow in response to events in object models. Secondly, messages in object models imply a goal and a return value type so that the data flow in **both** directions along the arrows. Most importantly, in object modelling processes and data are combined, so that processes must encapsulate the data stores that they utilize. Even an early proponent of data flow diagrams, Ed Yourdon, said as long ago as 1989: 'Data flow is dead'; even though it sometimes seems to refuse to lie down, especially when it comes to business process re-engineering methods.

Comparison with entity-relationship (ER) modelling is also possible. The main difference is that in object models the entities have operations as well as attributes; they become abstract data types. In object models it is more natural to create entity subtypes to arbitrary depth; so that while inheritance was always possible in ER models, it is now a more important modelling tool. ER models lack, however, the other distinguished structures of object modelling such as composition structures. It is extremely important to realize that the attributes of objects can be non-atomic; attributes can contain lists and any other complex entity type. Thus object models are **not** usually in first normal form, though they may be organized into third normal form in some cases. Like entities, objects still have life histories that can be represented by state-transition diagrams or regular grammars *a la* JSD. Unlike entities, objects can send and receive messages. This should remind us that it is improper to separate the static and dynamic aspects of a model as completely as is done within structured approaches; and yet most object-oriented methods try their hardest to maintain this separation: offering different notations for each. Perhaps the most striking violation of object-oriented principles was the inclusion of pure dataflow diagrams in the OMT method (Rumbaugh *et al.*, 1991).

Another common legacy from structured approaches based on the relational data model is the use of bi-directional associations in class models. This is a feature of OMT, Shlaer/Mellor, UML and Martin/Odell to name but a few methods. This practice totally violates encapsulation as shown in Appendix A.

1.5.1 Responsibility-driven versus data-driven approaches

The greatest danger in adopting a method based too much on structured techniques is that of data-driven design. Two software engineers at Boeing (Sharble and Cohen, 1994) conducted an experiment with internal trainees with similar backgrounds. One group was taught the Shlaer/Mellor method of object-oriented analysis – a method consciously and deeply rooted in traditional entity-relationship modelling – while the other group was instructed in the Responsibility Driven Design techniques of Wirfs-Brock *et al.* (1990). The two groups were then asked to design a simplified control application for a brewery. The Shlaer/Mellor group produced a design wherein most of the classes represented static data stores while one class accessed these and encapsulated the control rules for most of the application: in much the same style as a main{} routine in C would do. The other group distributed the behaviour much more evenly across their classes. It was seen that this latter approach produced far more reusable classes: classes that could be unplugged from the application and used whole. It also demonstrated vividly that the method you use can influence the outcome profoundly. It is my firm conviction that data-driven methods are dangerous in the hands of the average developer and especially in the hands of someone educated or experienced in the relational tradition. Furthermore, I hold that the approach taken to requirements engineering can have a huge influence.

The study by Sharble and Cohen shows convincingly that data-driven methods **do** influence the thinking of designers and that they tend to produce un-reusable classes as a consequence. The usual effects are:

- behaviour is concentrated in controller objects that resemble the main routines found in C programs; this makes systems much harder to maintain due to the amount of knowledge that these controllers store about other objects;
- other objects have few operations and are often equivalent to normalized database tables: not reflective therefore of sound object-oriented design.

SOMA and OPEN insist upon and encourage responsibility-driven design and analysis, as we shall see in subsequent chapters. We will be concerned throughout this text to emphasize this in all we do, just as we shall stress adherence to the basic principles of object technology: encapsulation and inheritance. This is not the pedantic reaction of a purist but a stance of immense practical significance.

1.5.2 Analysis, design and seamlessness

Software engineering can be viewed as splitting into analysis and design, where analysis results in a description of the problem domain and design splits further into:

- Logical design: a description of the solution and definition of interfaces.
- Physical design: a description of the structure of the implementation.

Object oriented methods are often claimed to offer a more seamless approach than conventional methods. This is because object models can be used to represent knowledge at each stage, instead of using several representations. A traditional approach might use dataflow diagrams for the analysis, structure charts for the logical design and pseudo-code for the physical design prior to coding. With object technology, analysis models are viewed as being the same as design models but with less detail. My feeling is that, although this continuum of representation does apply to the transition between analysis and logical design (thus making object-oriented methods preferable) there is a discontinuity between logical and physical design – at least usually. This is because the semantics of a particular programming language, such as C++, have no equivalent in the world that is being modelled. Therefore, when we translate a logical model to a physical one we must perforce introduce a discontinuity; so that information would be lost if we were to convert the code back to the model.

There are three possible solutions to this problem. We can adopt some cumbersome additional traceability mechanism, we could stick to the strategy of generating code directly from the analysis or we could restrict the analysis and design language to the semantics of the programming language. The latter strategy is the basis for modelling languages like UML and the CASE tools that support it. The problem with doing that is that it restricts the ability of users and developers to communicate over requirements very badly indeed. The problem with code generation is that current technology does not permit the generation of sufficiently efficient code. Also decisions about how to allocate objects to physical processors or threads are tremendously difficult, requiring a creativity that computers do not possess. For these reasons SOMA recognizes that there will be a visible 'seam' between logical and physical design and that some traces will need to be kept. One solution is to store cross references between analysis and design objects and source code. This can be accomplished using a repository product such as the *SOMATiK* repository manager as we will see later in this book. Many CASE tools, including *SOMATiK*, support code generation. However, we must recognize that the code generated will often need to be modified by hand unless only an executable specification is required. We will study this topic in detail in Chapter 5.

Fortunately for the beginner, the principles of object-oriented analysis are exactly the same principles as those of object-oriented programming; so that there is little new to learn. These are the principles of encapsulation (leading to greater reusability) and inheritance (leading to extensibility). Along with this good news comes the less pleasing fact that by 1995 around 70 OOA/D methods or method fragments had been published. Worse still no method up to then gave complete coverage of all the issues that a method should address. Even MOSES and SOMA had pieces missing; MOSES lacking guidance on GUI construction and SOMA having no detailed techniques for physical design and relying on Booch for this. This was a serious issue because, as I have argued repeatedly, object-oriented analysis is **the essential** ingredient of any object-oriented project if maintenance costs are to be controlled.

1.5.3 Analysis and design soup!

The first paper to use the term OBJECT-ORIENTED DESIGN was written by Grady Booch (1982). Strictly speaking it was not about object-oriented design but introduced a method for designing Ada programs: not a fully object-oriented language in those days. Later Booch (1991, 1994) produced a proper object-oriented design method in book form. His method remains to this day, in my opinion, one of the best language-level object-oriented design methods to have appeared. Similarly, the first book to use the term OBJECT-ORIENTED ANALYSIS in the title (Shlaer and Mellor, 1988) was not about object-oriented analysis in any recognizable sense; it described a method for entity-relationship modelling, mentioning neither behaviour nor inheritance. Later Shlaer and Mellor produced a second volume, adding state models to their 'objects' to rescue the behavioural aspects and substantiate their claim to the appellation 'object-oriented'. Therefore it is possible to claim that the first true object-oriented analysis method was published by Peter Coad and Ed. Yourdon (1989, 1991). The contribution of Coad's method was its great simplicity: a feature for which it was later criticised. But it did introduce many people to object-oriented ideas in an analysis context for the first time. Coad's approach was also rooted in the same traditions of data modelling and retained a clear data-driven focus, adding operations (services) to the description of entities. John Edwards' Ptech method had been around for some time when Jim Odell adapted it as an object-oriented method (Martin and Odell, 1992) designed to be upward compatible from Information Engineering – and therefore data-driven.

OMT (Rumbaugh *et al.,* 1991) copied Coad's approach of adding operations to entity-type descriptions to make class models but used a different notation from all the previous methods. Not only was OMT thoroughly data-driven but it separated processes from data by using data flow diagrams separately from the class diagrams. However, it emphasized what Coad had only hinted at and Shlaer and Mellor were yet to publish: the use of state-transition diagrams to described the life-cycles of instances. It also made a few remarks about the micro development process and offered very useful advice on how to connect object-oriented programs with relational databases. Just as Booch had become popular with C++ programmers because of its ability to model the semantic constructs of that language precisely, so OMT became popular with developers for whom C++ and a relational database were the primary tools – as was mostly the case in the early 1990s.

Blaha and Premerlani (1998) confirm this with the words: 'The OMT object model is essentially an extended Entity-Relationship approach' (p10). They go on to say, in their presentation of the second generation version of OMT that the 'UML authors are addressing programming applications; we are addressing database applications'. Writing in the preface to the same volume, Rumbaugh even makes a virtue out of the relational character of OMT/UML. I feel that a stricter adherence to object-oriented principles and to a responsibility-driven approach is a necessity if the full benefits of the object-oriented metaphor are to be obtained in the context of a fully object-oriented tool-set. In the context of requirements engineering this is even more true.

In parallel with the rise of the extended entity-relationship and data-driven methods, Wirfs-Brock and her colleagues were developing a set of responsibility-driven design (RDD) techniques out of experience gained more in the world of Smalltalk than that of the relational database. The most important contributions of RDD were the extension of the idea of using so-called CRC cards for design and, later the introduction of the idea of stereotypes. CRC cards showed Classes with their Responsibilities and Collaborations with other objects as a starting point for design. These could then be shuffled and responsibilities reallocated in design workshops. The idea had originated from the work of Beck and Cunningham at Tektronix, where the cards were implemented using a hypertext system. Moving to physical pieces of cardboard enhanced the technique by allowing designers to anthropomorphize their classes and even consider acting out their life-cycles – an idea we exploit heavily in SOMA.

Objectory is a proprietary method that has been around much longer than most object-oriented methods. It originated in the Swedish telecommunications industry and emerged in its object-oriented guise when Jacobson *et al.* (1992) published part of it (OOSE) in book form. The major contribution of this method was the idea that analysis should start with *use cases* rather than with a class model. The classes were then to be derived from the use cases. The technique marked an important step forward in object-oriented analysis and has been widely adopted, although we are able to make some fairly severe criticisms of it in Appendix B. Objectory was the first method to include a *bona fide* development process, although it was never placed in the public domain as the use case technique was.

OBA (Object Behaviour Analysis) originated from Smalltalk dominated work at ParcPlace and also included a process model that was never fully published although some information was made available (Goldberg and Rubin, 1995; Rubin and Goldberg, 1992). One interesting feature of OBA was the use of stereotypical scripts in place of use cases.

Coming from the Eiffel tradition Waldén and Nerson's (1995) BON (Business Object Notation) emphasized seamlessness and hinted at a proto-process. However, this approach (and indeed its very seamlessness) depended on the adoption of Eiffel as a specification language throughout the process. It made important contributions to the rigour of object-oriented analysis as did Cook and Daniels' (1994) Syntropy. BON improves rigour using the Eiffel idea of class invariants while Syntropy does this and further emphasizes state machines.

Thus far, to the eyes of the developer there appears a veritable soup of object-oriented analysis and design methods and notations. It was an obvious development to try to introduce some kind of unification and the Fusion method (Coleman *et al.*, 1994; Malan, *et al.*, 1996) represents one of the first attempts to combine good techniques from other published methods, although some commentators have viewed the collection of techniques as poorly integrated. There is a process associated with Fusion although published descriptions of it appear incomplete compared to the proprietary versions sold by Hewlett Packard.

MOSES (Henderson-Sellers and Edwards, 1994) was the first method to include a full blown development process, a metrics suite and an approach to reuse management. SOMA (Graham, 1995), which appeared in its mature form roughly contemporaneously with MOSES and was influenced by it, also included all these features, as well as attempting to fuse the best aspects of all the methods published to date and go beyond them; especially in the areas of requirements engineering, agent-based systems and rigour.

The modern object-oriented developer had to find a way to pick out the noodles from this rich soup of techniques. Because of this and because there were many similarities between methods it began to be felt by most methodologists that some sort of convergence was in order. At least two groups of methodologists began work towards this end. Booch, Rumbaugh and (later) Jacobson joined forces at Rational Inc., a CASE tool vendor, and produced the Unified Modelling language (UML): a notation and metamodel based largely on OMT. The OPEN Consortium is an informal group of about 30 methodologists, with no common commercial affiliation, that wanted to see greater method integration but felt strongly that methods should include a process, should be in the public domain, should not be tied to particular tools and should focus strongly on scientific integrity as well as pragmatic issues. The founding members of OPEN were Ian Graham and Brian Henderson-Sellers who began to integrate the MOSES and SOMA process models. The result was published as Graham, *et al.* (1997a). They were soon joined by Don Firesmith who started work on an integrated notation (OML) with the aim of a more pure object-oriented character than the OMT-influenced UML and one that would be easier to learn and remember (Firesmith, *et al.*, 1997). I will have more to say about these notations in Chapter 4.

My view is that notation is of only the most minor importance. In fact, I have used *SOMATiK* to present examples of the implementation of many of the ideas of this book. The advantage of doing this is that *SOMATiK* automates nearly all diagram production making any notation superfluous in the sense that one need not remember icon shapes to produce the pictures and because the context always makes the meaning of icons clear. However, it should be made clear that the use of the method in no way depends on the use of the tool, I merely use it out of convenience and to illustrate the sort of thing that is possible with modern software.

1.6 Bibliographical notes

More detail of the history and origins of object technology is given by Graham (1994), who also surveys many object-oriented analysis and design methods and method fragments that were in existence at that time. That work also contains a survey of many object-oriented programming languages and databases, including some of those mentioned in this chapter.

Graham (1995) gives a more detailed discussion of migration strategies and application of object technology along with a detailed, but early, description of the SOMA method, which is the subject of this text.

Readers may also wish to consult Booch (1994) on the subject of object-oriented design and for his excellent discussion of the issue of using object technology to control the complexity of software.

For a high level management-oriented overview of object technology consult Taylor (1997).

2

Approaches to requirements engineering and rapid development

Ours is a world where people don't know what they want and are willing to go through hell to get it.
Don Marquis (quoted in the Treasury of Humorous Quotations)

I n this chapter we review existing requirements engineering approaches to see if there is anything in them that should be salvaged for use within an object-oriented approach. We also survey approaches to rapid application development and give a very brief summary of the OPEN/SOMA development process model.

Rapid application development (RAD) or joint application development (JAD) is becoming widespread in industry. These phrases sum up a combination of notions including prototyping, evolutionary development and incremental delivery. Requirements engineering (RE) also has a number of connotations ranging from requirements elicitation to requirements analysis and proof of correctness. In this chapter we survey and explain both fields with a view to preparing the reader for the synthesis of these ideas with those of object technology and business process modelling that suffuses most of the remainder of this book.

⊟ 2.1 Approaches to requirements engineering

Pohl (1993) defines requirements engineering as 'the systematic process of developing requirements through an iterative co-operative process of analysing the problem, documenting the resulting observations in a variety of representation formats, and checking the accuracy of the understanding gained'. This definition, while it leaves some questions unanswered, is a good starting point because it suggests that there is more to requirements engineering than just writing a functional specification. By contrast, the IEEE (Dorfman and Thayer, 1990) define a requirement as one of the following.

1. A condition or capacity needed by a user to solve a problem or achieve an objective.
2. A condition or capability that must be met or possessed by a system or system component to satisfy a contract, standard, specification or other formally imposed documents.
3. A documented representation of a condition or capability as in 1 or 2.

This leaves out the issue of context completely and emphasizes the presence of a requirements document but is notable for the inclusion of the idea of a contract.

Macaulay (1996) suggests that the Pohl definition raises a number of important questions, including whether one can be systematic in the face of vaguely understood requirements, how one can know whether the requirements are complete in the context of iteration, how to define co-operation among agents, what representation formalisms can be used and, finally, how can a genuine shared understanding be reached. The approach laid out in this book offers answers to all of these questions but specifically in the context of object-oriented, rapid development.

We distinguish two aspects of requirements engineering: requirements elicitation and requirements analysis. Requirements elicitation is the process whereby a development agency discovers what is needed and why. It is a branch of the discipline of knowledge elicitation and will use many techniques developed within that discipline. Requirements analysis, on the other hand, is the process of understanding the requirements that have been or are being elicited. This is where the requirements engineer will ask questions about the completeness and consistency of the knowledge discovered. This distinction is represented by the division of most work on requirements engineering into two fairly distinct camps. One group focuses on knowledge elicitation techniques and is represented by work that uses *inter alia* ethnomethodology, human factors theories, soft systems methods and ergonomics. A second group emphasizes formal methods of systems analysis. Examples range from traditional systems analysis approaches such as JSD (Jackson, 1983) to overtly mathematical formal methods such as VDM and Z. In the context of object-oriented development there have been several attempts to extend object-oriented analysis with formal theories.

One of the problems with formal specification is that it can actually ignore the true requirement just as easily as an informal document-oriented approach. An example will suffice to illustrate this. An infamous case occurred in the case of aircraft undercarriage design. A requirement was stated that an aeroplane's reverse thrusters should not cut in until the aircraft was in contact with the runway. The designers reasoned that one could only be sure that the plane had touched down when its wheels began to spin forwards; which would be the case when in contact with a runway or similar. Therefore they arranged the system such that the thrusters would fire automatically when the wheels so span. This worked very well ... until the first time the plane had to land on a runway covered with water and aquaplaned! The plane overshot the runway. So, even if the system can be proved to meet its specification – and there is no principled reason why this could not have been done in our aircraft example – then there is still no guarantee that the specification meets the true requirement. This is especially the case when there are conflicting requirements. In the example just given the conflict was between the need to eliminate human error and the need to land safely in all conditions. In the succeeding chapters we will see how SOMA offers help in this area.

Formal methods emphasize proving the correctness of the code against the specification. This is achieved by writing the specification in a language based on some variant of formal logic. Mathematical proofs of correctness may then be constructed. There are two major problems with this. First, the proofs require great mathematical skill and for large systems can be quite intractable. On the other hand the effort may be worthwhile for safety-critical systems or systems upon which mission-critical systems depend. One of the largest projects of this kind involved the specification of the CICS transaction monitor. The second defect is, in my opinion, far more damning. The problem is that using logic as a specification language is tantamount to programming in logic. All the formal proofs can do is to show the equivalence of the two programs; they say nothing at all about whether the specification meets the users' requirements. The approach presented in this book addresses precisely this problem, as we shall see.

Examples of object-oriented approaches to formal specification include Object Z (Carrington *et al.*, 1990; Duke *et al.*, 1991) and Paul Swatman's work on the FOOM modelling language based upon it (Swatman and Swatman, 1992). In this work the formal language is used to express contracts in the form of logical assertions. Catalysis (D'Souza and Wills, 1997) is another method that emphasizes formality but without the extensive use of mathematical notation. Syntropy (Cook and Daniels, 1994) uses state-transition diagrams to achieve similar ends. What all these approaches have in common is that they are chiefly concerned with analyzing requirements that are already known and understood. The methods say little about the knowledge elicitation process.

A similar comment can be made about the approach of Wieringa (1996) who provides extensive guidance on how to analyze requirements using functional decomposition, entity-relationship models and JSD; and emphasizing the production of written requirements specifications. The approach is basically an extension of Information Engineering or SSADM and, as such, would not suit either an object-oriented or evolutionary approach to development.

In contrast, approaches such as ETHICS (Mumford, 1986) stress participation and the optimization of the social and the technical aspects of systems. ETHICS (Effective Technical and Human Implementation of Computer-based Systems) advocates 12 main steps:

1. Specify the Work Mission.
2. Describe current activities and needs.
3. Consider and measure job satisfaction.
4. Decide on changes needed.
5. Set objectives for job satisfaction, efficiency and effectiveness.
6. Consider the organizational options.
7. Reorganize.
8. Select computer solutions.
9. Train the staff.
10. Redesign jobs.
11. Implement.
12. Evaluate.

ETHICS thus is strongly echoed by more recent work on business process re-engineering and workflow analysis, though it is less associated with rigid and bureaucratic workflow systems of the sort commonly implemented in Lotus Notes and the like. I feel that all the above 12 issues must be addressed during requirements engineering and systems analysis, though not necessarily in that order. Implicitly ETHICS encourages the empowerment of teams and the use of formal inspections to facilitate self-correction of defects. The major problem with ETHICS is that it provides no guidance on how to go about modelling itself, which is the critical success factor for step 8. Nor does it integrate ideas from business process re-engineering, rapid application development or object technology into its approach. Thus, while not ignoring the advances of ETHICS, we must go well beyond it.

Jackson (1995) emphasizes the use of problem frames in requirements understanding and analysis. His approach is fundamentally that of an analyst but he pays far more attention to the human issues than is traditional in requirements analysis. He stresses formality but without using the kind of alienating symbolism found in the formal methods tradition. Most importantly of all Jackson points out that the generality of a method is in inverse proportion to its applicability. To this end he proposes the building of a library of problem frames to cover commonly encountered problem types and appropriate methods to go with them. I shall have more to say about problem frames in Chapter 7 in the context of logical design.

Ethnography and ethnomethodological techniques, deriving from Anthropology, have been applied to requirements engineering in order to recognize that task analysis based on studies of individuals is flawed if it fails to recognize that all business activity takes place in a social context. The behaviour of groups is studied over some time and conclusions about requirements drawn. Suchman (1987) provides an excellent case study: applying the method to the design of photocopying machinery. We adopt an approach in Chapter 5 which focuses on networks of social commitments but does not require extensive observational studies; though these are by no means ruled out.

Participatory design is a general label for approaches that emphasize user involvement throughout the specification and design process. Leading proponents include Ehn (Ehn *et al.*, 1990, 1991). Requirements are not fixed at some arbitrary point as in conventional structured approaches. This view is consistent with the evolutionary process model outlined in this chapter. Also important to the advocates of participatory design is that systems should not be used to downgrade and de-skill users' work. Webster (1996) provides some pretty horrifying counter-examples in the context of the degradation of work when looked at from a gender specific viewpoint – and that includes the degradation (or elimination) of the work of both sexes. I believe that all relevant social factors should be taken into account when designing systems (including perhaps, age, gender, race and physical ability) and that designers have a social responsibility at least to *predict* the effects of their technology.

Research into human computer interaction has led to approaches based on user-centred and task-centred design. These can utilize direct user involvement, observational studies or even questionnaires and surveys. Eason (1989) is a leading exponent of user-centred design whose approach has much in common with ETHICS although socio-technical design and cost benefit analysis get more emphasis. The task-centred approach descends from the educational technology movement of the 1950s and 60s. User task analysis is a key influence on the approach presented in subsequent chapters but we combine these ideas with those of use cases, semiotics (part of ethnomethodology) and script theory from artificial intelligence. SOMA advocates the use of a number of other techniques, such as Kelly grids, derived from knowledge engineering. Chapter 5 presents several such techniques.

Quality function deployment or the so-called 'house of quality' has been put forward as a way of discovering users' requirements based on correlating them pairwise with product features. I believe that the techniques described in this book make this kind of approach superfluous.

The CREWS approach to requirements engineering (Maiden *et al.*, 1997) emphasizes techniques based on scenarios for checking that specifications are consistent and – more especially – complete. This important work is discussed further in Chapter 5, Section 5.8.

An approach to the analysis of workflow systems developed by Winograd and Flores (1986) has much to recommend it and is integrated into our approach as described in Chapter 5. It emphasizes the network of commitments that exists between the agents in a business and their sequenced conversations. However, the approach has been criticized for leading to over rigid work practices in the implementations that it arrives at. I believe that this can be overcome by delving deeper than the workflow aspects of the conversations and analyzing the users' tasks as well. We will return at length to the subject of Flores nets, as they are known, in Chapter 5.

ORCA (Object-Oriented Requirements Capture and Analysis) (MacLean *et al.,* 1994) represents one of the few attempts to make requirements engineering for object-oriented development rigorous in any way. It advocates the use of soft systems style 'rich pictures' as a starting point and then, like SOMA and Syntropy, makes a clear distinction between models of the world and models of intended systems. ORCA's approach relies on the differentiation of *purposive* and *behavioural* entities and provides two distinct notations to represent each aspect of its models. Purposive entities are things not directly observable, such as countries, and correspond to the SOMA agents that will be introduced in Chapter 5. Behavioural entities correspond to SOMA classes. MacLean *et al.* (1994) point out that the two may coincide, as in the case of organizational structures. Here the correspondence is with the agent classes of SOMA that internalize agents in the computer system. Clearly, ORCA has some points in common with SOMA, not least in addressing requirements engineering at all – unlike most other object-oriented methods. However, there are differences, among which is ORCA's inability to provide a formal link between its two modelling languages and its reliance on a good deal of modelling techniques derived from entity-relationship approaches; e.g. bi-directional associations and even SSADM-style exclusion arcs are permitted in ORCA.

ORCA emphasizes business process re-engineering and the environment in which systems are embedded. In this sense it is innovative and powerful. However, its use of object modelling techniques is somewhat pedestrian. Workshops and rapid development are not stressed, but business objectives are discussed as part of the knowledge discovery process.

ORCA's world model consists of objects that represent purposive entities and the contracts that exist between them, expressed in term of services with pre- and post-conditions and constraints (class invariants). These classes may also embed non-functional requirements (to the credit of the method). From this model a behavioural model (basically a conventional object model) is intuited and then described using a mixture of extended entity-relationship diagrams and diagrams that are essentially an extension of UML sequence diagrams, though with clearer semantics and less related to the program code. A key contribution of ORCA is the provision of formal syntax for both its modelling languages. This enables the models to be checked more easily for consistency and errors and is the main basis for ORCA's claim to be rigorous. ORCA cannot however, and despite this rigour, prove that its system model meets the requirements as stated in the world model. We will see in the Chapter 5 that it is the ability to do precisely this that lays the foundation for the claim that SOMA is rigorous – though SOMA has no formal syntax defined currently.

Soft systems research (Checkland, 1981; Checkland and Scholes, 1991) is concerned with apprehending an entire, situated problem in the context of an organization and the purposes of the whole problem solving activity. Emphasis is on elicitation of behaviour and problem dynamics from multiple perspectives. The foundation of soft systems work was in general systems theory and Cybernetics. Clearly, the same traditions are at the root of approaches to business process re-engineering such as that of Senge (1990). The approach usually begins by drawing a so-called rich picture of the problem situation. Such a picture is not unlike a freehand, annotated SOMA business process model.

RE AND SOMA

This section has only provided a brief and fairly cursory review of approaches to requirements engineering (RE), since my main purpose is to present my own approach. Many of the techniques for requirements engineering described only briefly in this section have been incorporated into SOMA and I acknowledge my debt to them. In Chapters 4 and 5 we begin to construct a rounded approach based on the use of object models to represent knowledge about requirements and businesses. The approach will emphasize the need to prove that system specifications actually do service the requirements as represented. This is the basis of my claim that the approach is rigorous. Mathematical formalism is possible within SOMA but we choose not to go down that route in this book – and indeed in the vast majority of practical problems that we face from day to day.

We conclude with a brief digression, comparing the features of SOMA with those of soft systems, since I am often asked what the connexion is. It may be safely omitted at a first reading since it assumes some knowledge of SOMA concepts not yet defined in the text.

COMPARING SOMA WITH SOFT SYSTEMS METHODS

It is possible to make a number of specific remarks concerning the relationship between Checkland's (1981) soft systems method (SSM) and SOMA as there are evident similarities. Checkland's famous mnemonic, CATWOE – standing for: Customers, Actors, Transformation processes, Weltanschauung, Owners and Environment – is used within SSM as a guide to what the components of a system model should cover. These items have a direct correspondence with SOMA concepts as shown in Table 2.1. Furthermore, Checkland's concept of a root definition for the system problem corresponds to our mission statement in a direct manner.

In SOMA, as a system modelling approach, we are not concerned with the fine distinction Checkland and Scholes (1991) make between the system as a model of the world and the world as a system. It is not relevant here precisely because we are modelling. Also, I agree with these authors on the importance of the active rôle of the subject in cognition but disagree that there is no objective basis to cognitive acts.

The world is a system in some objective sense but 'system' is also a subjective idea imposed on it. However, in SOMA we do have a 'world model' in the form of the Agent and Task Object Models and a 'system model' in the shape of the

Business Object Model. This text is not the place to explore these important philosophical ideas further. In practice there is no problem in using SOMA as a method for modelling soft systems and its fuzzy extensions are particularly apposite.

The SSM requirements engineering process is also remarkably similar to SOMA. In the former there are seven stages which have been annotated with their SOMA equivalents in Table 2.2.

Table 2.1 SOMA and the Soft Systems Method

SSM	*SOMA*
Customers = victims or beneficiaries of T	External agents = Stakeholders, Users, sponsors, regulators, external systems, etc.
Actors = those who would do T	Actors, Internal agents
Transformation process (T) = conversion of input to output	The System
Weltanschauung = Worldview that gives meaning to T in context	Goals, Objectives, measures, assumptions, exclusions, etc.
Owners = those who could stop T	Sponsors
Environmental constraints = elements outside the system over which we have no influence	External objects, timers, assumptions, etc.

Table 2.2 SSM stages and SOMA techniques

SSM	*SOMA*
Find out about problem situation	Mission grid, Objectives, Agent Object Model
Express the situation (rich picture)	Agent Object Model
Select viewpoint and produce root definitions	Mission grid, Objectives, Agent Object Model
Build conceptual models of what the system must do for each root definition	Agent Object Model
Compare the conceptual model with the world	Task Object Model, Business Object Model, Walkthrough/Event trace
Identify feasible and desirable changes	Objectives, Workshop discussions

2.2 The need for incremental development

One way to assist developers to elicit requirements is for them to build prototypes. Such activity has become associated with a more iterative style of development. This section examines such approaches with a view to integrating them into the process model developed in the next.

According to a report by the Standish Group, published in 1995, of some 250,000 development projects in the US in 1995 one third were cancelled, costing $80,000m with a further $60,000m estimated for cost and delivery overruns. Why is this so? The report advances several reasons reported by survey participants as follows:

- a lack of user involvement throughout projects;
- no clear statement of requirements agreed at the outset;
- no ownership of the project by the business;
- no clear vision and objectives agreed and shared between the business and the development organization;
- a lack of project planning disciplines.

In this book, we characterize rapid or joint application development as a technique that uses joint user and developer workshops to establish clear, prioritized objectives and outline requirements at the start of a project, involves users throughout it and delivers increments of useful behaviour at regular intervals. Large programmes are decomposed into smaller projects involving no more than about six people and lasting no longer than about six months. The process is managed by a rigorous régime of time-boxes, ensuring that delivery deadlines are met even if there is negotiation on the scope of what is delivered – based on the agreed priorities of course. The benefits of a workshop-based approach are manifold:

- Workshop costs are often lower than those for multiple interviews.
- They help to give structure to the requirements capture and analysis process.
- Workshops are dynamic, interactive and co-operative. They involve users and cut across organizational boundaries.
- They help to identify and prioritize needs and resolve contentious issues.
- If properly run, they help to manage users' expectations and attitude to change.

According to Rush (1985) requirements workshops are up to five times more efficient than the traditional interview-based approach.

For me, having facilitated something like 50 RAD workshops over the last ten years, the one message that shines through about this approach is that it builds a concrete, shared understanding of the problem and its solution among all the stakeholders: users and developers. However, nearly all my experience recently has been with an approach that combines object-orientation with rapid application development. The reason that this works in building this shared understanding is predicated on the nature of the modelling technique itself. That is to say that we should believe that people from all backgrounds can think naturally in terms of objects – and this insofar as I have found that starting a session with an explanation of the object-oriented approach is actually counter-productive. Users especially tend to think in this way about their world. They do not think naturally and without a lot of guidance in terms of data flow diagrams or entity-relationship models.

⊟ 2.3 Principles of dynamic system development

The Dynamic Systems Development Method (DSDM) is a 'framework of controls for rapid application development' (Stapleton, 1997). Unlike OPEN or SOMA, there are no prescribed techniques. DSDM has a rudimentary and high level process model that can be tailored for individual organizations' requirements. It was developed as a potentially standard approach by a consortium of 17 UK user organizations in 1994 that now has over 1,000 members world-wide. It eschews affiliation to any particular style of development and Version 2 removed any reference to object technology for this reason. This was perhaps fortunate because the few remarks that the Version 1 manual made about object-orientation (OO) were largely wrong. On the other hand the view taken by the DSDM Consortium – that OO is a mere technique – is arguable from my point of view that characterizes OO as a general method of knowledge representation. DSDM has nine fundamental principles, all of which SOMA adheres to totally. They are:

1. Active user involvement is imperative.
2. Teams are empowered to make decisions.
3. The focus is on the frequent delivery of products.
4. Fitness for business purpose is the essential criterion for acceptance of deliverables.
5. Iterative development and incremental delivery are necessary to converge on an accurate business solution.
6. All changes during development are reversible.
7. Requirements are defined at a high level.
8. Testing is integrated throughout the life-cycle.
9. A collaborative and co-operative approach between all stakeholders is essential.

These principles enable an organization to determine whether a particular project is suitable for the approach. For example, if you know perfectly well that under no circumstances will a representative sample of users be available, then forget it. Of course under many circumstances it may be permissible to make do with representatives of users, rather than the users themselves. Although this is not ideal, it is usually better than returning to the old, rigid, ineffective way of doing things.

Figure 2.1 illustrates the DSDM development process model. The approach starts with feasibility and business studies, which are followed by three iterative and overlapping phases: essentially based on the spiral model.

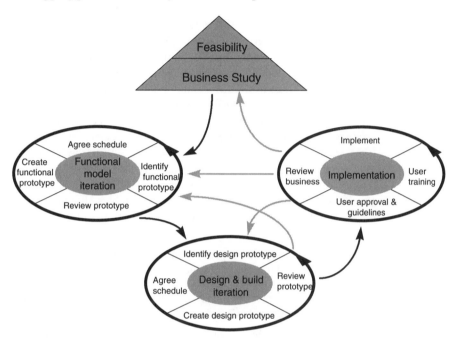

Figure 2.1 The DSDM development process model (after Stapleton, 1997)

DSDM is not entirely suitable for object-oriented development because it cannot perforce assume the kind of flexibility that an object-oriented approach gives. Nor does it support any notion of contract-driven or responsibility-driven design or development. It is necessary to modify the life cycle to take full advantage of object technology. DSDM has no model of reuse management. Nor does it have a formal notion of a 'programme' decomposing into smaller 'projects' as do, for example, both OPEN and SOMA. Furthermore, DSDM fails to distinguish adequately between process and product life-cycles. These issues are discussed in Section 2.4, where we will see that DSDM phases can be reconciled with the object-oriented contract-driven life-cycle model of SOMA and OPEN.

What DSDM does give is a framework that can be informed with the concrete political and organizational characteristics of a project. The commitment to time-boxing (principle 3) means that milestones are equated with deliverables, making the approach very product oriented. Testing is performed throughout the life-cycle, rather than as an end-stage activity, and this leads to far higher quality and far fewer implementation surprises. Very importantly, the products and documentation mandated by DSDM are as minimal as possible, while still ensuring adequate quality and progress towards delivery and maintenance. Unfortunately, if an object-oriented approach is not adopted there can be no guarantee that the resultant system will be easy to maintain in the face of further evolution of the requirements – as was explained in detail in Chapter 1.

We have already noted that DSDM is product oriented. However, SOMA is stricter than DSDM in enforcing the frequent delivery of operational components than DSDM. The latter has to compromise slightly because the products of conventional development are typically coarser grained than those of object-oriented development. Thus, in DSDM a data model might be the end product of a time box. In an object-oriented RAD method we can argue that all the object models produced are, at least potentially, executable – as we shall see later. In either method, this product focus is far more flexible than a task-oriented approach whereby low level tasks are assigned to individual team members. With the latter regimen it is much harder for a team to modify tasks to meet a deadline and it is here that principle 2 (empowerment) finds its apotheosis.

Principle 9 not only implies that team members should include both users and development staff, it mandates certain organizational principles too. As Stapleton (1997) points out:

> 'Some organizations put up artificial barriers between different parts of the IT department. *It is useless* for the application development staff to put a system together quickly, if the operational staff do not view its take-on as important and delay it because of their own conflicting set of priorities.' (*emphasis added*)

Thus, an organization that maintains traditional mainframe-oriented user acceptance testing (UAT) and roll-out practices or one that has maintenance and engineering teams that report to a different line management from that of the developers will find RAD far more difficult to implement and far less beneficial.

DSDM, like OOSE (Jacobson *et al.,* 1992), restricts users' attention to the user interface. This is perfectly valid for simple MIS systems or for the specification of machinery such as vending machines or telecommunications switches, but it is far from adequate for more complex systems as we shall see in Chapter 5. SOMA's requirements engineering techniques allow the analysis to 'penetrate' the user interface in order to build a shared understanding of how the system will actually work. Recognizing this limitation perhaps, DSDM is not advanced as suitable for applications with any computational complexity. That this need not apply, at least, to an object-oriented RAD method is evinced by my experience in the financial services industry where there are often complex calculations behind option pricing or the generation of yield curves or volatility surfaces and where SOMA has proved successful.

DSDM, in common with SOMA, recommends an approach to prototyping that parallels our approach to knowledge discovery in general. We proceed with a broad and shallow analysis (prototype) covering all the key features of the target system in outline. This is followed by an in depth analysis (prototype) of one area of the problem. Here there are three possibilities:

1. tackle the easiest area first to boost developers' confidence;
2. tackle the area that solves 80% of the business need first; or
3. tackle the area with the greatest technical challenge first.

The first approach is seldom the right one, because there can be some nasty shocks awaiting the team downstream and because it is not a good way to impress users with the team's skills. A combination of the other two approaches is ideal. With an object-oriented approach to the analysis, far more emphasis must be placed on the search for potentially reusable components as each successive functional area is attacked. The focus too is on the essential requirements early on, rather than those features that the users (or developers) would like the system to have ideally.

DSDM recommends the use of specialist human computer interaction consultants. I disagree fundamentally with the separation of the user interface design from the design of the system as a whole. It is not possible to design a good interface to a system with an inappropriate architecture. My solution is to ensure that sufficient developers are skilled in user interface design.

Finally DSDM introduces a fourfold categorization of prototypes as follows:

- business prototypes (or demonstrators);
- capability/design prototypes;
- performance and capacity prototypes;
- usability prototypes.

This reflects the separation of functional and design iterations in the DSDM life cycle (Figure 2.1) and is incompatible with a more seamless object-oriented approach such as the one described in this book. We instead distinguish only research, throwaway and evolutionary prototypes. This also reflects my view that it is quite wrong to separate functional and non-functional requirements.

⊟ 2.4 How and why object technology helps

A tradition of prototyping has long been associated with object-oriented programming and, indeed, with 4GLs and artificial intelligence. Unfortunately, many practitioners in these fields were prone to a fairly undisciplined style of development that focused on issues of technical elegance at the expense of more commercial considerations. This gave prototyping and even incremental development something of a bad name. As we will see in the next section, it is now possible to control and manage projects that use this approach and to do so in a manner totally compatible with object-oriented development.

The features of object-oriented programming languages that make them particularly suitable for a rapid application development approach are precisely those that we examined in Chapter 1: the reusability that arises from tight encapsulation and the extensibility which inheritance makes possible. Systems can be added to without destabilizing already working components. In an ideal situation we can also build initial prototypes very quickly indeed by reusing existing components. Anyone who has used a modern development environment (such as Delphi, Visual Age or MS Studio) will have been the grateful recipient of this benefit.

Encapsulation protects prototypers from needed changes to implementations caused by the need for efficiency improvements and other exigencies arising from non-functional specifications. Inheritance guards them from functional changes because they can add a new subclass instead of changing and re-testing an existing component. However, this will only work – as I have argued – if the interfaces are well designed in the first place. This is the apotheosis of object-oriented analysis and design.

Prototyping and rapid development will benefit from the use of existing components but there are some dangers. Components are not fully specified by their signatures but need rulesets to complete their description. Although methods such as SOMA and Catalysis recognise this, most object-oriented programming languages do not. Therefore, organizations that are serious about the approach need to adopt and understand a suitable method, or hazard that their developers will not be able to reconcile component oriented development with rapid delivery and high rates of system evolution.

Another, completely different way in which object technology helps is precisely in the area of requirements elicitation and analysis. It is one of the key arguments of this book that an object-oriented approach to requirements engineering is natural for users and can be made so for developers. In Chapters 3 and 5 we will begin to explore this issue in detail. Before doing so we will examine a process whereby object-oriented projects can be managed with speed, flexibility and confidence.

2.5 The development process

The development process of SOMA is compliant with the OPEN process (Graham *et al.*, 1997) and refines the wisdom to be found in DSDM. In this section I give a brief summary of the SOMA object-oriented development life cycle. The reader who requires more detail is referred to Graham (1995) and Graham *et al.* (1997a).

2.5.1 Managing projects by contract

Waterfall models are inherently unsuitable for rapid development, as has been widely recognized. Attempts to replace them with spiral models are unconvincing mainly because the latter are essentially 'wound up' waterfall models. Also, we should be aware of the need for some special guidance in the context of object-oriented development.

It was probably Brian Henderson-Sellers who first observed that while software engineers with an interest in measurement have always distinguished process metrics from product metrics, no-one had ever clarified the equally important distinction between the product and process life-cycles. This elementary observation allows us to assert a **product life cycle** that is a simple waterfall with three stages: Plan; Build; Deliver. We simultaneously assert a **process life cycle** which is nothing like a waterfall, a spiral or any other conventional model.

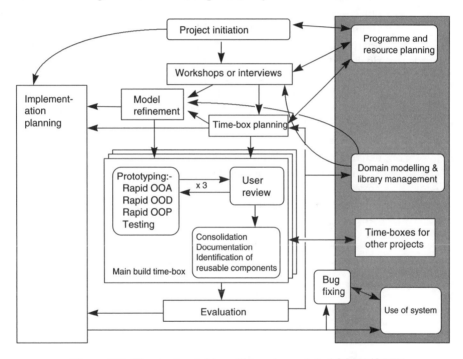

Figure 2.2 The contract driven life cycle model of SOMA/OPEN

When we discuss the nature of modelling in Chapter 4, we will see that object models can be applied to many topics other than software. It follows that we can model the stages of the waterfall model as three objects representing overlapping **stages**, connected by messages (usage links) representing permissible transitions. We can do the same in the process dimension and build a *bona fide* object model of the development process. The process life cycle object model realizes the build stage of the product life cycle object model.

Figure 2.2 illustrates SOMA's contract-driven process life cycle. In this diagram, the rectangles are objects that represent project **activities**. The arrows that connect the activity objects are messages that represent valid 'transitions' between activities; specifically such a message will trigger or enable a method of the target activity object: a **task**. Thus the operations (methods) of activities are system development tasks that the project team must or may execute. All such transitions are guarded by pre-conditions that represent contracts between activities. For this reason the model is called the **contract driven life cycle**.

TIME BOXES

A **time-box** sets a rigid limit to prototype iterations to ensure management control over prototyping. A small team is mandatory and the tested prototype is both end point and deliverable. Time-boxed development is highly beneficial, whether object-oriented tools are in use or otherwise, and there is a growing amount of empirical evidence for this. There is some evidence that maintainability is improved but only when throwaway prototypes are not allowed to evolve into the final product. There is little empirical support for the idea that rapid prototyping cannot be used for developing large systems.

The time-box technique offers the following benefits. It imposes management control over ripple effects and uncontrolled iteration. Control is achieved by setting a rigid elapsed time limit on the prototyping cycle and using a small project team. Furthermore, it has a usable system as both the end-point of the process and its deliverable. There is no distinction between production, evolution and maintenance as with conventional approaches, which usually ignore maintenance costs during project justification.

The time-box tackles the following management issues:

■ Wants *versus* needs: by forcing requirements to be prioritized by negotiation between users and developers. Users and the project team are forced to concentrate on the real needs of the business.

■ Creeping functionality: in the traditional life cycle the long delay between specification and delivery can lead to users requesting extra features. The use of a time limit reduces this tendency.

■ Project team motivation: the developers can see a tangible result of their efforts emerging.

■ The involvement of users at every stage reduces implementation shock.

The approach reduces time to market, not by a magic trick that makes difficult things easy, but by delivering an important, usable subset of the entire system in no more than a few months.

It is absolutely critical to maintain credibility; build on success and manage expectations during the development process. This is achieved by several means. Users should be warned that a quickly developed prototype may conceal much complexity. A working system will take time in proportion to the complexity of the tasks that it assists with. Equally, users should be stimulated by many small, incremental deliveries. With SOMA, they agree prioritized objectives and developers should show that corners that are cut to keep within time limits are low priority corners. Developers can thus afford to accept reasonable changes to requirements, provided that existing, low priority requirements can be eliminated by mutual agreement based on the priorities. This expectation management is a key task for the project manager. If it is neglected the project will usually fail. The technique prevents paralysis by analysis, errors due to delay, spurious requirements and implementation shock. It usually motivates teams better than the waterfall approach.

SOMA, like DSDM, insists of the use of time-boxes to control projects. Figure 2.2 thus distinguishes unbounded from bounded activities. Unbounded activities have no elapsed time limits and are represented by rounded rectangles. As objects they are merely stereotyped as 'unbounded'. Bounded activities, or time-boxes, are shown by proper rectangles. They are subject to a defined end date as soon as they are first entered. The entire project is to be regarded as bounded by a **project time box** (not illustrated), although project initiation will usually overlap its boundary.

The project time box is normally limited to a maximum of six months, although it could be much shorter. Clearly this would exclude many major development efforts from the use of SOMA if we did not assert some way of decomposing large problems to a scale suitable for rapid development. Therefore we distinguish between a project and a programme. A **programme** is an aggregate of one or more projects.

The grey area to the right of the diagram shows extra-project activities that are outside the project and its encompassing time box. Its first activity is programme and resource planning. This activity involves the break up of the definition of the programme vision and its decomposition into scheduled projects, together with the sourcing and allocation of the resources that these projects will need.

To help understand the model of Figure 2.2 let us walk through its activities in a typical order. Project initiation always begins a project and often starts within programme and resource planning. It has no time limits because sometimes thinking up new ideas can take years. Typically it consumes few resources but it could involve substantial effort in certain cases; such as building a proof of concept demonstrator or writing a detailed proposal and business case. In SOMA our philosophy is to test everything as it is produced. One consequence of this principle is that transitions between activities are also guarded by post-conditions; usually by requiring the existence of a deliverable, tested product. The only such test applied to project initiation is the existence of a Project Initiation Form signed by an executive sponsor with appropriate financial authority. That's all! How the project team obtain that signature is another matter entirely. It may be necessary to produce a 500 page cost-benefit analysis or it might be obtained just by saying: 'trust me, I'm a developer'. Either way the project can only proceed when the signature is dry on the page.

Signing the project initiation document triggers or enables several other activities, the most crucial of which is the primary requirements elicitation activity. SOMA, in particular, insists on workshops to help build shared understanding. Therefore we usually label this box Workshops, although interviews may be used in extreme necessity. The details of the workshop activity are described in detail in the next chapter. The product of the activity is a report describing the requirements together with the various object models to be described in subsequent chapters. The other activity that might start once initiation is definite (and it could be cancelled by the outcome of the workshop) is the implementation planning activity. This is where the commissioning of hardware, office accommodation and the like is planned and expedited. It may include the procurement of such items as a user acceptance testing environment or the planning of high volume stress testing prior to live operation.

After the workshop passes its post-condition hurdle – the sign-off of the workshop report – we can activate time-box planning and model refinement. Time-box planning is a conventional project management activity that produces and publishes plans for the Main Build time-box. Model refinement takes the Business Object Model produced in the workshop and refines its logical analysis and design, incorporates architectural standards and includes components from the reuse repository along with those already imported during the workshop. A systems analysis report is produced and agreed with the project steering committee as the post-condition on this activity.

Now we are ready to roll with the main Build. The prototyping sub-activity rolls up analysis, design, coding and testing but in no particular order. If you like to design carefully before doing any coding, then so be it. If, on the other hand, you are the kind of developer who likes to design while coding, then that's OK too. All that matters is that the results of tested code and design documentation are produced to the agreed standards. Also the user review activity embeds a level of user acceptance testing into the process. The diagram indicates that about three iterations between these two sub-activities is appropriate but this is not a hard and fast rule. Notice that the final iteration may demand the creation of a realistic user acceptance testing environment, depending on organizational circumstances. Note also that the activities labelled Rapid OOA and Rapid OOD are essentially the same as the model refinement activity. Finally, when the users on the team are happy or the time-box is due to expire the work must be consolidated with results from earlier or parallel time-boxes and the documentation checked for quality and completeness. At this stage the team may nominate some of the classes that it has produced as potentially reusable, though it will not try to make them up to reusable levels of quality, because this would take too long.

The team has full authority to negotiate on the scope of the application to be delivered. As we will see in Chapters 3 and 5, this negotiation is based on a set of prioritized objectives obtained during the initial requirements workshop. These objectives are not meant to be negotiable, but their relative priorities provide an objective basis for deciding what system components can be omitted in order to do two critical things:

- meet the time-box deadline; and
- modify the requirements according to the users' most current understanding.

The latter point is crucial in distinguishing the rapid application development approach from more bureaucratic methods; requirements are **not** fixed but business objectives and delivery dates **are**.

If everything is in order, we proceed to Evaluation. This is a meeting attended by the team and third parties that were nominated during time-box planning. It can only make one of three decisions:

1. Deliver the system into use.
2. Abandon the project as infeasible.
3. Rework the entire project.

Absolutely no other decision is allowed. There is to be no whinging about details of how the system might be improved and most certainly the evaluation team is not empowered to introduce any delay short of complete cancellation of delivery. I have found that this is the biggest source of misunderstanding about the SOMA process. If enforced properly it works well; but it must be clearly understood by all concerned: users, managers and developers.

The bug fixing activity will be discussed below in the context of reuse management.

The full specification of the activities of the contract-driven model, their tasks and pre- and post-conditions is beyond the scope of this text. It is given in Graham (1995) and Graham *et al.* (1997). We will only note that each task is classified by one of the following five levels of 'duty':

- Mandatory   You must always perform this task.
- Recommended   You must formally justify not performing this task.
- Optional   You can perform this task or not according to your own judgment.
- Discouraged   You must formally justify performing this task.
- Forbidden   You should never perform this task.

Similarly, each task is associated with a number of techniques which may also be mandatory, recommended, forbidden and so on in relation to a specific task. For example, the design activity has a task called 'construct design level class model' and the Booch design method is a recommended or optional technique, depending on the views of the organization concerned.

PARALLEL TIME BOXES   Combining results from different projects and time-boxes presents some additional problems to the project manager. It is rarely completely straightforward for large (e.g. five month) projects. A simple but effective rule of thumb is to double the estimates when a large parallel time-box is used. Merging and consolidating can take nearly as long as building something from scratch and is quite likely to lead the users to modify some of their requirements when they see the combined results. Where very small (e.g. one week) time-boxes are involved this is less of a problem, although some extra time should still be allowed for.

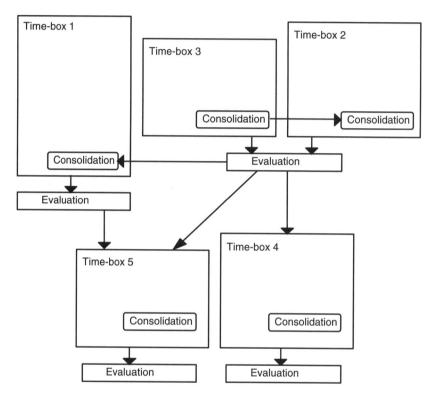

Figure 2.3 Combining results from multiple projects

Figure 2.3 shows a schematic of how the results from parallel projects and time-boxes combine.

2.5.2 Reuse management

As I have said, making objects of sufficient quality to be genuinely reusable with good, stable well-defined interfaces, is not possible within the constraints imposed by rapid and time-box oriented development. I advocate the establishment of a separate reuse team to do this. However, commercial experience of such separated teams has been generally poor. The reason for this is that they quickly become isolated from the businesses and development teams that they serve and ossify into ivory towers with concerns of their own and less and less knowledge of what is really needed. To overcome this Graham (1995) advanced the idea of the 'hairies and conscripts' model for reuse management.

Figure 2.4 shows two alternative resource profiles for a software project. The dotted line shows the true resource loading during the lifetime of the project but the solid line shows how the typical project manager allocates resources: grabbing all he expects to need at the outset and holding on to them until the end of the time-box. This dichotomy has a number of interesting effects. First, the under-utilization indicated by the area marked A may be used for learning and generally getting up to speed. The area marked B indicates a period of hard work, long hours and often heightened angst. But the under-utilization labelled C is not the ideal way to relax and recuperate; it is usually a boring time and is always wasteful. Developers deserve a genuine break after the high intensity work and stress that characterizes time-box based development. Adopting the view that a change is as good as a rest, we can advocate that the developers so under-utilized can take one of two routes. They can be assigned to hand-holding and fixing the inevitable post-implementation bugs: the bug fixing activity. Or, they can be 'conscripted' to a sabbatical with the reuse or library team for a period.

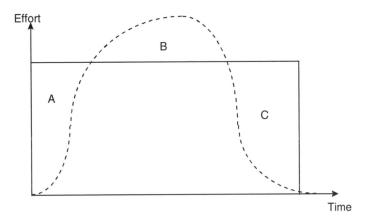

Figure 2.4 Project resource profiles

This reuse team must be populated by permanent staff too: people dedicated to software excellence who are responsible for the architecture of the library and knowing its contents inside out. Unfortunately perhaps, such skills are not always to be found in the same individuals as the customer facing skills that RAD developers need so crucially. Graham originally characterized the library staff as 'hairies' by analogy with the IBM systems programmers of the 1960s, who were often bearded, besandled and replete with anorak and train spotters' manual – but *very* good at their job. The resultant 'hairies and conscripts' model of reuse management is then a model of knowledge interchange designed to prevent the reuse initiative becoming a separate ivory tower. Developers (the conscripts) take the business knowledge that they have acquired on their projects into the library domain along with the new classes that they will help make more reusable. During their sojourn in the library they learn reuse and architectural skills from the librarians and, what is more important, learn what is in the other parts of the library. When they return to their next project they then act as reuse ambassadors and mentors to other team members.

REUSE LIBRARY MODELS

The outstanding specific issues raised by reuse that we must discuss concern co-ordinating products from the repository, managing updates to the repository and releasing updates to the repository.

Henderson-Sellers and Pant (1993) describe four different models of reuse co-ordination. In their **end of life cycle** model the generalization activity is carried out after projects complete. My observation has been that there is a severe danger that this activity is omitted due to the demands of new projects for the newly released personnel who are the ones expected to carry out the generalization. Even if these resources are made available, as Henderson-Sellers and Pant point out, it is unlikely that the customer will be altruistic enough to fund the apparent extension to his project after he has taken delivery of a satisfactory end-product. The obvious alternative is to make developers responsible for creating reusable classes during the project. Menzies *et al.* (1992) call this the G-C1 model. I refer to it as the **constant-creation** model. The arguments for this approach are strong. The costs can be attributed to the customer during development. Furthermore, good developers have a tendency to produce reusable code 'as a silk worm produces silk'; as a by-product of what they are doing anyway. However, in practice this increases costs and increases time to market and is often the victim of time pressures within projects. Obviously, nothing should be done to discourage the production of high quality, reusable classes during projects but it cannot be enforced in practice. When this régime is in place we tend to observe a lot of source code copying and improvement rather than subclassing. To overcome problems with both these approaches Henderson-Sellers and Pant suggest two models, appropriate for small to average and very large companies respectively: the **two-library** model and the **alternative cost-centre** model.

The SOMA version of the two-library model is illustrated schematically in Figure 2.5. Here there is a library of potentially reusable classes identified during projects and another of fully generalized and adopted classes maintained by the domain team. How an object's potential for reuse can be determined is almost impossible to legislate for. Business knowledge and development skills combine to determine the result in concrete circumstances. Developers will typically ask if the concept is important to the business, likely to be used in other systems, fundamental to technical components of applications and so on. Attentive readers will have already noticed that SOMA uses a two-library approach. In *SOMATiK*, the two-library model is represented within a single repository database by introducing the concept of **signing**. Additions to the repository may be viewed, and may be edited. However, they cannot be downloaded until a duly authorized accessor of the repository has *signed* the element. This locks the element (preventing further editing) and at the same time enables it for downloading into other projects.

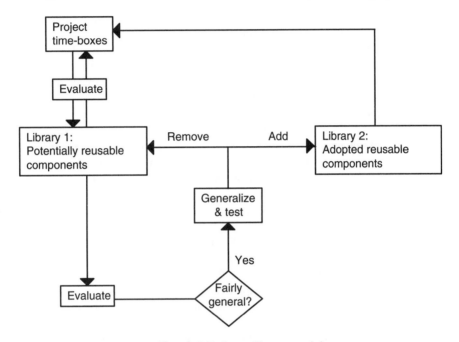

Figure 2.5 A two-library model

The only additional effort specific to the project in this approach is the recognition of potentially reusable classes and the extra cost is almost nil. As we have seen, early on in projects, from RAD workshops to prototyping in the time-box, library components are scanned. If the classes identified in this way happen to reside in Library 1 then an additional generalization cost is incurred by the project, but this is entirely as it should be and the costs can be happily borne by the sponsor. The two-library model directly addresses the danger of over-generalization alluded to earlier.

The alternative cost-centre model involves creating and funding a separate cost-centre centrally. It is not funded by projects and initially runs at a loss, costs being recovered by selling classes to projects long-term. This model is only thought to be appropriate for very large organizations. SOMA is compatible with this approach too, as long as the hairies and conscripts technique is firmly applied.

2.5.3 Project rôles and responsibilities

This subsection details the responsibility to the project of each rôle in which people interact with the project. It provides definitions of all rôles referred to elsewhere in this book.

PROJECT RÔLES

The **project sponsor** is the individual who is responsible for the project, has authority to approve initial and continued expenditure on it and authority to approve implementation of any changes to production systems. The sponsor pays the bills and is thus of key importance. S/he should be kept informed of all significant milestones and involved in review points, especially evaluations. The sponsor will sign off each workshop, analysis document, time-box deliverable and change of plan.

Responsibility for day-to-day management of a project is given to a **project manager** or **project leader** from either the development department or a user department. The project manager may be a developer as well. S/he should possess all key project management skills and be responsible for steering committee and sponsor liaison. Project leaders are responsible for the technical and commercial success of the project, and for maintaining quality standards through the development. Both may act as **time-box managers**.

Specific responsibilities of project managers include: ensuring all work carried out is covered by defined tasks as contained in the plans for the project; reviewing the proposals with specific reference to exposure to risk, ensuring all methods used by the individual are appropriate and are consistent with the project's overall objectives for quality, cost and duration; checking the quality of their own work before indicating its completion; ensuring that all necessary communication channels with other groups have been established; identifying and resolving issues and problems which influence the quality, duration or cost of the project as a whole; considering the implications of the new system on the production environment; managing changes requested by users; and diagnosing and resolving problems.

DEVELOPERS

The **developer** has a key rôle in the process. The developer's skill set may/must include C++, Java, Smalltalk, operating system skills, client management, finance, pragmatism, GUI design, project management, database techniques and object-oriented analysis/design. In SOMA the developer is **not** responsible for making classes reusable but only for spotting opportunities for reuse. Evidence shows (Henderson-Sellers and Edwards, 1994) that practice helps developers do this earlier in the process. There are not analysts, designers, coders, etc. There are just developers. This implies that horizontal stratification is the order of the day rather than vertical structuring. Standard career grades are obsolete. This does not imply that there is no division of labour or that special skills are not exploited. It does imply a flat organizational structure and a flexible approach.

A key developer sub-rôle is that of system **architect**. This rôle provides the overall technical vision for the system and ensures that standards and issues such as extensibility and reusability are properly attended to. The DSDM rôles of technical co-ordinator and visionary are usually subsumed into this rôle.

Domain analysts in the reuse team need broad business knowledge and the skills and dispositions of the systems programmer; an impossible combination it seems. The job should rotate until suitable staff are discovered by trial and error. Domain analysis for reuse is a long term investment that will pay off when RAD workshops begin to use its products. At the outset there may be only small visible benefits. Subsection 2.5.2 outlined the rôle of the domain analyst in the context of the hairies and conscripts model.

USERS

Best practice in system development places emphasis on rapid application development; hence the degree of user involvement will be high. In order for the RAD process to be successful, users must also supply a number of devoted resources, ones that are aware of the business requirements relating to the development.

Users are responsible for approving progress at major project milestones, in that the project sponsor has to sign off documentation at the end of each activity. Users have to perform acceptance tests, having previously written the acceptance test plan based on the event traces produced in workshops. They should be made responsible for generating test data for this activity.

Users agree to the project being migrated to the production environment by a mutually agreed date and decide whether the cut-over has been successful.

The user is no less important than the developer. Users ideally need computer awareness, management skills, enthusiasm and commitment. However, we recognize that only unskilled users are not busy and that project involvement will not always be full time. It must however be a committed and planned involvement.

A **lead user** should be appointed to resolve disputes. This person will be one respected by other users and need not always be the most heavily involved in terms of time spent. Our lead user corresponds somewhat to what DSDM calls an *ambassador* user. Many users will only be consulted on an *ad hoc* basis and these then correspond to the *adviser* users of DSDM.

The project manager should possess all key project management skills and be responsible for user and sponsor liaison.

WORKSHOP RÔLES

The participants in a workshop are the sponsor, the users, the facilitator, the requirements engineer or scribe, the project leader and the team members. The rôles of the sponsor, facilitator and requirements engineer are discussed fully in the next chapter.

MENTORS

When an organization is beginning the move to object technology as a whole or just to a new technique, method or language, it is highly likely to benefit from employing a **mentor**. This is someone who understands the new skill, can explain it and, preferably, has done it before. This person is often a consultant from outside the organization but this need not be so. A mentor must be prepared to teach by doing and by demonstration as well as by running courses. The developers must also be prepared to learn by apprenticeship to mentors.

Particular classes of mentor include language specialists, system architects, methodologists and integration specialists. A number of companies offer mentoring services.

A project with a mentor on it may not produce an ideal product. The mentor may not be perfect. However, the key benefit comes from the learning experience itself and even if the mentor's ideas and the product produced are totally discarded and rewritten successfully at a later stage, then the mentoring can be seen to have been a success. Without it the results would have been worse and the staff would be incapable of even making this kind of critical observation.

OTHER ROLES

The **change controller** has the key rôle of ensuring the continuing integrity of systems as they are upgraded. Other key rôles include the **support** team that provides backup, assistance, continuing training and ensure that the required infrastructure is present. Representatives from other functional areas such as the security and legal areas may also become involved.

Evaluators need reuse awareness and both technical and business skills. Some evaluators must not have been part of the project team and can benefit from training in inspection techniques such as Fagan's inspections if these are used. It is of paramount importance that evaluators are appointed at the *beginning* of a project.

2.6 From project initiation to workshops

One of the main problems that worries developers is how to proceed from project inception to the build. No RAD method, whether SOMA or DSDM, can provide guarantees on navigating through the often tortuous political process that this involves, although we can offer some help and guidance.

As discussed in Section 2.5.1, project initiation usually starts within programme and resource planning. It has no time limits because we cannot place limits on creative thinking or organizational learning (*cf.* Morgan, 1997; Senge, 1990). Typically it consumes few resources but it could involve substantial effort in certain cases; such as building proof of concept demonstrators or writing a detailed proposal and business case.

Applying a DSDM style suitability filter as discussed in Section 2.3 helps to increase management confidence in the approach. Sometimes employing external consultants or mentors for a short time will also increase credibility, on the basis that a prophet is often without honour in his own house; people tend to believe advice that has cost them real money. However, it is usually a grave error to hand over the project entirely to consultants because of the need to build lasting and intimate relationships with the users. Perhaps the critical success factor is having a project visionary on the team. Such a person listens to and understands the needs of the business and can visualize an outline solution and sell it to the key beneficiaries. S/he must also be able to convince those people that giving up time to be involved in the project will benefit them far more than a 'hands off' approach. What developers don't do often enough is stand back and say to users: 'if you haven't got the time to get involved then maybe the project just isn't worth doing'. The difficulty here is where the users are not the sponsors and a different approach is required in such cases. For example, the thousands of Year 2000 projects that are underway as I write are seldom consciously inspired by user needs. Fortunately, such projects rarely involve object-oriented development and a conventional waterfall approach can be used. SOMA is designed for user-driven projects and I would argue that these are the projects that bring the biggest business benefits and *should* constitute the majority of non-infrastructural projects within any organization.

In SOMA we test everything as it is produced. Therefore transitions between activities are guarded by post-conditions; usually by requiring the existence of a deliverable, tested product of some sort. The only test applied to project initiation is the existence of a Project Initiation Form signed by an executive sponsor with appropriate financial authority. How the project team obtains that signature is a different matter. It may be necessary to produce a cost-benefit analysis or it might not. Either way the project can only go on when the document is signed.

Completing project initiation with a signed document triggers, among other activities, the workshop. Sign-off from the workshop usually guarantees organizational commitment to the project because of the way it builds a shared understanding of the problem and solution among the participants. To explain this, we focus on how to organize and run workshops in the next chapter.

⊟ 2.7 Bibliographical notes

Macaulay (1996) provides a concise survey of conventional approaches to requirements engineering and many of the techniques used within these including workshops, focus groups, quality function deployment, future workshops, cost-benefit analysis and learning by apprenticeship. Wieringa (1996) presents an approach based chiefly on Entity-Relationship modelling and JSD.

MacLean *et al.* (1994) present the ORCA method in detail and is well worth reading for the many interesting ideas that it contains. A rich discussion of scenario-based approaches to requirements engineering is provided by Carroll (1995). Maiden and Rugg (1996) present desiderata for choosing requirements engineering techniques appropriate for different problem classes, including observational studies, protocol analysis, interviews, workshops, card sorting, prototyping, brainstorming, ethnography, scenario analysis, laddering and repertory grids.

Jackson (1995) provides a huge number of insights into the problems of requirements engineering in a series of alphabetically ordered topics.

The Springer journal *Requirements Engineering* is a useful source of current research papers on the topic.

Stapleton (1997) provides a concise and readable summary of DSDM. Although she claims that the official DSDM manual adds necessary detail to her exposition, I think that most readers will not need to buy it.

A great deal of material on the nature and benefits of object-oriented rapid application development and on specific techniques for knowledge elicitation appears in Graham (1995) and has not been repeated here.

The contract-driven life cycle model was first described in detail by Graham (1995) and later adopted by the OPEN Consortium. The specification of the process was completed and published by the consortium in 1997 (Graham *et al.,* 1997). SOMA continues to extend and improve on the OPEN process.

3

Organizing and running workshops

They claim no thrones, they only ask to share
Arthur Penrhyn Stanley (The Gypsies)

everal times in the last chapter there have been references to the use of 'RAD
Workshops'. Here we wish to look in detail at how these workshops, an
important component of the SOMA process, should be organized and
managed. There are a number of different ways of structuring workshop sessions,
so this chapter is not so much a prescriptive tutorial on how precisely to execute
workshop events, but rather a set of guidelines, based on my experience of running
workshops over the last two decades.

The focus of the chapter is on the organization and management issues
involved in setting up and executing a successful workshop. Details on the stages
that a workshop passes through are (in this context) implicit in the SOMA method,
as described in Chapter 5. The process within which workshops are held was dealt
with in the previous chapter.

3.1 The benefits of a workshop based approach

Historically, system requirements were captured from users during a series of
interviews. Systems analysts would interview individual users, or sometimes small
groups of users, on an aspect of the required system. The results of these interviews
would be collected into a systems analysis report, which would then be circulated
for comments. Based on the comments received, a revision would be issued for
further comments, and so on. Such reports were usually very large and often quite
unreadable. It is difficult to believe that anyone ever both read and understood them
all. One suspects that they were often signed in default of a full understanding,
rather than provoke a fruitless confrontation.

There are several problems that arise from this approach:

- Each user being interviewed is inclined to focus on the system seen from her own perspective. This is natural and proper but the absence of comments from other users involved in using the system being proposed means that trade-offs in function and ease of use by the various members of the user group are not made visible until after the report has been circulated – and then only if it was read and understood thoroughly.
- The approach is inclined to inculcate into people an 'us and them' attitude for the users and the developers, and sometimes between different groups of users. The users ask for features and state requirements. The developers go away and produce something. That which is produced never exactly matches the users', perhaps not properly articulated, original requirements. Blame and finger-pointing inevitably follow.
- Setting up a complete interview round, recognizing that each user has a busy diary of her own, can be a lengthy process. Two or three months may be spent on the initial round of interviews, particularly if users are geographically dispersed. A second round of interviews for elaboration or clarification is often necessary. All this increases the elapsed time of the overall project, and in a shifting environment this in its own right causes problems with the delivered system. The requirements the users claimed at the beginning of the process will inevitably change as the business circumstances change. The longer the development process, the greater the guarantee that the delivered system will fail to match the requirements current on the delivery date – a phenomenon commonly characterized as: requirements drift.

In contrast, workshops offer the following advantages:

- They reduce the elapsed time needed to establish the requirements.
- They ensure that all participants have heard at first hand the contributions of other users, which eases the problem of arriving at compromises where these are necessary.
- Developers gain a first hand appreciation of the real goals of the users implicit in their requests, as opposed to a mediated set of requirement statements.
- They develop a shared ownership of the project between and among the developers and users.
- The monetary and other costs of the requirements elicitation and refinement process can often (but not always) be reduced.
- The tempo of a rapid development process is established. Introducing RAD ideas into an organization where users have experienced the all too familiar pattern of projects being delivered late, over budget and under specification can be met with a not unjustified degree of scepticism. Visibility of a documented requirements specification produced by

cooperative effort in a matter of a few days can go far to overcome this response.

3.2 Rôles within a workshop

The participants in a workshop are the sponsor, users, domain experts, the facilitator, the requirements engineer, the project manager and the team members. Some of these were discussed in Chapter 2. In addition, observers may attend the workshops (which provide excellent opportunities for training) where they may have contributions to make in specific but limited areas of expertise.

The **requirements engineer** (sometimes also called the **scribe)** is an experienced systems analyst – who must understand SOMA and object modelling – who documents the requirements during workshops using *SOMATiK* or otherwise. I dislike the term 'scribe' because the word tends to diminish the importance of the rôle, the contribution being made and indeed the very high levels of skill required to carry out the task effectively. For a large workshop, it can be useful to have two individuals allocated to the rôle, to assist each other and spread the burden of typing.

The **sponsor** is a senior executive responsible for the business area under review. Her rôle is to approve the cost and results of the workshop, resolve issues that cannot be resolved during the event itself and ensure that the appropriate participants are selected and committed to the project. The sponsor should attend the scoping session but does not need to attend the detail sessions.

The core team is made up of developers and between two and twenty key business users who are experts in the business area being analysed. Their rôle is to provide the business requirements, as elicited by the facilitator, and to verify that requirements are correctly documented.

The **facilitator** is almost the key determinant of the success of a workshop. S/he is an experienced business analyst who:

- conducts the scoping and detail sessions;
- ensures the requirements are captured in a complete and consistent way;
- ensures the right level of detail is achieved for input into the next project activity.

3.3 Who should attend

Not everyone affected by a proposed new system can always be present at requirements capture workshops. A good, and oft-quoted example is dealers in financial trading rooms who are reluctant to leave their investment positions unattended. Furthermore, such events would be too large and unwieldy to be managed comfortably. Therefore, some users act as delegates for their immediate colleagues, managers and subordinates. In the example given, dealer management often stand in for actual dealers. The selection of the right delegates for the task is a key determinant of the success of the event and the participants must at least include representatives of both the users of the proposed system and the development team.

USERS
The presence of key users is both more important and potentially more difficult to organize than one might think. Surely the identity of the correct participants from the user side is obvious and unarguable. Not necessarily! There are several factors to weigh:

- Seniority: more senior people may have a better grasp of the wider business issues being addressed in the workshop (or maybe just think they do) but the devil is always in the details, and operational level staff are more likely to be familiar with the detailed intricacies of operations, which will be the things that will break a proposed system if they are not taken into account. So we need people from different levels of seniority – but then we need to be aware that some people will not like to be seen to contradict their boss in public. This is where the facilitator's job of setting ground rules and ensuring fair play becomes important.
- Every stakeholder present *must* have delegated signatory authority to commit to the findings of the workshop. There is an escape path in the shape of the open issues which we will discuss later; but it is not acceptable for someone to say at the end of the session when the sign-off sheet is going round that they do not have the authority to sign it. Apart from causing delay, this vitiates the purpose of a workshop in gaining consensus; it makes the deliverables the subject of editing by people who were not present. Ensuring that this signatory authority is in place is a key job of the sponsor.
- The number of people present: the complexity of the interactions will rise exponentially with the number of participants, so life is easier the smaller the number – and the workshop is cheaper to run. Everyone affected by the proposed system should be represented; but, in the limit, this could mean half the company. What must be avoided is the situation of somebody feeling later that they were improperly overlooked. When the delivered system has a flaw, you do not want to be told that that some stakeholder or user was never consulted in the first place.

The above list indicates that before setting up the workshop, the sponsor, project manager and facilitator should have a prior meeting, generally led by the facilitator, to establish the participant list. They should examine all the options in terms of inclusions and exclusions, probe the emerging list for weaknesses and seek to rectify them and document the reasons for the final invitation list. It can be useful to develop a matrix of candidates, enumerating all the people who could conceivably attend, and then compare possible combinations of candidates from the grid in terms of the impact on the workshop's success. Start with the company's organization chart, and collapse the relevant components into a matrix where the rows are the organizational units, the columns represent approximate seniority levels within the organization, and the cells contain names of logical job descriptions and possible candidates. Note especially that this document is **not** a formal deliverable, because the logical rôles may be the subject of discussion and change during the workshop, as discussed in Chapter 5, Section 5.1.

	Strategic management	*Tactical management*	*Operational management and clerical staff*
Sales	Sales Director National Sales Manager	Account managers Regional managers	Sales staff Clerical and telesales staff
Marketing	Marketing Director	Product managers	Marketing assistants
Production	Distribution Director	Production engineers	Warehouse supervisors Machinists

Figure 3.1 Workshop participation grid

As an example, consider a system to support a new process for product presentation, sales, order taking, and manufacturing. This would affect *inter alia* the Sales, Marketing and Production divisions. A possible workshop participation grid is shown in Figure 3.1. One should ensure that the grid reflects the actual organizational structure, then fill in the names of the candidates for participation. Considering the options, one representative for each group may make the workshop too large. Beware of the dangers of arguing that a manager can always speak for the troops as well – because he used to be one. This may be true, but it is difficult for people to represent their own needs sincerely as well as those of someone else. The inevitable exceptions that do occur, as with the dealers alluded to above, should be handled with extra care and sensitivity. Otherwise, if any rôle is not to be represented at the workshop, then there is an assumption this rôle will not be affected by the new system – and this should be documented. Some sensitive issues can arise if this is a business process re-engineering project: some rôles may disappear altogether, and asking possible victims of reorganization to contribute enthusiastically to planning the wake may be regarded as unproductive, or in bad taste at the very least. The aim is to produce a participant invitation list along with a supporting document justifying the rôles represented and not represented, and the reasoning behind the choices made.

Users should attend the entire workshop. This is often easier said than done. Freeing people from important work, even for a few days, can have a significant business impact and cost implications. It is also sometimes the case that people will not wish to appear in any way 'dispensable'. Having people attending for a couple of hours, disappearing for a while, then coming back can be very harmful to the progress and ultimate value of a workshop. The sponsor and project manager must work hard with departmental managers to ensure that a block of time is made available to run the event as a block and not as a set of piecemeal sessions with a floating population of participants.

DEVELOPERS Where at all possible, the complete development team should attend the workshop(s). An absolutely central idea in RAD (or JAD) is that of a *joint* development team, made up of users and technical people. The challenge is to avoid the development of an 'us and them' attitude: where the user group states its requirements, the developer group goes away and produces something with little contact with or reference to the users. Only later do the users have the opportunity to tell them where they went wrong, when it is often too late to avoid project deadline pressure freezing the mistakes into the end product. The reason for having the whole development team present at the workshops is to help gain *shared* ownership of the system requirements: to understand more fully the content of the formal documents they may be dealing with later in the project. Importantly, all developers should feel involved in all parts of the project. Of course, someone may be on the team because of specialist skills, say in network design and management, because it is known that this will be a key component of the delivered system; but that person should not have the feeling that their contribution is just at the level of their own narrow specialism – they should be regarded as significant contributors to the system as a whole.

3.4 Selecting the location

Having decided to run a workshop rather than conduct interviews, a major choice faced by the organizer of a requirements engineering workshop is whether to hold the session on or off the site where the users normally work. There are arguments for and against both strategies as summarized in Table 3.2

The most usual off-site location is an hotel. Choose one that is not near to the normal work place, preferable in an idyllic country setting that offers comfort and suitable recreational facilities. Alternatively, if a software house is building the system and has a suitable location, that may suffice if there is no chance that the developers will be interrupted by their company; and if the users can be so persuaded.

.

Table 3.2 Comparison of on-site and off-site workshop location strategies

	On-site	*Off-site*
For	It is easier to persuade users and domain experts to attend	A change of environment often relaxes the participants, especially if they normally work in a stressful environment
	On-site space is usually less costly	There is less opportunity for the users and domain experts to be called away for meetings, fire-fights, 'urgent' jobs, etc.
	Travelling costs may be lower	Catering facilities are usually better
		You have more control over the allocation of rooms and facilities
Against	There may be constant interruptions and users may be called back to their work often. This is really the most important and common reason for workshops failing apart from poor facilitation	Accommodation costs are usually higher
	Users are less likely to be able to take their minds off their normal duties	There may be significant extra travelling costs

▤ 3.5   Logistical requirements

Ideally, arrange to have a main room, as discussed below, and a break-out room which can be quite small, containing only a table, chairs and a flip-chart. More than one break-out room may be needed if the workshop is a large one. The breakout room may be useful if a sub-group needs to split off to resolve some important but not necessarily mainstream point. Coffee and refreshments can be served in the breakout room, but in any case should be served outside the main room, even if this is in the corridor outside. This ensures that a break really is a break, giving people a chance to stretch their legs, cool down if things are getting warm, or just refocus in a different environment for a few minutes. Even more importantly, the arrival of coffee is de-coupled from the session in progress; this sounds like a minor point, but so often you find when facilitating that the group are just reaching towards some important consensus or insight when a hardworking hotel employee comes clanking in with the tea-trolley and fractures the flow and concentration just at the wrong moment.

Figure 3.2 Facilitator's-eye view of a typical room layout

The layout of the room or rooms in which the sessions are conducted is important. Figure 3.2 shows a typical but not necessarily ideal layout. For example, in many circumstances it is an extremely bad idea to allow coffee to be served in the main room as this can distract from the proceedings. On the other hand if there is no other room available then in-room coffee is better than no coffee. The main table is U-shaped to support the walkthrough sessions when bean bags are thrown about and the facilitator needs quick and easy access. All the participants can have eye contact too. This is important. A horseshoe table like this is easily the best layout; a boardroom style table is second best, and not as good because the facilitator must then either stay at the head of the table at all times, or lose contact with participants by walking behind them as s/he moves around. Separated tables should not be used. People sitting at a table for two, and from the same department, inevitably get the subconscious feeling that this is their turf which they will defend against all comers – the reaching of group consensus becomes more difficult.

The other table in the figure should really be several tables to support the printer and other items. At least two flip charts are needed and a white board is useful too, especially one that can produce hard copies of what is drawn or written on it. Get plenty of marker pens, check they all work before you start, and make sure they are erasable or water-soluble before you write all over the whiteboard. Figure 3.2 shows an ordinary white board and flip-chart pages 'blue-tacked' to the wall at the rear. Some hotels don't permit fixing paper to their walls like this: avoid them.

On the right we can see the requirements engineer with the computer, which is equipped with a copy of *SOMATiK* and/or other CASE tool(s) and probably a standard suite of office automation software such as MS Office. This machine is connected to a fast laser printer and to an LCD palette set atop of the overhead projector that projects on the screen to the right.

Not shown are all the little items needed but catalogued in the checklists below. Nor do we see the video or audio recording equipment that it is advisable to use sometimes.

SOMATiK can print out class cards and intermediate and final workshop reports in real time for distribution among the participants, but whatever tools you use some artefacts will need to be distributed during the workshop. Therefore, make sure that the hotel can provide adequate photocopying facilities. At break times, the current state of the project document should be printed and photocopied, so that after the break participants sit down with the absolute current state of the workshop in front of them. You need to check that the hotel understands this time schedule. Often, the management may quite sincerely say they offer photocopying, when in practice this means you can hand a couple of sheets in at the desk and get a single copy in an hour or so when someone gets round to it. Make sure the management is clear that you may need 20 copies of a 30 page document prepared on demand in a 20 minute period (and you are prepared for one of the team actually to do the copying). And if they can't service the requirement, use somewhere else.

Get set up and tested in good time, and preferably the night before. This is particularly true if you are using hired equipment. Check everything; has the computer got the printer driver for the printer? Does the printer have adequate paper and toner? Do you have a splitter cable for the projector so the scribe can see the terminal as well as project on the screen?

There will also need to be the rooms allocated for break-out sessions and syndicate work. These sessions are used to resolve specialized issues and especially to allow the users to work on the first cut at class descriptions (class cards). I find that keeping the development staff away from the early stages of this process of discovery is beneficial in terms of getting a good, business-oriented model. The developers should look over the resultant model later to apply solid object-oriented design principles. Another useful approach is to split the users into two teams and then merge the resultant class cards in the plenary session. This can appear to take longer, but often reveals important conflicts and alternative approaches. Also small groups usually get results faster than large ones. The layout for these secondary rooms can be much simpler: just a large table, chairs, one flip chart and stationery such as blank acetates. Figure 3.3 illustrates a typical layout.

Figure 3.3 Typical syndicate room layout

3.6   Workshop organizer's and facilitator's checklists

The checklists on the next three pages are intended to help the organizer of workshops and the facilitator. They are to be treated as reminder lists and not adhered to slavishly. Look at each item and think: 'Do we need (to do) that?'. These checklists have been used by the organizers of many projects and may be considered tested; but I would be interested to hear readers' views on whether anything useful could be added.

The first two checklists cover the suggested order of business for scoping and detail workshops respectively. The third list is perhaps the most useful; it is a list of useful or essential items to procure before the workshops starts.

Checklist 1: Running scoping sessions

Introduction to approach
Mission statement
Objectives
Measures
Voting
Priorities
External process model
       External agents and communication paths
Internal process model
       Actors
       Messages
       Triggers
       Return values
       Goals
Exclusions
Assumptions
Outstanding Issues – who will resolve?
Implementation priorities
Reuse candidates?
Next steps
Obtain sign-off

Checklist 2: Running detailed analysis sessions

Introduction to approach (if needed)
Scoping session output
  Goals and messages
  Mission, objectives, measures and priorities
  Candidate classes
Process modelling
  For each message analyze
  Goal – Offer/Request – Negotiation – Root task – Handover
  Triggers for external agents
  Top level tasks for each message
  Decompose task scripts into sub-scripts to atomic level
  Exceptions: side-scripts
Examine business process re-engineering opportunities
Is there a task for each objective?
Is there an objective for each task?
Syndicate work
  Textual analysis to find candidate classes
  Class cards
  Layers
  Structures (classification, composition, association and usage)
  Card sorts or repertory grids to refine structures
  Assign attributes to classes
  Assign operations to classes
  Rules
  State models if necessary
Confirm associations (by drawing 'entity' model) – optional; ten minutes
  maximum
Rôle play – record event traces for each task trigger
Objective/message matrix
Review library classes
Discuss implementation priorities
Reuse candidates
Have open issues from scoping been resolved?
Operational aspects dealt with?
Legal aspects dealt with?
Security policy dealt with?
Disaster recovery dealt with?
Sign off document

Checklist 3: Organizers administration and logistics checklist

Book the hotel/rooms
Number of participants
  Room big enough?
  Enough syndicate rooms?
Specify room layout(s)
Catering arrangements
  Meal/drinks schedules?
  Meals/drinks/special diets?
  Coffee taken outside the main room
Photocopying arrangements
Inform the participants, facilitator(s), analysts
  Have they confirmed availability?
  Travel arrangements
  Facilitator briefed?
Book computer equipment and install and test software
  Computer, printer, RGB adapter, display screen, palette or projector
  Software installed and tested?
      MS Office or similar
      SOMATiK
      SOMATiK Repository (if available)
      Other CASE?
      Existing repository classes and class cards
      Sufficient disk space?
      Appropriate printer driver installed?
Video/audio equipment ordered, installed and tested
Flip charts, pens, overhead, blank foils, video/audio, blank tapes,
  paper for printer and participants, pencils, glow pens, post-its,
  blue tack, Sellotape, coloured stickers, etc.
Spare bulbs, batteries, etc.
Is there a (copy generating) white board?
Prepare foils, handouts
  Handouts duplicated?
Collect and take documents from earlier sessions
Collect class and task descriptions from earlier workshops (if not using
  SOMATiK Repository)
Prepare agenda
Create sign-off document (produced automatically by *SOMATiK*)

⊟ 3.7   Facilitation skills

Effective facilitators require a rare combination of talents.   They must be knowledgeable in the method – SOMA in this case – and about the business, at least to the extent of being comfortable with the terminology and familiar with the main ideas. Presentation and communication skills are key. They must be assertive but know when to keep in the background and just listen. They have to be able to encourage diffident participants and give them confidence while knowing how to deal with troublesome personalities, often very senior ones, without upsetting or belittling them. Setting up and agreeing ground rules for the workshop (discussed below) is a very helpful technique.

A sense of humour helps put people at ease and the facilitator should not be afraid of quips and even risqué remarks, as long as this does not get out of hand. The key skill is that of being able to pull out the essence of an argument and see its principal contradictory elements quickly. My approach is always to look for two opposites in analyzing anything and then explore the dialectic and mediations between them. With practice this can be done very quickly. Probably, the only way to learn to be an accomplished facilitator is by apprenticeship. Perhaps some people are just born and grown as natural facilitators. I have never had formal training in facilitation; I learnt through practice, theory and imitation. Perhaps a study of group dynamics would be a useful background; it is certainly very important.

Importantly, the facilitator must be neutral with respect to groups of participants, and moreover be *seen to be* neutral. There must be no perceived bias towards any user group, and no perception that the facilitator 'represents' in any sense the development group. This is important because occasionally the facilitator will be a member of the development organization. Life's experience will often have left users with a feeling that they are going to get what the developers want to deliver, rather than what they asked for.

Voting is an important way of reaching consensus but should be handled carefully. A vote may not indicate the truth, merely the current conjuncture of opinion. The results of voting should be presented as such: softly and as a guide only. The facilitator is responsible for obtaining the sponsor's and other user's sign-off. This too requires a combination of tact and determination. We present the group with a form offering a single choice between 'I agree that this model is a good representation of the requirements' and 'I **strongly** disagree ...'; nothing in between will do.

The facilitator is responsible for maintaining the time-box discipline within the workshop and should have approximate time targets for each step on the agenda. S/he should also have a clear mental model of what will happen and where delays are likely. The facilitator must be aware of the tasks of the requirements engineer and clarify issues or slow the pace for him when necessary. A good rapport between these two is essential and telepathy would be a distinct advantage – although subtle hand signals and nods usually suffice.

Potential indicators of a poor facilitator include any tendency to be a bully or autocrat, timidity, lack of confidence when presenting, fixed ideas, inability to sit back and listen, any tendency to sycophancy in the face of senior management, lack of awareness of general and specific business issues and general lack of authority or charisma. Curiously, you cannot discover these faults reliably without watching the person actually do the job. Interviews and – especially – psychometric tests are of little use.

3.8   Who should scribe?

As I have remarked above, the word 'scribe', frequently used in the literature, demeans both the importance and the difficulty of the task of correctly recording the proceedings. This is why I prefer the term REQUIREMENTS ENGINEER. There are two basic prerequisites: absolute familiarity with the selected documentation tool and its underlying method, be it *SOMATiK* or some other product; and fluency and accuracy in typing (not necessarily touch typing though). But there is much more. The engineer must be able to turn shorthand notes thrown up on the board or flip chart by the facilitator into grammatical connected text; but without recording every jot and tittle of conversations that, while they may lead to important conclusions, may also contain much that is irrelevant. On the other hand, if there is any doubt about relevancy, it is better to record it than not. The text can be amended later.

3.8.1   Recording the event

It is sometimes useful to record the proceedings of a workshop using audio tape or even video. In this section I want to present, very briefly, a few guidelines and rules of thumb on the use of such technology.

Having a taped record is mainly useful for the scribes and analysts who may have failed to understand or record some nuance of the argument or detail of a required feature. This applies to completing the RAD report and refining the analysis into a more detailed specification or systems analysis report. I have found that the difference between audio and video recording is of little significance when using the tapes for this purpose. I therefore feel that the additional cost of video can really only be justified if the physical actions of users are being studied in some way. Of course the organizers of the workshop may wish to impress the users with all their high-tech equipment, but that is another issue.

My experience, and indeed common sense, tells us that there is hardly ever any point in having tapes transcribed into typescript. No-one ever reads such documents and the process is time-consuming and expensive. The exception to this rule is when the users have described a complex knowledge-based task and a protocol analysis is to be applied.

Whether using audio or video, the facilitator must always ask the group's permission to record the proceedings and offer to turn the tape off at anyone's request, perhaps if a particularly sensitive issue is being discussed. The group should be assured that the tapes will be confidential to the project team and that they will be destroyed after use or, if required, returned to the lead user for destruction.

🗄 3.9   Running the workshop

A SOMA workshop can last from one to five days. A workshop taking longer than a week should be broken down into separate workshops. Apart from the difficulty of taking people away from their normal jobs for so long, if the workshop will last longer it means that there is too much to do in the time for the technique to work properly. Half-day workshops do not usually work well for detailed sessions but can be used to define scope and partition the job among subsequent detailed workshops.

Deciding on how much time should be allocated for a particular workshop is still something of a black art. After all, we are asking how much time will a group of people, who have perhaps never worked together before in this way, take to agree on an unquantifiable number of points. But we are obliged to come up with some sort of estimate, in order to allocate people for the requisite time. Taking three days as a norm we might allocate half-a-day to a day scoping and two to two and a half days on the detail; the more people involved, the longer it will take. If the scoping indicates that there will not be enough time to cover everything in detail, it is important to cover all the issues discovered at a reasonably high level, and then schedule further workshops for the detail, rather than to exhaust the detail on some areas and not cover some at all.

The facilitator should have a mental model of the temporal structure of the workshop and the issues that must be covered. The checklists provided in Section 3.6 provide a useful *aide memoire*. Usually I find it best not to publish this in too much detail in advance. Certainly publish and review the *sequence* of the agenda – but refrain from a blatant announcement of specific times. It is easier to estimate the time requirements for the entire workshop than for each session. Often, extra time spent on one issue will ease the discussion and reduce the time taken on a subsequent one. Furthermore, the iterative nature of developing consistency at each level means that no stage is necessarily complete until all stages have been covered. But if there exists a piece of paper saying something like:

  9:30 Mission Statement
10:00 Objectives
11:00 Business Process

12.30 … etc.

then people will feel uncomfortable if the workshop is straying too far from the (rather arbitrary) timings that were assigned at the outset, and they may wonder if things are growing successfully to a point. Sometimes, for example, the sponsor may already have thought through the mission statement in some detail, and be able to state it to everyone's satisfaction in a couple of minutes. On other occasions, the real mission may only become clear after analyzing an initially diffuse set of more detailed issues. So, as facilitator, give yourself enough leeway in timings so that no-one can question whether the workshop appears to be running early or late. An exception to this must be made when there is a need to schedule slots for specialists such as legal or security experts to participate.

If people are genuinely engaged in the event, a 9am-5pm day should be regarded as the norm. There is a temptation to maximize the use of the day by scheduling sessions in the evening, but this should be avoided. People run out of stamina and the results are degraded. Take a definite one hour break for lunch. Plan for this and keep to the schedule – it is a courtesy to the participants to let them know that they can rely on a break say between twelve-thirty and one-thirty to be available for phone calls and other commitments. Schedule coffee and tea breaks mid-morning and mid-afternoon but, for these, do not guarantee the precise time; come to a suitable break-point and then stop for 20 minutes. Remember also the need for regular comfort breaks – especially when there are smokers present.

3.9.1   Setting and enforcing the rules of engagement

The facilitator can make her own job easier, and the workshop experience more satisfactory for everyone involved, by laying down some ground rules right at the start – and inviting participants to specify their own rules, add them to the list and then agree to follow those very rules. If things get a little emotional later on, it can help to defuse the situation by referring to the abstract rules, rather than heightening tension further by the facilitator becoming involved on a personal level. If a rule is established saying that only one person to speak at a time, and not be interrupted; and two people start having a highly vocal argument then pointing out that the rule has been violated is a more emollient intervention than telling people to shut up. The 10 minute rule is possibly the most useful rule in this respect. Having said all this, the facilitator must have the *gravitas* to take charge in a positive way, if that is what it takes. Here are some rules that have proved useful:

- One speaker at a time and no private, parallel conversations.
- No hogging the floor; ten minutes is the maximum and the facilitator can instruct offenders to stop after that time.
- Politeness dictates that interrupting other speakers is not on.
- Personal reflections are to be avoided strenuously.
- Job titles and grades are left outside the room; the participants are here to work together.

- Mobile phones are switched off. Pick up messages during breaks.
- Everyone gets a chance to speak on any point of discussion. That's the facilitator's responsibility. This can be quite a tricky issue for the facilitator. In a big workshop, one cannot ask everyone in the room every time a topic arises. In such a case, one should encourage people to raise their hands or make some signal that they have something to say – but be sure to be alert enough to notice and include them. Otherwise the more vociferous individuals will dominate while the more taciturn will rarely get a chance to comment.

An important technique for closing down redundant discussion and ensuring wider participation is to explain at the beginning of the workshop that there will be a ten minute rule. This means that, at the facilitator's discretion or on the request of other participants, any topic that has been discussed for too long is placed on the open issues list for later resolution by fewer people. The ten minute rule can be applied to defuse group dynamics conflicts. If consensus on a topic is not emerging after ten minutes, the facilitator, or anyone else, can point this out and have the topic shelved. The issue should be noted as open for subsequent resolution. This requires judgment and discipline on the facilitator's part. After all, looked at from one viewpoint, the whole event relates to one topic. When does one topic segue into another? This is why it is so important to keep the current focus clear in everyone's mind – keeping a keyword on the whiteboard until this area has been exhausted helps here.

Enforce the rules fairly, consistently and thoroughly. Being seen to be prepared to enforce the rules early on, perhaps on a minor issue, can serve as an object lesson and in itself reduces the need to enforce the rules later.

3.10 Keeping up momentum

As with ordinary interviewing, there is a difficult path to tread between the pastures of rambling but productive discussion and the quagmire of the unfocused talking shop. It can be useful to write the current topic of discussion on the whiteboard, to refer to when someone is wandering off track. Use a flip-chart to note down topics that are raised but are divergent from the current issue on the whiteboard. This allows you to abort some branch of discussion without being negative towards the person raising it. An interesting point can be returned to later.

Make a point of telling people the *time* that the meeting will be reconvened after breaks. It is useful to have a clock in the room. It helps to get the meeting restarted on time after such interruptions. If you announce a ten minute break people will tend to extend their off-line activities to the next round half hour. At least a few minutes will be lost at every break. If you can point at the clock and say that the much-needed ten minute leg stretch will bring us up to 11:20 (a nice round number even though it's actually 11:06 now) then people will tend to return and be ready at the appointed time.

If people appear to be losing concentration, do not be afraid to take short (five to ten minute) breaks at unscheduled times – other than the planned refreshment points.

3.11   Concluding the workshop

After several days hard work, the time comes for everyone to return to their normal jobs and various locations. It is central to the philosophy of SOMA that workshops are used to build shared understanding between the user and development groups. As we will see in Chapter 5 the construction of object models has a key rôle to play in this, but the way in which the facilitator closes the workshop is also critical.

It is vital that before concluding the proceedings, a sign-off sheet is circulated to all the participants and their signature obtained. They can either sign as being in agreement that the project should proceed based on the high-level object model developed, or as being in **strong** disagreement with the final report produced. No intermediate position can be countenanced. Strong disagreement, it should be explained, is tantamount to signing the 'project delay form'. Remembering that the workshop report is a document covering the results agreed during the workshop, there is usually no legitimate reason why anyone should be in disagreement. This is particularly true if the facilitator and requirements engineer have ensured that the developing document has been re-circulated and reviewed at various key breakpoints during the event, so that people have had a chance to review it as it develops and raise any divergent issues at the time.

The open issues section of the report offers an escape valve for divergent opinions, so that people in violent disagreement over some aspect can still agree to sign the document as agreeing with the fact that the open issue has been recorded and awaits resolution. When an open issue is recorded, it is important to record who is responsible for resolving it and by when.

It is important that everyone goes away with the warm fuzzies. Nobody should be left with the feeling that the event has been a waste of their time. At close, review the progress made, summarize the findings and talk about the next stages and the next key milestones that can be expected.

⊟ 3.12   Other knowledge elicitation techniques

Many techniques that can be used in normal interviews can be readily extended for use in workshops once they are well understood. This section discusses just a few of the techniques that I have found particularly useful.

3.12.1   Interviewing techniques

It is usual to divide interviews into structured and focused interviews. Typically structured interviews are at a high level of generality and take place earlier in the discovery process. A structured interview aims to grasp an overview of the topic which is broad but shallow. It will result in elicitation of the key objects and concepts of the domain but not go into detail. In a workshop this corresponds to running a scoping session, where the same techniques can be used.

Focused interviews or detailed workshops go into the detail of one area and are typically narrow and deep. During the elicitation process it is essential to search for reusable elements – the grey rectangles in Figure 3.4. Analysts should select the area that gives either 80% of the benefit or 80% of the predicted complexity or reuse potential as the first area to explore – preferably both. This corresponds, ideally, to about 20% of the scope of the system. This broad and shallow followed by narrow and deep scenario corresponds closely to the approach that should be followed during prototyping.

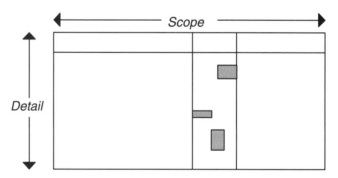

Figure 3.4 Narrow and deep *versus* broad and shallow approaches to interviews and prototyping

Structured interviews follow a plan that should be prepared in advance and state the objectives of the interview. At the start of the session, participants should agree an agenda. Then, for each agenda topic, interviewers or workshop facilitators ask questions, put out **probes**, review the results at each stage and move to the next topic. Finally, one must review the overall results and compare them with the plan, asking whether the objectives have been achieved. If not, the exercise can be repeated. It is essential that questions are open rather than closed. Open questions do not permit an answer such as 'Yes' or 'No' that closes further discussion or elaboration. Probes are merely particularly useful types of open question. Table 3.3 sets out some probe types with examples. Probes use all six question words: what, why, when, how, where and who.

Table 3.3 Types of probe

Probe type	Example
Definitional	What is a ...?
Additive	Go on ...
Reflective	What you're saying is ...
Mode change	How would your colleagues view that?
	Can you give a more concrete example?
Directive	Why is that?
	How?
	Could you be more specific?

Focused interviews are less easy to describe in abstract. Their form depends more on the domain in question. However, techniques such as teachback, repertory grids and task analysis are commonly the ones used. Teachback involves interviewers presenting their understanding to the users formally and receiving corrections thereby. The other techniques are described below.

A good interviewer or facilitator plans and prepares sessions and sets clear objectives. However, adaptability is the key skill and one must be prepared to adapt or even abandon a plan that is not working. Some domain knowledge is prerequisite to facilitate open discussion as is a good understanding of object-oriented technology itself, especially object modelling.

3.12.2   Repertory grids and laddering

One of the most useful knowledge engineering techniques for eliciting objects and their structures is that of Kelly, or repertory, grids. These grids were introduced originally in the context of clinical psychiatry (Kelly, 1955). They are devices for helping analysts elicit 'personal constructs'; concepts which people use in dealing with and constructing their world. **Constructs** are pairs of opposites, such as slow/fast, and usually correspond to either classes or attribute values in object-oriented analysis. The second dimension of a Kelly grid is its **elements**. These usually correspond to objects. Elements are rated on a scale from 1 to 5, say, according to which pole of the construct they correspond most closely to. These values can then be used to 'focus' the grid; a mathematical procedure which clarifies relationships among elements and constructs. In particular, focusing ranks the elements in order of the clarity with which they are perceived and the constructs in order of their importance as classifiers of elements. The details can be found in any decent book on knowledge acquisition; e.g. Hart (1989) or Graham and Jones (1988).

To illustrate the usefulness of Kelly grids, suppose we need to interview a user. The technique involves first identifying some 'elements' in the application. These might be real things or concepts, but should be organized into coherent sets. For example, the set {Porsche, Jaguar, Rolls Royce, Mini, Driver} has an obvious odd man out: Driver.

The use of the Kelly grid technique in its full form is not recommended. However questioning techniques based on Kelly grids are immensely powerful in eliciting new classes and attributes and extending and refining classification structures. There are three principal techniques:

- asking for the opposites of all elements and concepts
- laddering to extract generalizations
- elicitation by triads to extract specializations.

Considering Figure 3.5, we might have discovered that SportyCars was a key class. Asking for the opposite produced not 'Unsporty' but 'Family' cars; not the logical opposite but a totally new class. Thus, asking for the opposite of a class can reveal new classes.

In laddering, users are asked to give names for higher level concepts: 'Can you think of a word that describes all the concepts {speed, luxury, economy}?' might produce a concept of 'value for money'. This technique is known as laddering, and elicits both composition and classification structures. It generally produces more general concepts. Asking for a term that sums up both Fast and Sporty we might discover the class of 'ego massaging' cars for example.

| | ----------------- ELEMENTS ---------------------- | | | | | |
CONCEPT	Rolls Royce	Porsche	Jaguar	Mini	Trabant	OPPOSITE
Economical	5	4	4	2	2	Costly
Comfortable	1	4	2	4	5	Basic
Sporty	5	1	3	5	5	Family
Cheap	5	4	4	2	1	Expensive
Fast	3	1	2	4	5	Slow

Figure 3.5 A Kelly grid. Scores are between 1 and 5. The left hand pole of the concept corresponds to a low score for the element and the right (its opposite) to a high one. The grid is not focused.

Elicitation by triads is not a reference to Chinese torture but to a technique whereby, given a coherent set of elements, the user is asked to take any three and specify a concept that applies to two of them but not to the third. For example, with {Porsche, Jaguar, Mini}, top speed might emerge as an important concept. Similarly, the triad {Mini, Jaguar, Trabant} might reveal the attribute CountryOfManufacture: or the classes BritishCar and GermanCar. As a variant of this technique, users may be asked to divide elements into two or more groups and then name the groups. This is known as card sorting.

These techniques are first rate ways of getting at the conceptual structure of the problem, if used with care and sensitivity. Exhaustive listing of all triads, for example, can be extremely tedious and easily alienate users.

3.12.3 Textual analysis

Task scripts constitute a form of written requirements specification and so can be analysed using the textual analysis technique introduced by Abbott (1983) and widely used by object-oriented analysts ever since. In a nutshell the technique says that nouns describe candidate objects and verbs indicate operations. This is of course only a first cut at the identification of objects, but it always gives the discovery process a useful kick start. More detailed guidelines are given by Graham (1995) but the noun/verb idea is usually enough to begin with. The next, harder, step is to assign the operations to the appropriate classes and organize the latter using the four object-oriented structures of classification, composition, usage and association discussed in the next chapter. This process will undoubtedly reveal errors in the assignment of operations, missing classes and classes that must be decomposed differently. This in turn will lead to re-structuring, so that the process is highly iterative. Textual analysis of this kind is our main initial method of going from a Task Object Model to the Business Object Model.

3.13 Using *SOMATiK* to prepare a workshop report

This section will only be relevant if the reader has access to a copy of *SOMATiK*. Otherwise it may be safely skipped over.

The workshop report can be prepared using an ordinary word processor, but this usually means that the requirements engineer must give up evenings and a weekend to pull the document into shape. It also implies that the workshop participants may have departed before they have a chance to read the report and sign off on its models, conclusions and recommendations. *SOMATiK* allows the report to be produced by the requirements engineer in real time during a workshop. This report includes a valuable sign-off sheet.

Normally the requirements engineer will prepare the title sheet and list of participants in advance of the workshop. To do this run *SOMATiK* and start a new project (**File|New**). Select **Project Details** from the view menu or toolbar and click on participants when you have filled in the front of the project details tab card. Click the add button to add a new participant. Note especially that you must check the Signatory box if you want this person's name to appear on the sign-off sheet.

Once the workshop gets under way, the next step is to complete the mission and objectives sections and any other appropriate sections in the project details area as the discussion goes on. When the facilitator begins to elicit the agent model the Internal Context view (which lets one draw an Agent Object Model) is used.

Select **Print Preview** from the File menu to see what the default report will look like.

⊟ 3.14   Bibliographical notes

For a very readable overview of requirements capture in group sessions, evidently based on a lot of practical experience, see Gause and Weinberg (1989). Macaulay (1996) lists several approaches to the management of group sessions and gives checklists and guidance for each approach. Graham (1995) gives a few additional, useful techniques that I did not see fit to repeat here because of our focus on workshops and rapid development.

Some of the material in this Chapter was provided by Peter Jones based on his extensive experience of facilitating workshops. Peter developed the idea of the participation grid in the course of this work. Jones (1999) provides further detailed discussion of the best way to organize and run workshops in the context of complete development projects.

4

Object modelling

To find and explain a definition best fitting natural phenomena ...
Galileo Galilei (Discourses and Demonstrations
Concerning Two New Sciences)

Object modelling is a technique for describing human knowledge about the things and concepts we encounter in the world and in our thoughts, and the relationships between them. In this chapter I will set out a comprehensive language for object modelling sufficient for this purpose and show how it can be applied to modelling business objects: specifications of objects that can be implemented on a computer but are also models of real-world artefacts. In subsequent chapters we will see how exactly the same language can be used to model human and system agents, users' tasks and even the software development life cycle itself – as we anticipated with the contract-driven life-cycle model of Chapter 2, Section 2.5.

In this chapter I lay the details of the semantics of the SOMA object modelling language before the reader. Before doing that we must turn to the nature and status of models in general and ask how object modelling should be used in software development and requirements engineering.

4.1 The nature of models

Arguments about whether object-oriented development is seamless or not, whether transformational approaches are better than round trip gestalt design or disputes about the difference between essential and system models have beset attempts to explain object-oriented requirements engineering. I believe that lack of clarity about modelling is at the root of these disputes and has also led to a great muddle concerning the concept of a business object. In this section I want to explain my understanding of the meaning and status of modelling within object-oriented development. Then it will be possible to explain what a business object really is.

Modelling is central to software engineering practice and especially to object-oriented development. A **model** is a representation of some thing or systems of things with all or some of the following properties:

- It is always **different** from the thing or system being modelled (the *original*) in scale, implementation or behaviour.
- It has the shape or appearance of the original (an iconic model).
- It can be manipulated or exercised in such a way that its behaviour or properties can be used to predict the behaviour or properties of the original (a simulation model).
- There is always some correspondence between the model and the original.

Examples of models abound throughout daily life: mock-ups of aircraft in wind tunnels; architectural scale models; models of network traffic using compressed air in tubes or electrical circuits; software models of gas combustion in engines. Of course **all** software is a model of something, just as all mathematical equations are (analytic) models.

Jackson (1995) relates models to descriptions by saying that modelling a domain involves making designations of the primitives of the domain and then using these to build a description of the properties, relationships and behaviour that are true of that domain. For example, if we take the domain of sending birthday cards to one's friends, we might make designations:

p is a friend;
d is a date (day and month);
$B(p,d)$ says that p was born on d.

Then we can make descriptions like: For all p, there is exactly one B. Jackson suggests that modelling is all about ensuring that the descriptions apply equally well to the model and to the original domain. In the context of computer models this might mean that the instances of a class or the records of a database are made to correspond uniquely to domain instances of our friends. Most usefully, Jackson presents this concept as the M configuration shown in Figure 4.1.

The Domain and the Machine are different; in the domain friends do not reside in disk sectors. There are many things in the domain that are not in our model, such as our friends' legs or pimples. There are also things that go on in computers that we are not concerned with in a model, such as time sharing. The model comprises the features shared between the domain and the machine.

This understanding of what a model is can be applied to the problem of object modelling. We must understand clearly that a so-called Business Object Model is both a model of the domain and a potentially implementable machine model. But we must begin with a model of the domain to understand and validate the requirements.

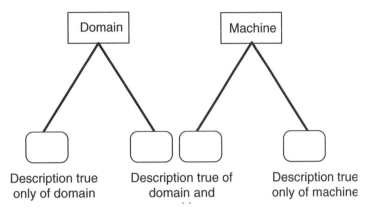

Figure 4.1 M is for 'model' (after Jackson)

It is my thesis that object modelling is a very general method for knowledge representation. There is little that cannot be modelled with objects – provided, of course, that we do not restrict ourselves to the semantics of some particular object-oriented programming language. We can model both the domain and the machine using objects. This is not to say that the world consists of our model objects, but it is to say that we can almost always model the domain as if it was made of objects. A good example is provided by Cook and Daniels (1994), who make a strong distinction between *essential* (i.e. domain) and *specification* models. They argue that the world is not made of objects citing by way of example the fact that the sun does not wake the birds up each morning by sending each one a message. However, if we want a correspondence between our domain and specification models, it is quite permissible to model the sunrise event as recorded on a 'blackboard' object in which each instance of the class Birds has registered interest. That is not what happens physically but it is a good model insofar as object semantics do not include a broadcast metaphor. There are of course many exceptions where object modelling is inappropriate, but the sheer discipline of trying to model with objects is beneficial in terms of scientific parsimony and ordered thought. For example, I doubt whether the solution of a differential equation is best modelled with objects. Here another idea promoted by Jackson (1995) may be useful. He argues that one can recognize analysis patterns (which he calls problem frames) that recur and which imply suitable modelling methods. This classification-based approach provides references for solving future problems of the same or similar types. One example is the 'simple IS frame', which indicates that a JSP approach is suitable. The arguments in this case are convincing, but generally I find that object modelling gives more chance of success than any other general approach and that JSP can be accommodated as a technique within an object-oriented approach. Kristen (1995), for one, does this within his KISS method. Jackson's problem frames can be criticized for being *post facto* rationalizations of only a few well known situations, so that they do not help much with the discovery of solutions to new problems. Nor does Jackson provide a concrete process for applying the approach. However, this can be said of any pattern oriented approach and the power of such approaches is widely recognized.

Jackson's M metaphor provides us with an understanding of the correspondence between two worlds – the domain and the machine in the example above. However, if we are to apply object modelling to a realistic business problem it turns out that this is often too simplistic a view. In practice we must build a linked series of models more reminiscent of a tasty *mmmmmm* than single M. de Champeaux (1997) offers some support for this view. He distinguishes between two approaches to object modelling that he characterizes as constructivist (neat) and impressionist (scruffy). Scruffies do not emphasise the precise semantics of object modelling. They opine 'the design fleshes out the analysis' without being precise about what this means. Precision is only introduced in the implementation models when the semantics of a programming language has to be faced. The neats are different. They want to 'exploit the analysis computational model' and observe that analysis models are 'nearly executable'. Examples of approaches close to the spirit of the neats include those of Cook and Daniels and of de Champeaux himself. In both cases precision relies heavily on the use of state models, but this is not necessarily always the case. In SOMA, for example, there is a defined sequence of model transformations but state machines are only an optional technique. We model the business mission and objectives, the interactions among the agents involved in the business, the tasks that they perform and the business objects that they use and refer to before implementing a system. Each of these models is transformed into the next using procedures to be discussed in the next chapter.

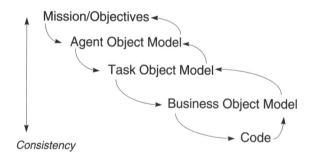

Figure 4.2 The SOMA validation pattern (after Bezant, 1997)

At each model transformation we validate the consistency of the models as suggested by Figure 4.2. Doing so guarantees that the resultant system meets its users' objectives. As we will see in Chapter 5 some of these models are object models and some are not.

4.1.1 The need for multiple models

The normal approach of object-oriented analysis and design methods is to offer a notation for object modelling and possibly a semantic meta-model. This notation is then used to construct a model of the computer system to be built, either at the level of business objects or in a way more closely attuned with a programming language. This technique may be preceded by various other, usually non-object-oriented techniques for requirements capture (such as use cases) or user interface design (such as Browne's (1994) STUDIO). It is my view that object-orientation both can and should be used throughout the life cycle. This is more parsimonious in terms of the number of modelling techniques that have to be learnt or understood. It is also more seamless as I shall show later.

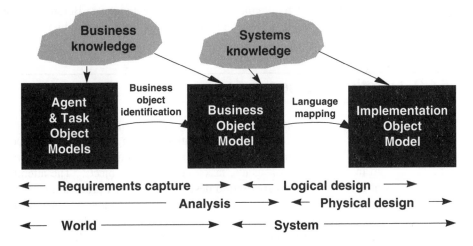

Figure 4.3 Object model sequence

SOMA therefore advocates the construction of a linked sequence of object models as indicated in Figure 4.3. First we build a model of the concrete, real-world business. This is done by using our standard object modelling semantics to construct an object model where the objects are the 'agents' – human and otherwise – that operate and connect to our business. These agents, of course, communicate by message passing as in any standard object model. This is the Agent Object Model.

The operations of an agent object are the tasks performed by that agent. We can also construct an object model of these tasks: the Task Object Model. Finally, we can extract business objects from the descriptions of these tasks and refine the resultant model using normal object modelling skills. This leads to the Business Object Model, which for the first time begins to look like a model of a computer system. We then have a choice. If we only want to produce an executable version of the specification, perhaps as a prototype, then we can employ a code generator to do this directly from the Business Object Model. Alternatively, we may wish to engage in more careful physical design to exploit the features of a particular language or special hardware. In that case we must convert the Business Object Model into an Implementation Object Model that takes account of the features of such a language. SOMA is language independent and therefore cannot be used directly for this purpose. The developers can use a technique of their choice. Typical choices at the time of writing would be Booch or UML. A SOMA Business Object Model stored in *SOMATiK* can be converted automatically into a UML class model in Rational *Rose*. *Rose* can print such a model using the UML, Booch or OMT notations. A reverse link to convert a *Rose* model to a *SOMATiK* model is also available. Alternatively, *SOMATiK* can generate C++ directly.

In the next chapter we will examine this sequence in detail and present a complete set of requirements engineering techniques. Before we can do that, we must understand better what an object model consists of and how to build one.

4.2 Notation and semantics

The basics of object modelling were explained in Chapter 1. Now we present the details. This section defines our notation and language for object modelling and the equivalent UML notation. We will use it to formulate all the object models referred to in Section 4.1: of agents, tasks and business objects. The attentive reader will note that it was already used to describe the SOMA process life cycle in Chapter 2. However, in this chapter I ask you to think of the language as applied to a business object model in the normal way. We show that the language must have certain features before it can be sufficiently expressive while still supporting encapsulation and expose some defects of UML in this respect. The section is fairly dense in order that we may get on to the book's main topics more quickly.

We begin, in this chapter, to introduce the reader to the *SOMATiK* software insofar as it enables developers to create and store business object models. The use of the SOMA method does not depend at all on the use of *SOMATiK*, but the latter does provide a useful existence theorem for a type of tool different from conventional CASE and well-suited to illustrating the ideas of SOMA.

4.2.1 Describing individual objects

The basic concept that we will work with is that of an object. An **object** is anything with unique identity throughout its lifetime. All objects consist of an interface and an implementation, with the implementation hidden. The interface shows the identity and features of the object and can be represented textually or graphically. There are two standardized graphical notations: UML (Fowler, 1997; Rational, 1997) and OML (Firesmith *et al.*, 1997). We will use an extension of OML but always give the UML version as well, where one exists. The resulting notation is known as the SOMA Modelling Language. We will see as we proceed that neither OML or UML is quite rich enough to represent the semantics required to model the business functions that we will consider, although OML is richer than UML. For example, UML sequence diagrams cannot represent concurrency, looping or branching while OML uses logic boxes to this end. Also OML distinguishes three kinds of inheritance while UML has only one. This is useful in relation to programming languages such as Java that distinguish specialization from interface inheritance. The reader may choose freely which notation to adopt for subsequent work, making the necessary modifications as needed.

The **features** of an object's interface are divided into **responsibilities** and **rulesets**. Responsibilities divide further into **responsibilities for knowing** about the object's state and **responsibilities for doing** things: either to change that state or to send messages to other objects.

Uniquely, the interfaces of SOMA objects include rulesets: unordered sets of if/then rules and assertions concerning the object's other responsibilities. Rulesets generalize the class invariants of other methods because they can be chained together, giving the object the ability to make inferences.

Rulesets could be regarded as responsibilities for being: being coherent in a certain sense. Normally, object modelling languages do not insist that class invariants or, more generally, rulesets are encapsulated by objects. I prove in Appendix A that encapsulation **implies** the need for this. In other words objects without rules are not really objects, or as Desmond D'Souza has remarked (D'Souza, 1997) a signature is not enough to specify an object.

An object always has the following responsibilities for knowing:

- a list of its superclasses;
- a list of its components;
- its attributes;
- its associated classes (associations).

Its responsibilities for doing are called its **operations**. Operations are specifications for methods. Methods implement the behaviour of the object.

Objects may be classes or instances. Both satisfy the definition of object given above. Messages may be sent to classes or to instances. **Classes** are collections of several instances and are thus always named in the plural. **Instances** represent individual things and are named in the singular. For example, Marco Polo is an instance of the class of all People. This is consciously and deliberately different from the naming convention adopted by approaches descended from relational technology where the opposite convention is normally used and the class would be called Person. The latter conventional makes for database queries that read nicely but is confusing when it comes to cardinality and the class/instance distinction. Strictly speaking a class implements a **type**: the idea or intension behind the class that is extended through its instances. Being a single idea, a type should be named in the singular; so that Person is a type, People the class that implements it and

Marco Polo is an instance of this class. Types can be thought of as interfaces. As Fowler (1996) points out correctly, the analyst is mostly concerned with types. However, we shall deal with classes in this text, since our specifications will be executable. If you prefer to think of what we are discussing as types, then by all means do so. What I refer to as an object in this book is referred to in OPEN as a **CIRT** (Class, Instance, Rôle or Type), signifying that a precise determination is not necessary at this stage in the analysis process (Graham *et al.*, 1997). UML restricts the term OBJECT to mean only instance.

Graphically, we can represent classes as shown in Figure 4.4 where the icon on the left is in the SOMA notation (which in this case is the same as that of OML). In UML there is no notion of rulesets, so the best that can be done is to attach a textual 'note' as shown on the right, or perhaps a stereotype – either solution is slightly awkward because notes and stereotypes have many other uses; and this one is rather special. OML, as presented by Firesmith *et al.* (1997), would have to present an icon, with three 'drop-down boxes' for the attributes, operations and rulesets. This is clearly only appropriate if a CASE tool is in use.

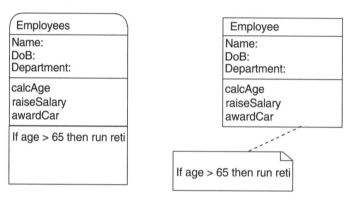

Figure 4.4 Classes in SOMA, OML and UML

Actually, I have a made a small *faux pas* in Figure 4.4 by choosing **Employees** as a class. This would perhaps make sense in a payroll system but, normally, we should regard **Employees** as a rôle rather than a class. The difference is that the instances of a rôle may come and go, while instances of a class are for life. To be clearer, once you become a Person (either at birth, 28 days after conception, at conception or as soon as your parents first stare at each other across that smoky bar – according to your religious bias) you stay one till you die (or beyond – according to …). However, being an employee is a temporary and sometimes precarious business. One can pass from being a student to being an employee and terminate that state for several causes: retirement, redundancy, resignation, etc. Most object-oriented languages have no features that support this kind of dynamic instantiation. It can be modelled using state attributes (see below) or using a pattern such as the

State or Visitor patterns of Gamma *et al.* (1995). In this text we will use classes to model rôles. A detailed discussion of rôle modelling would be out of place in this work. A more complete treatment is given by Reenskaug *et al.* (1996).

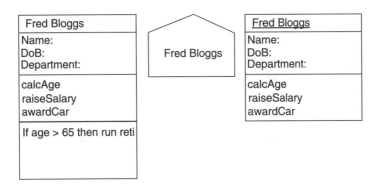

Figure 4.5 Instances in SOMA, OML and UML

Instances are shown in SOMA with sharp corners as shown on the left in Figure 4.5. OML has a slightly different notation that I regard as unnecessarily difficult to draw and do not therefore use it. It merely gives the instance icon a pointed top. UML uses the same icon for classes and instances, merely underlining the instance name.

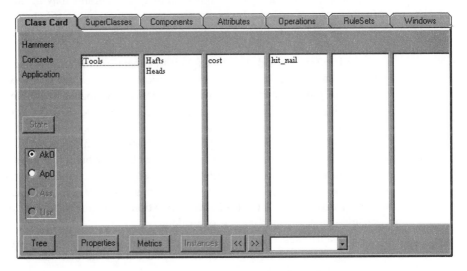

Figure 4.6 Classes in *SOMATiK*

All the notation introduced so far is intended for use on paper or perhaps in a simple CASE or graphics tool that helps its users to draw simple two-dimensional pictures. We can also represent a class using the rather more powerful and active notation of *SOMATiK* shown in Figure 4.6.

Figure 4.6 shows a summary of information stored about a class called Hammers. If you have a copy of *SOMATiK*, to create such a class click the ObjectLists tool or find its equivalent on the View menu. Now click on the Classes tab on the right of your screen and type Hammers in the list box. After two carriage returns you will see a summary view of a *SOMATiK* class card as shown in the figure. This has exactly the meaning of the notation in Figure 4.4 but is a little more powerful. Hammers is a subclass of Tools; click on the superclasses tab, add this superclass and return to the summary (Class Card) tab. As a further exercise, add Hafts and Heads as components and then add some attributes such as cost.

FACETS A feature of an object is either an attribute, association, operation or a public ruleset. Private rulesets are not features because they are not part of the object's interface. But all features and rulesets may have **facets**. Attributes are placeholders for values. They may also be regarded as pointers to primitive types: Reals, Chars, Dates, etc. Indeed, the difference between attributes and associations is quite arbitrary. An attribute is merely an association to a class that represents a primitive type. We need to make the distinction to avoid cluttering up our diagrams with classes such as Reals or even dates. What is designated as primitive is up to the discretion of the analyst or designer, so that the diagrams may be easily adjusted to fit the purpose at hand by converting associations into attributes. In *SOMATiK*, they may be readily promoted back to associations later, with no loss of information because the tool remembers the cardinality constraints.

It is often claimed that the explicit treatment of attributes violates the principle of information hiding and thus encapsulation. However, the complexity of the data structures present in most commercial systems – compared to simple programming abstractions like windows or stacks – leads to the need to make attributes explicit and visible. Thus, in this method we retain attributes in the interface. To retain some object-oriented purity, we regard each attribute in this window as a shorthand for two standard methods. For example, the attribute name is short for the operations getName and putName (or setName). Special versions of these operations may be included in the operations list, in which case they override the standard operations. Each of these operations is regarded as containing standard security checks, which may be overridden.

All attributes may have facets, which add details such as type, ownership, defaults, valid ranges, etc. Validation and other conditions must be specified for each attribute as facets.

An operation may contain (along with facets for the details of the method's function, parameters and type information) invariance, pre- and post-condition facets: conditions that must hold when the method is running, fires and terminates respectively. These are called **assertions**. In this way, a part of the control structure is encapsulated in the object's methods. Note that these definitions extend the Eiffel notion of assertions with the idea of invariance conditions. The latter are important when concurrency is an issue and should not be confused with Eiffel class invariants. Invariance conditions apply to individual operations whereas class invariants refer to the whole object. Class invariants are also a kind of assertion.

Another important facet of an operation is its list of servers and the messages sent to them. Some operations may be sequentially nested, where several operations are executed together in a fixed sequence. These should be represented as 'subroutines' of an operation representing the combined effect. Such subroutines can also be invoked directly by messages unless otherwise indicated by a 'private' facet. The facets of a ruleset are its rules and its inference régime as explained later.

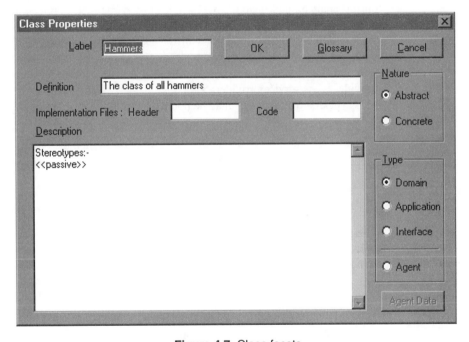

Figure 4.7 Class facets

Objects may also have facets that are universally called stereotypes nowadays. For example, we distinguish between application and domain objects. **Domain objects** are those considered to be generally useful throughout an enterprise and which are likely to be servers for other objects. **Application objects** are more contingent; they arise in specific applications and may never be used again. Classes such as Orders or Products are likely to be domain objects. Rôles such as Students may be domain objects in an educational context but application objects elsewhere. This distinction is imprecise but is intended to assist with assessing the need for generalization for reuse and with providing a form of data independence. A third category available is that of **interface objects**. These are the new objects introduced during logical design that are not strictly business objects at all. The complete details of a class, including its stereotypes, are recorded on a **class card** either in *SOMATiK* or on paper (see Figures 4.6 and 5.18 respectively). We will use the class cards later to support model validation walkthroughs.

As an example of these distinctions in most business domains, Products and Transactions are unarguably domain objects, while DiscountCalculators might be a special application object. Classes like Sensors and InputValidators are likely to be interface objects.

Other stereotypes that are sometimes useful include controllers, co-ordinators, information holders and service providers. As Wirfs-Brock and McKean (1996) point out, these classifications are intentionally over-simplifications to be refined during analysis and design. *SOMATiK* class cards (see Figure 4.6) provide radio buttons for a few common stereotypes, such as Application/Domain/Interface or Agent. Others must be recorded in the Description field of the Class Properties dialogue box illustrated in Figure 4.7. We adopt the UML notation in adding stereotypes to the class description whereby the indication that a class is a service provider is: <<service provider>>.

Typical attribute facets may be notated as follows:

■ Every attribute has a type, which is either a primitive type (integer, date, etc.) or a user defined object type or class. When the type is a class, there can be cardinality information indicated. This is an association (see below).

■ An attribute may have a list of allowed values (if it is of enumeration type).

■ An attribute may be declared as a state variable that represents one of a number of enumerated states that the object may occupy. Ideally there should be only one such attribute per class.

■ Types are qualified as either {set}, {bag}, {ordered set} or {list}.

■ Initial values and default values are shown as follows: attrib(type,n,m); init=x; default=y.

■ Attributes can be variable/fixed/common/unique. **Fixed** means that the value may not change during the lifetime of the object. Different instances may have different values and we need not know what these values are. **Variable** is the opposite of fixed and is the default. **Common** attributes require that all instances have the same value, again without necessarily knowing what it is. **Unique** attributes are the opposite of common ones; each instance has a different value. A well-known example is a primary key in a database table. The default is neither common nor unique. The notation is one of the following: {variable}, {fixed}, {common}, {unique}, {fixed,common}, {fixed,unique}, {variable,common}, {variable,unique}.

■ Security level may be specified.

■ Ownership may be specified.

- Null values may be permitted or not. If not, the facet NON-NULL is set true. For associations this is shown by a minimal cardinality of 1; e.g. WorksFor(Depts.,1,n).
- Valid range constraints may be specified; e.g. age>16.
- $ before an attribute name indicates a class attribute. Its absence indicates an instance attribute. A class attribute is a property of a collection of the class's instances such as the maximum height of People. An instance attribute may have a different value for each instance such as the height of a person.
- × before an attribute name indicates that it cannot inherit its value.
- / before an attribute name indicates a derived (i.e. inherited) attribute.

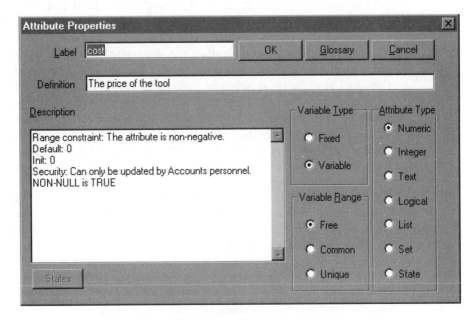

Figure 4.8 Attribute facets

Facets are a gloss on each feature together with information on ownership, nullity, valid range, defaults, computation, derivation, security, visibility, class/instance applicability and so on. Attribute facets include also pre- and post-conditions on get and put operations.

4.2.2 Structural links between objects

Of course, objects are related to each other. The number of different types of relationship between objects is potentially infinite and we could regard a web of such interconnexions as a semantic network. Indeed, this is the term adopted by OML (Firesmith *et al.,* 1997). However, in my view there are four especially important kinds of linkage between object, which we discuss in this section: inheritance, composition, usage and undifferentiated association. The first three are all strengthenings of the idea of an association.

INHERITANCE If we wish to represent the idea of inheritance discussed in Chapter 1, we need a way of encapsulating the knowledge about a class's superclasses. Let us be clear that we should not do the opposite, because for a superclass to know its subclasses would violate encapsulation. This is because if we want to add a new subclass, to modify the function of a component say, then we do not want to have to modify the component's list of subclasses.

Strictly speaking, the idea behind inheritance refers to several different things. An instance can be a member of a class; so that we can say that Fido is a Dog. This is called **classification** and abbreviated IsA. All Dogs are a kind of Mammal, including Fido, and all Mammals are Vertebrates. This latter relationship is known as **generalization** or **specialization** and abbreviated AKO (a kind of). Inheritance is often only used to refer to the implementation of AKO in a program, where it can be used to enforce the semantic subtype as per an analysis model or to merely borrow (inherit) some features from a class that is not a true supertype. The latter is referred to as implementation inheritance. There is also a difference between black-box and white-box inheritance, whereby the subclass can inherit only the public (interface) features or the private ones respectively. OML and UML have plenty of notation to represent such notions and details. However, such matters are usually of little interest or relevance to the requirements engineer or analyst and we can safely ignore them in this text. When we talk about inheritance we shall always be speaking of semantic classification or generalization and when we want to distinguish the two ideas we will use **IsA** and **AKO**. We will also lump all these together by routinely using the term CLASSIFICATION STRUCTURE to include classification and generalization links.

Classification relationships can, of course, be shown graphically. This relationship is a very close one because it can give a subclass access to the implementation of a superclass. For this reason both SOMA and OML use a thick arrow for specialization (AKO) and a thin arrow for any other kind of relationship or structural link. A dotted thick arrow represents classification (IsA). Figure 4.9 (a) shows how the idea could be used to represent a simple retail banking idea wherein all Bank accounts have responsibilities for printing statements and storing customers' details. Current accounts (checking accounts in American English) are specializations that can send a new cheque book when they detect the customer is running out of cheques. Deposit (savings) accounts cannot do this but can calculate monthly interest accruals. In UML an empty triangle is used to signify inheritance, as shown in Figure 4.10.

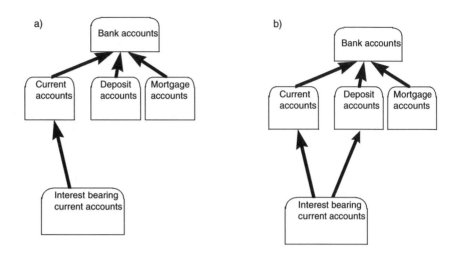

Figure 4.9 Single and multiple inheritance in SOMA or OML notation

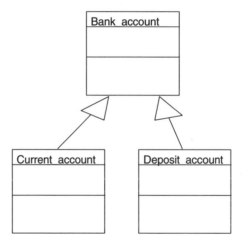

Figure 4.10 Inheritance in UML notation

Many years ago, UK banks did not offer current accounts that paid interest but were gradually forced to introduce them in the late 1970s. In fact, they incurred major system re-writing costs as a result. If they had been using object-oriented techniques back then, they could have merely added a new subclass of Current accounts as shown in Figure 4.9, obviating the need to change existing code or code new behaviour other than that concerned with the interest computation. If they had been using a language that supported it, they could have been even smarter and used **multiple inheritance**: the ability of a class to inherit from more than one generalization. In that way they would not even have had to code the interest calculation: inheriting it instead from Deposit accounts. This strategy is shown in Figure 4.9 (b).

Of course, there are problems with multiple inheritance; two operations with the same name but different implementations may be inherited by the same object. Therefore multiple inheritance, although a powerful modelling tool, can be a little dangerous in inexperienced hands. Multiple inheritance is at its most useful when building libraries of reusable components. The arguments for this are given convincingly by Meyer (1994).

To illustrate further how inheritance makes systems flexible for the programmers among you, consider the problem of error trapping. In the conventional style of a language like C we might write something like:

```
Switch (n)
{case 1: error = 49;
      print("Warning - Error 49");
 case 2: error = 71;
      print("Execution halting due to Error 71");break;
 case 3: continue;
}
```

With this style of coding, the documentation cannot really be any simpler than the code itself. Adding a new case means recompiling and linking the system and of course such code is seldom reusable. Now imagine what an object-oriented programmer would do using the simple classification structure for errors shown in Figure 4.11. If our programmer were suddenly to uncover a totally new type of error – let's call it a fawning error – he could merely add a new subclass somewhere in this structure and create an instance of it. In some languages he would not even have to stop the system running to do this. The argument illustrated by this rather artificial example is that inheritance makes systems inherently more extensible.

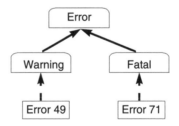

Figure 4.11 Object-oriented error trapping

ASSOCIATION Every structural link between objects that is not a classification, composition or usage link is called an association. In fact, classification, composition and usage are all just special kinds of association. In SOMA associations are represented as pointers and state that the object that stores the pointer knows about some feature of the object that it is pointing at. We already have the notion of the interface to an object containing an attribute and its facets. We view associations as generalized attributes. An attribute contains zero or more values of a nominated type; an association stores values of a nominated user defined (or library) type. The only difference is that attributes point at 'primitive' types. What is primitive is up to the analyst and a key criterion for making this decision is whether the type (class) should appear on the class model diagrams.

Typical associations in an HR application might include ones that show that employees must work for exactly one department while departments may employ zero or more employees. These are shown as follows.

WorksIn: (Depts,1,1) is an attribute of Employees.

Employs: (Employees,0,n) is an attribute of Depts.

We regard attributes as split into two sorts: **pure attributes** and (attributes representing) **associations**. The associations of pure attributes are not shown in the association structure diagrams, mainly to avoid clutter. The default cardinality for a pure attribute is (0,1); if the attribute is non-null this is shown as a facet. In *SOMATiK* the Attributes tab on a class card expands to show both attributes and associations.

My definition of associations is radically different from that of methods such as OMT, Shlaer/Mellor, Coad or UML. These methods view associations as external to objects and their metamodels require a new primitive to accommodate them. This shows up most clearly when bi-directional associations are used.

As we have seen, one of the two basic and characteristic features of object-orientation is the principle of encapsulation. This says that objects hide the implementation of their data structures and processing and are used only via their interface. An object-oriented model uses object types to represent all concepts and divides these types (or their implementations as classes) into a public interface representing the type's responsibilities and an implementation that is hidden completely from all other parts of the system. The advantages of this are that it localizes maintenance of the classes and facilitates their reuse via calls to their interfaces alone. Modifications to classes are avoided by creating specialized subclasses that inherit basic responsibilities and can override them and add new ones.

Bi-directional associations violate encapsulation. Stating that class A is associated with class B in some way or other is a statement of knowledge that concerns BOTH classes. There are three obvious approaches to storing this knowledge:

■ If the knowledge is separated from either class then we must return to a system of first and second class object types such as the one that plagued semantic data modelling. This means that, when we reuse either A or B, we have to have knowledge that is external to both of them in order to ensure that important coupling information is carried into the new system. Since this knowledge is not part of the classes it is quite conceivable that it could be lost, forgotten or overlooked by a hasty developer.

■ Alternatively, we could place the knowledge inside one of the object types, A say. This will not work either, because now B will have lost track of its coupling with A and could not be reused successfully where this coupling was relevant.

■ Finally, we could store the knowledge in both A and B. This last approach leads to the well-known problems of maintaining two copies of the same thing and cannot usually be tolerated.

Thus, separating objects from relationships violates encapsulation and compromises reuse. However, I will demonstrate in Appendix A how the knowledge can indeed be split between the two types without loss of integrity, using rules encapsulated in the objects.

One other way in which UML violates encapsulation is the use of its constraint language. Constraints on the way objects are related are written on UML diagrams near the associations that they refer to and connected to them by unadorned dotted lines. Clearly no class encapsulates them. For a particularly striking example of how foolish and unnecessary this is, consider the {or} constraint shown in Figure 4.12. This example is actually taken from the UML documentation. It shows that a bank account can be held by a person or an organization, but not by both.

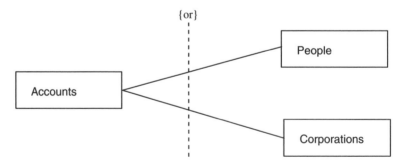

Figure 4.12 A UML constraint violating encapsulation

The amazing thing is that any object-oriented designer should know perfectly well that, instead of this bad design, one should utilize inheritance polymorphism to represent the disjunction, as in Figure 4.13. Here exactly the same information is conveyed and encapsulation is preserved. In addition we have forced the discovery of a very reusable class and − I would assert − a new analysis pattern.

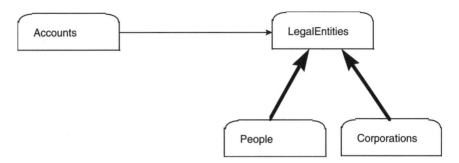

Figure 4.13 Polymorphism makes constraints unnecessary (OML)

As I have said, inheritance is not the only structural link between objects that is possible. In SOMA there are three others. In both SOMA and OML the most fundamental link is called an association or mapping. This is represented by a thin arrow connecting two classes or instances (the third picture from the left in Figure 4.14). This says that A stores information about the existence of some feature of B's interface. Inheritance makes a stronger statement: that a subclass has privileged access to the implementation of a superclass.

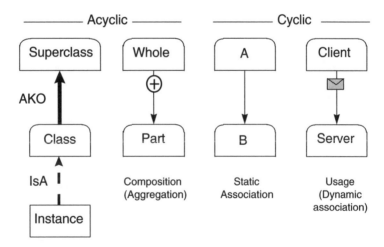

Figure 4.14 OML Light notation

APO   Apart from inheritance (classification) there are two other ways in which we can
strengthen an association.   These are known as composition and usage.
Composition indicates that a whole is made of (physically composed of) its parts.
A good heuristic test for whether a relationship is a composition relationship is to
ask: 'if the part moves, can one deduce that the whole moves with it in normal
circumstances?'.   For example, the relationship 'is the managing director of'
between People and Companies is not a composition because if the MD goes on
holiday to the Alps then the company does not. On the other hand if his legs go the
Alps then the MD probably goes too (unless he has seriously upset some
unscrupulous business rivals). The arrow is adorned with a plus sign in a circle
indicating addition or assembly (the icon represents the head of a Philips or
posidrive screw). This is a semantic notion that should not be confused with the
notions of aggregation or composition in UML. These are represented by empty
and filled diamonds respectively as shown in Figure 4.15 and represent
programming language level concepts. In UML the empty diamond of aggregation
designates that the whole maintains a *reference* to its part, so that the whole may
not have created the part. This is equivalent to a C++ reference or pointer
construction. The filled diamond signifies that the whole is responsible for creating
its 'parts', which is equivalent to saying in C++ that when the whole class is
allocated or declared the constructors of the part classes are called followed by the
constructor for the whole (Texel and Williams, 1997). It is clear to me that this has
little to do with the analysis of business objects. We continue to use the terms
composition and aggregation interchangeably and the OML screwhead symbol to
represent the common-sense notion of assembled components. The semantics of
this notion were explored in detail by Odell (1994) whose argument may be
summarized as follows.

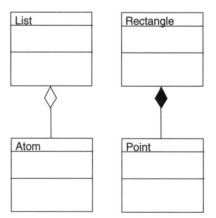

Figure 4.15 Aggregation and composition in UML

Odell classifies composition relationships according to three decisions: whether they represent a structural relationship (configurational), whether the parts are of the same type as the whole (homeomeric) and whether the parts can be detached from the whole (invariant). This evidently factors APO into eight types. He then discusses six of them and names his different interpretations of composition as follows:

1. Component-integral (configurational, non-homeomeric and non-invariant).
2. Material (configurational, non-homeomeric and invariant).
3. Portion (configurational, homeomeric and non-invariant).
4. Place-area (configurational, homeomeric and invariant).
5. Member bunch (non-configurational, non-homeomeric and non-invariant).
6. Member-partnership (non-configurational, non-homeomeric and invariant).

In SOMA we only use configurational, invariant composition. All other types of so-called composition (such as the manages relationship alluded to above) are handled by either associations or attributes (which are merely a special case of associations in SOMA).

Some authorities regard the notion of composition as undefinable and others definable only in terms of some specified set of operations defined on the whole. I recommend that composition is used sparingly in business object modelling but we will see that it is absolutely essential when modelling tasks as objects, as we do in Chapter 5.

USAGE   **Usage** relationships signify that not only does a client know about the existence of a feature of a server but that it will actually send a message to exercise that feature at some point. Ordinary associations might never be exercised. This is not, as many of my critics have claimed, an implementation concept but a key part of the semantics of a model. Saying that two classes are associated does not imply that the structural link between them will ever be traversed. For example, there may be many relationships in a database that are there to support *ad hoc* queries that may never be made by any user. A usage link on the other hand states that there will be some interaction or collaboration. The existence of usage links removes the need for a separate notion for collaboration graphs as found in RDD (Wirfs-Brock *et al.*, 1990). This kind of relationship is also extremely important in requirements engineering and business process modelling, as we shall see in Chapter 5 when we come to modelling agents in businesses as objects. It is a concept missing from both OML and UML, although in UML one could use a dependency labelled 'uses' to represent the idea. Henderson-Sellers (1998) argues for the inclusion of a 'uses' relationship in OML.

In SOMA terms, one class 'uses' another if it is a client to the other class acting as a server. This specific usage relation is an important feature of the SOMA approach. Any associations introduced may subsequently be replaced by more specific usage or (more rarely) composition relationships.

```
/* example operation script for Orders.order */

BeginWindow ('Order Dialogue')
      OnChange 'orderNo'
              GetInstance('Orders','orderNo')
      EndHandler
EndWindow
Operation: 'sendInvoice' of Class 'AccountsWrapper'
      Send: ;
  Receive: ;
Operation: 'deliver' of Class 'DispatchAgents'
      Send: ;
  Receive: ;
```

Figure 4.16 An operation script sending messages to other classes

Usage relationships between one class and another are defined in *SOMATiK* by the encapsulating a message passing operation in an operation script of the sending class. The example given in Figure 4.16 shows how such an operation is defined. The script in this highly simplified example, which is part of the class **Orders**, sends only two messages: one calling the operation **sendInvoice** of a class called **AcctsWrapper**; the other calling the operation **deliver** of class **DispatchAgents**. The usage structure implied by these operations, like any other, can now be generated automatically and is shown as Figure 4.17.

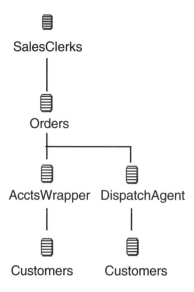

Figure 4.17 A usage structure

Note that the usage structure is complete in the sense that it shows the entire collaboration that will take place among the five classes in this very simple model. In this case the focus is currently on SalesClerks.

4.2.3 Building object models without drawing pictures

In *SOMATiK* the SOMA Business Object Model is implemented as a set of classes from which all the diagrams can be constructed. The classes are discovered from general domain knowledge and from an examination of the scripts of the task objects covered in Chapter 5. It is to be expected that building the class model and examining the structures generated during model construction will lead to further refinement of the model.

To create a class in *SOMATiK* you must fill in a 'class card' of the form shown in Figure 4.6. The class card has slots for specifying attributes, associations and operations. Inheritance links are created by specifying the superclass that the current class inherits from. Similarly, components of the current class can be specified. Once this information is present diagrams showing classification, composition and association links can be drawn automatically using the Tree button on the class card, as we saw for usage. Various facets of attributes, operations and rulesets can be specified. If operation scripts are added as facets of an operation then instances of the class can be created. These may be examined using the Instances button. I will explain how the model can be animated in the next chapter.

DRAWING STRUCTURES SOMA eschews class diagrams that draw association, classification, composition and usage arrows on the same page. We will see later that diagrams of large models involving all four structures quickly become impenetrable and unhelpful. They are very hard to read as soon as anything more than trivial is represented. In *SOMATiK* the structure diagrams are therefore drawn in a four dimensional space with only one kind of link permitted in each dimension. This makes a model's structure far easier to understand and navigate. Each kind of structural linkage is orthogonal to the others in the sense that separate diagrams can be generated for each type of relationship.

Where a node (a class) participates in more than one structure, the view may be flipped from one structure to the other as if we were operating in a four-dimensional space. Thus we have four orthogonal structures two of which, inheritance and composition, are acyclic, as indicated in Figure 4.10. Acyclicity means that cycles in the structure are not permitted, so that we cannot tolerate the situation when A is a kind (part) of B and B is a kind (part) of A. Cycles in the other two structures are permitted but note that we discourage recursive aggregation and association of the type found in UML. This is because an association with oneself should be described in the class's interface and not on an external inter-object diagram. To do the latter violates the principle of encapsulation somewhat.

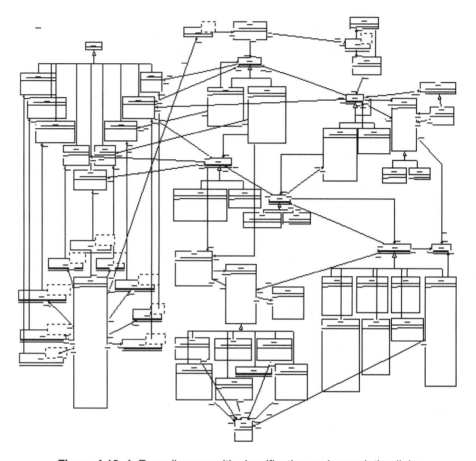

Figure 4.18 A *Rose* diagram with classification and association links

MULTI-
DIMENSIONAL
BROWSING

Many of the problems in representing the relationships among classes arise because we are dealing in a multidimensional space. To represent all relations on a single two-dimensional piece of paper requires the definition of a complex convention of notations to distinguish the various kinds of linkages. This in turn leads to the possibility of error and confusion in developing the diagrams, and down-right bewilderment on the part of users if they are asked to validate a static diagram.

To illustrate this Figure 4.18 shows a UML diagram generated by Rational *Rose*. The diagram consists of class icons (with their features suppressed to protect confidentiality) and inheritance and association links. This diagram was produced by reverse engineering an existing piece of C++ code from an important, live financial engineering application, and the associations are derived from usage relationships in that code. The purpose of doing this for the major investment bank concerned was to enable a new member of the development staff to understand the code and take over its maintenance. The details are not important and the diagram is far too small to see clearly (in actuality the printed version covered an entire desk) but it is immediately clear that it is impossible to say very much about the design. The diagram fails to expose whether the design of the code is bad or good.

SOMA and *SOMATiK* take a different approach to the problem. Recognizing that the computer is an intrinsic tool in the system design and development process, we aim for an almost invisible standard of notation, and instead use the capability of the computer to allow us to create projections across the various dimensions onto the plane.

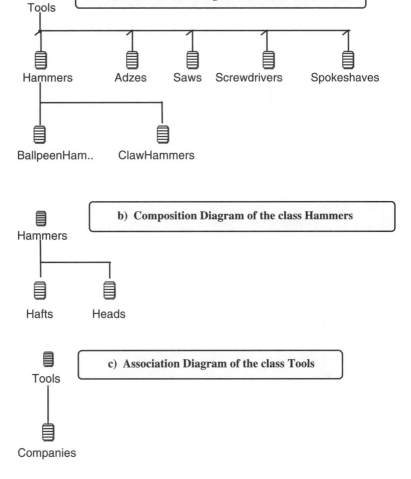

Figure 4.19 Automatically generated structure diagrams

The classification, composition, association and usage relations are therefore displayed as special cases of the overall collaboration of a class. The presentation is also a browser, so the user can leap from one dimension to another from the face of the diagram. By automatically generating the diagrams from the semantic description of the classes, we ensure that a consistent view of collaboration is maintained – something which is difficult to ensure if independent, bottom-up diagrams are being created to define the relationships in the first place.

In *SOMATiK*, the question of notation arises less sharply because the tool draws diagrams of all four structures automatically. Returning to our examples of hand tools, choosing the AKO radio button on the Tools class card and clicking Tree produces the classification diagram shown in Figure 4.19 (a). Clicking on the icon for Hammers in this diagram displays a pop-up menu that allows us to select the composition view in place of the current classification view. This is shown in Figure 4.19 (b). Alternatively, we could have navigated to the association view shown in Figure 4.19 (c).

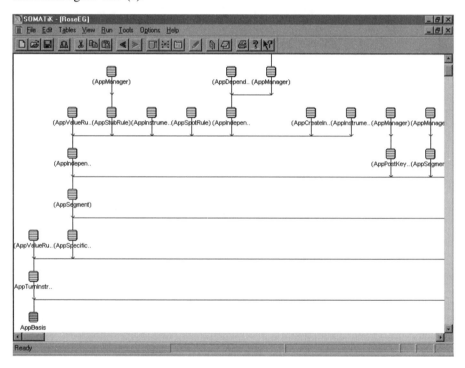

Figure 4.20 Usage dependencies in a C++ program

The tree diagrams discussed above can be switched between two views – an outline view which shows the maximum amount of structural information on the screen; and a detailed view that expands each class icon to show the attributes and operations of the classes.

In the case of the financial C++ application discussed above, the *Rose* model was converted to *SOMATiK* using the bridging technique built into *SOMATiK*. The *SOMATiK* user is then presented with an alphabetical list of classes. Let us suppose that the class AppBasis catches the attention first. We can ask *SOMATiK* to present the usage structure for this class, a fragment of which is shown in Figure 4.20. This form of presentation shows immediately that there are many classes that are dependent on AppBasis. Perhaps there is a fundamental design flaw. Before we can proceed with this example and find out if this is the case we must first understand the significance of the brackets that appear around some of the class names.

DERIVED DEPENDENCY It is important to realize that although classification and composition structures are orthogonal, they do interact with each other. A subclass inherits the components of all its superclasses. Few graphical case tools are able to make this properly clear, because diagrams are usually drawn by developers fron the bottom-up, and can be incomplete. Therefore, there is a risk that a subclass could be burdened with extra copies of components which have already been inherited.

Consider a class A with subclasses B and C. A has components AC1 and AC2. Class B has components BC1 and BC2. The correct composition structure for Class B is as shown in Figure 4.21. Note that components AC1 and AC2, which are inherited from the superclass A, are shown correctly in the diagram, showing their names enclosed in brackets indicates that they are inherited .

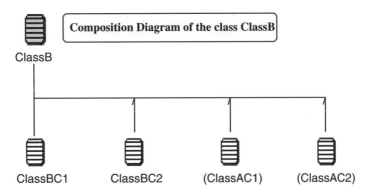

Figure 4.21 Inheriting components

Figure 4.22 shows the classification and composition structures for the class A. The fact that *SOMATiK* auto-generates all the diagrams ensures that the diagrams are both complete and consistent.

These structure, or 'tree' diagrams provide a useful tool for exploring the structure of a model. All directly and indirectly related classes can be reached within a single complete and coherent hyperdiagram.

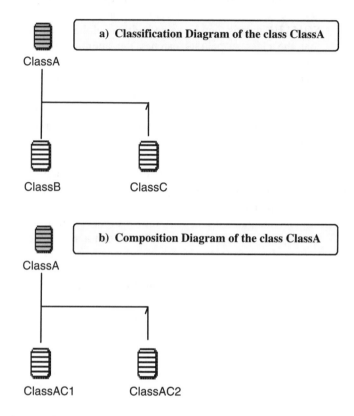

Figure 4.22 Classification and composition structures for class A

Returning to our financial example, we can ask *SOMATiK* to redraw the usage dependency diagram for AppBasis without the derived dependencies. The result is shown in Figure 4.23. It can be seen that the situation is not nearly as bad as it appeared, with only three clients now shown.

The next thing to be done is to look at the inheritance diagrams for the classes that produce the derived dependencies: AppDBCommon. This is easy to discover by merely switching to the classification view from any of the three clients. The offending tree is shown in Figure 4.24. My interpretation is that the author of this program has fallen victim to the use of implementation inheritance, which is easy to do in C++ especially where a framework library is in use. Also the very broad structure might well compromise the reusability of some components in a distributed environment. Other parts of the design revealed similar flaws and the application was successfully redesigned: starting off with a SOMA workshop of course!

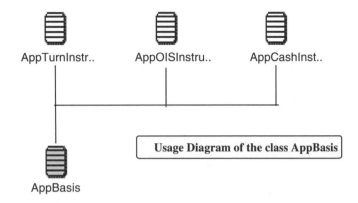

Figure 4.23 AppBasis usage without the derived dependencies

The conclusion we drew from this exercise was that two-dimensional visualization of complex object models is woefully inadequate except for the highest level of documentation. The power of modern graphical user interfaces makes multidimensional browsing possible and effective.

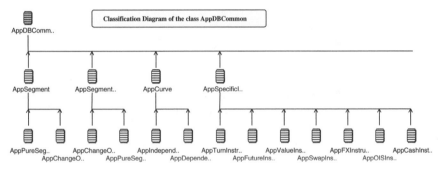

Figure 4.24 Inheritance tree for AppDBCommon

4.2.4 Rulesets and class invariants

As I prove in Appendix A, it is quite insufficient to specify only the attributes and operations (the signature) of an object. To specify the object completely we must say how these are allowed to interact with each other and what rules and constraints must be obeyed by the object as a whole to maintain its integrity as such. Some languages, such as Eiffel, and some methods, such as BON or Syntropy, achieve a partial solution by using assertions. Assertions in such systems are of two kinds: assertions about the operations and assertions about the whole object. The former are typically pre- and post-conditions while the latter are called class invariants. SOMA adds invariance conditions to the operational assertions and generalizes class invariants to rulesets. There are also assertion facets representing attribute constraints. Here are the definitions:

Attribute assertions

- **Range constraints** give limits on permissible values.
- **Enumeration constraints** list permissible values.
- **Type constraints** specify the class that values must belong to. Type constraints are always present.

Operational assertions

- A **pre-condition** is a single logical statement that must be true before its operation may execute.
- A **post-condition** is a single logical statement that must be true after its operation has finished execution.
- An **invariance condition** is a single logical statement that must hold at all times when its operation is executing. This is only of importance for parallel processing systems (including business process models).

The facets of an operation may include more than one assertion of any of these types. Assertions may be represented by state-transition diagrams as we shall see later.

Object assertions and rulesets

- A **class invariant** is a single logical statement about any subset of the features of an object that must be true at all times (in Eiffel this only applies to times when a method is not executing).
- A **ruleset** in an unordered set of class invariants (or **rules**) and assertions about attributes together with a defined inference régime that allows the rules to be chained together. **External rulesets** are part of the interface and express second order information. **Internal rulesets** are merely (first order) private operations. They may be written either in natural language or in the executable SOMA rule language.

The normal assumption behind the above definitions is that the logic to be used is standard first order predicate calculus (FOPC). In SOMA we make no such assumption although FOPC is the default logic. Other logics that can be used include temporal, fuzzy, deontic, epistemic and non-monotonic logic. Each class in a system determines its own logic locally.

Rulesets generalize class invariants and permit objects to do several things:

- Infer attribute values that are not stored explicitly.
- Represent database triggers.
- Represent referential or semantic integrity constraints (*cf.* Appendix A).
- Represent operations in a non-procedural fashion.
- Represent control régimes.

The last application of rulesets is by far and away the most esoteric. Object-oriented methods must obviously deal with multiple inheritance. This extension must include provision for annotating the handling of conflict arising when the same attribute or operation is inherited differently from two parent objects. One way to deal with this is to use rulesets to disambiguate multiple inheritance. One can then also define priority rules for defaults and demons. (A demon is a method that wakes up when needed; i.e. when a value changes, or is added or deleted.) That is, these rules can determine how to resolve the conflict that arises when an attribute inherits two different values or perhaps specify whether the default value should be applied before or after inheritance takes place or before or after a demon fires. They may also specify the relative priorities of inheritance and demons.

Business rules specify second order information, such as dependencies between attributes; for example, a dependency between the age of an employee and her holiday entitlement. Global class invariants and pre- and post-conditions that apply to all operations may be specified as rules. A typical business rule in a human resources application might include 'change holiday entitlement to six weeks when service exceeds five years' as a rule in the **Employees** class. With rulesets the notation can cope with analysis problems where an active database is envisaged as the target environment.

Rulesets are composed of an unordered set of assertions and rules of either 'if/then' or 'when/then' form. This modelling extension has a number of interesting consequences, the most remarkable of which is that these objects – which are local entities – can encapsulate the rules for global system behaviour. Another consequence is that objects with rulesets can be regarded as intelligent agents for expert systems developments.

As with attributes and operations, the interface of the object only displays the name of a ruleset and, in the case of a backward chaining ruleset, the name of the value being sought: its goal.

Rules may be of several different types. For instance, we may have triggers, business rules and control rules. Business rules typically relate two or more attributes and triggers relate attributes to operations. For example:

```
Business rule:
        If Service_length > 5 then Holiday=25
Forward Trigger:
        When Salary + SalaryIncrement > 20000
              run AwardCompanyCar
```

The above simple business rule is interesting because we could evidently implement it in two completely different ways. We could place a pre-condition on getHoliday that always checks Service_length before returning the value. Alternatively, we could place a post-condition on putService_length that detects whether Holiday should be changed on every anniversary. Clearly, the former corresponds to lazy and the latter to eager evaluation. The important point here is that we should **not** be making design decisions of this nature during analysis. Using a rule-based approach defers these decisions to a more appropriate point.

Quite complex rules can be expressed simply as rulesets. For example an **InsuranceSalesmen** class might contain the rules for giving the best advice to a customer in the form shown in Figure 4.25.

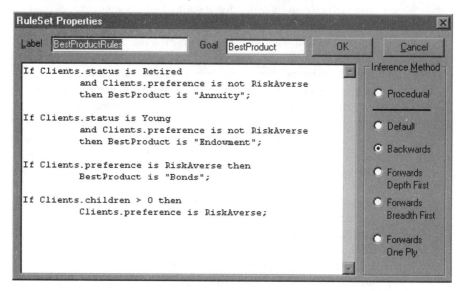

Figure 4.25 A ruleset

The rules fire when a value for **BestProduct** is needed. Note that these rules do not compromise the encapsulation of **Clients** by setting the value of RiskAverse in that object. The Salesman is merely making an assumption in the face of missing data or prompting the **Clients** for that information. If the Clients.preference attribute is already set to RiskAverse, these rules never fire. Note also the non-procedural character of this ruleset. The rule that fires first is written last. The ruleset executes under a backward chaining régime to seek a value for BestProduct. Thus, we can see that the language is non-procedural. That is, the ordering of a set of rules does not affect their interpretation.

Control rules are encapsulated within objects, instead of being declared globally. They may also be inherited and overridden. The benefit of this is that local variations in control strategy are possible. Further, the analyst may inspect the impact of the control structure on every object – using a browser perhaps – and does not have to annotate convoluted diagrams to describe the local effects of global control. Genuinely global rules can be contained in a top level object, called 'object', and will be inherited by all objects that do not override them. Alternatively, we can set up global rules in a special 'policy blackboard' object. Relevant classes register interest in **Policies**, which broadcasts rule and status changes to registrants as necessary. This uses, of course, a publish and subscribe *pattern* (see Chapter 7). Just as state transition diagrams may be used to describe the procedural semantics of operations, so decision trees may be found useful in describing complex sets of rules.

Rules are used to make an object's semantics explicit and visible. This helps with the description of information that would normally reside in a repository, such as business rules for the enterprise. It can also help with inter-operability at quite a low level. For example, if I have an object which computes cube roots, as a client of that object it is not enough to know its operations alone; I need to know that what is returned is a cube root and not a square root. In this simple case the solution is obvious because we can characterize the cube root uniquely with one simple rule: the response times itself twice is equal to the parameter sent. If this rule is part of the interface then all other systems and system components can see the meaning of the object from its interface alone, removing thus some of the complexities of repository technology by shifting it into the object model.

Recall that assertions are also attached to each operation and are inherited. Another way of classifying rules and rule-sets is into the following six kinds:

1. Rules that relate Attributes to Attributes. Example: If Service >5 then Hols=Hols+1. This could be expressed as a post-condition on put.Service causing put.Hols(Hols+1) or as a pre-condition on get.Hols.
2. Rules that relate Operations to Operations. These are naturally expressed as assertions rather than rules anyhow.
3. Rules that relate Attributes to Operations. Example: These may be expressed as if_needed (pre.get) or if_changed demons (post.put) or as pre- or post-conditions.
4. Control rules for Attributes. Example: Behaviour under Multiple Inheritance conflicts and Defaults (pre-conditions on gets).
5. Control rules for Operations. Example: Behaviour under Multiple Inheritance conflicts (post-conditions on gets).
6. Exception handling rules. Example: Overheated sensor (invariance or post-condition on temp).

Control rules **concern** the operations and attributes of the object they belong to. They do not concern themselves. Thus, they cannot help with the determination of how to resolve a multiple inheritance conflict between rulesets or other control strategy problem related to rulesets. This would require a set of metarules to be encapsulated and these too would require a meta-language. This quickly leads to an infinite regress. Therefore, in SOMA, multiple inheritance of rules does not permit conflict resolution. A dot notation is used to duplicate any rulesets with the same name. Thus, if an object inherits rulesets called POLICYA from two superclasses, X and Y, they are inherited separately as X.POLICYA and Y.POLICYA. The case of fuzzy rules is slightly different since fuzzy rules cannot contradict each other as will be explained later. Therefore multiply inherited fuzzy rulesets with the same name may be merged. In both the crisp and fuzzy cases, however, the careful user of the method should decide every case on its merits, since the equivalent naming of the inherited rulesets could have been erroneous.

OMT's qualifiers may be expressed as rules. For example, consider the many-to-many association between DOS files and directories. The Filename qualifier reduces this to a many-to-one association. In general, qualification only partitions the sets. This is because qualification is relative; there is a degree of qualification. To avoid confusion SOMA uses rules such as 'Every file in the ListOfFiles attribute must have a unique name', a rule encapsulated in Directory. If FileNames is an attribute this can be avoided by writing FileNames[set of names] as opposed to [bag of ...] or [list of ...].

Rule based extensions to object-oriented analysis help enrich the semantics of models of conventional commercial systems. This makes these models more readable and more reversible; more of the analysts' intentions are evident in the model. SOMA also provides a truly object-oriented approach to the specification of advanced database and knowledge-based systems.

RULESETS IN SOMATiK   The class card also has a tab for entering rulesets of the sort discussed above and their facets, including a variable inference régime. The inference régimes available in *SOMATiK* are forward and backward chaining, opportunistic chaining (the default in *SOMATiK*) and procedural execution. Opportunistic chaining is the same as backward chaining except that whenever an attribute value is filled the inference system will infer forwards from this datum as far as possible before continuing backwards search. A procedural régime says that the ruleset is regarded as a conventional program or method. Effectively, procedural rulesets are used to represent private methods.

Rulesets in SOMA classes serve several different purposes. Firstly, they allow the documentation of business rules which will apply to the operations of the class when implemented. These may be documented in any convenient notation. However, *SOMATiK* offers a language for describing rulesets, and if the syntax of this language is used, the rulesets can be executed by *SOMATiK*. This supports the important *animation* and *event tracing* capabilities, which are described in the next chapter.

The syntax of the ruleset language is similar to the C/C++/Java model with the extension that attribute names can be made to include embedded blanks by enclosing them in quotes. The language provides all the control structures of C++, does not support pointers and compiles into and executes from p-code. Another syntactical difference from C is the notation for conditionals. By default, code executes procedurally. However, there are also a variety of underlying 'inference engines' or régimes which can be used to process a set of rules in the manner usually found in a knowledge-based or expert system product. The if-then notation must therefore support both a procedural and inferential style. The inference engine to be used is selected using a set of radio buttons with options including *Backwards Chaining, Forwards Chaining*, and a number of variants and a *Default* method, which is backwards chaining with opportunistic forwards chaining. This is not the place to digress into an extensive review and discussion on approaches to inference engine construction, but the interested reader is referred to Graham and Jones (1988) or Graham (1995).

Public rulesets form part of the published interface of a class. Private rulesets do not, so that they can be regarded as private methods of the class, and can only be invoked from the class's own operations.

EXECUTING MODELS

Diversion

SOMATiK provides many extensions to the SOMA method. One of these is the concept of class windows. The windows of a class exist to support animation by providing a capability for rudimentary user interaction when a model is animated. Windows for a given class can be created very quickly by selecting the attributes of the class which should appear in the window. The window layout is not under user control. This is deliberate, because the intention is to produce throwaway prototypes. The purpose is to provide a *very* fast method of getting operable windows in place with minimal functionality. The purpose is explicitly *not* to provide a tool that would encourage developers to extend their models with extensive user interfaces. Delphi, VisualAge, Visual Basic and the various Java environments all provide excellent facilities in this regard. The emphasis of *SOMATiK* is the support of requirements engineering and the validation of a class's collaborations, not user interface development.

Having specified a class in terms of its relationships, attributes, operations, rulesets, windows and stereotypes, a class may be tested by actually executing its specification. The testing is carried out against the tasks that were defined in the earlier part of the modelling exercise. This generates an event trace (or, in UML terms, an activity diagram) showing the collaborations that take place in support of the execution of a user's task. This topic is discussed further in Chapter 5.

4.2.5 State transition modelling

It is sometimes useful to make the behaviour of an object explicit in terms of certain key significant states and transitions between them. This can be done by drawing conventional 'bubble and line' state-transition diagrams using any drawing tool or a CASE tool that supports them. *Rose* for example enables the drawing of this kind of picture using the UML notation. Alternatively the same information can be presented in a 'fence' diagram as used by Martin and Odell (1998) for example.

The *SOMATiK* tool provides for the automatic generation of state diagrams from a set of pre- and post-conditions. If a class possesses a State attribute, then the state transition diagram for the class can be generated by pressing the State button on its class card (see Figure 4.6).

A class may have zero or more state bearing attributes but I recommend that there should be only one per class. These are created like any other attribute, but given the type *state*. Once so typed, it is possible to nominate the allowed values for this state attribute. (In C++ terms, a state attribute with its allowed values may be though of as an **enum**.) If there is more than one state bearing attribute in the class, a choice is offered as to which corresponding state diagram to display.

PRE- AND POST- CONDITIONS
Valid state transitions are defined by including assertions in the classes operation scripts: *PreCondition* and *PostCondition* statements. The value of a state attribute can change during the execution of an operation by calling a ruleset that computes the value. The value is tested on exit from the operation using a *PostCondition* statement. If the post-condition is not satisfied at this point the state condition is set to the corect value. Note that if the pre-condition is not met on entry to the operation, an exception will be raised and an message issued. Execution of the event trace is then halted.

EXAMPLE
A simple example of a class possessing state, LightBulbs, is given in the *SOMATiK* tutorial (Bezant, 1997). At its creation, an instance of this class is either 'on' or 'off', and may oscillate between these two states until it eventually dies and enters the 'broken' state – from which there is no escape. This state transition process is shown in Figure 4.26 by the diagram that *SOMATiK* generates. The class Lights here has a state attribute called *Condition*. This has permissible values of 'on', 'off' or 'broken'. Instances can be driven from one of these states into others by the operations of their class. The buttons in the diagram are active elements: clicking on an operation name pops up its description, as shown for the operation *SwitchOn* in Figure 4.27.

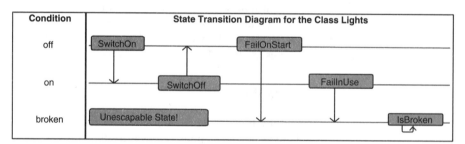

Figure 4.26 State transition fence diagram (after Bezant, 1997)

```
BeginWindow ('Switch Light ON')
      OnOK
                GetInstance ('Lights','Name')
      EndHandler
EndWindow
Precondition: 'Condition' = 'off'
Postcondition: 'Condition' = 'on'
Notify ('...Switched the light on.')
```

Figure 4.27 An operation script with pre- and post-conditions

To help follow the script shown in Figure 4.27, look at the *Window* block which opens the script. This lets the user interact via a window dialogue and create or choose an instance of the *Lights* class. Next, the *Precondition* statement defines the precondition that must hold before the operation can be legally executed. The post-condition that is true on exit from the operation is defined in the *PostCondition* statement. Finally there is a *Notify* statement to confirm the successful execution of the operation, if it gets that far. The pre- and post-condition statements can be positioned at any point in a script; they are global conditions on the operation.

The notation used for these state diagrams is that of fence diagrams. This simplicity is consistent with the *SOMATiK* approach of using the strength of the computer to auto-generate pictures. The more coplicated 'bubble and line' diagrams are used in other methods such as UML, showing triggers, guards and the like would clutter up the diagram, making the essentials harder to apprehend at a glance. It would also fail to provide a complete set of data. Popping up the operation that triggered the transition, provides *all* the information needed.

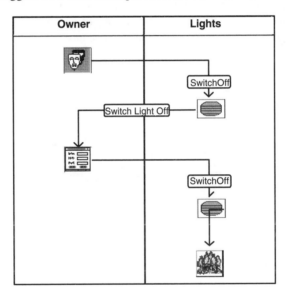

Figure 4.28 Event trace diagram showing a state transition failure

The state transitions are not solely provided for the purposes of documentation. If a pre-condition is not met then execution halts, as shown in the example in Figure 4.28 where the user who started the animation has attempted to switch off a light which is already in the *off* state. The animation is halted and the user may click on the script where the simulation crashed (in flames) to find out what went wrong and why. In UML event traces are referred to as activity diagrams. *SOMATiK* produces automatically (along with all the other diagrams) and therefore they cannot contain errors – unless the assertions are incorrectly defined of course.

4.2.6 Packaging strategy: wrappers

Any modelling language with ambitions to describe non-trivial systems or systems of great magnitude must adopt some sort of packaging strategy to reduce the complexity of its models. Many other methods have a fairly informal approach, so that the unit of packaging is only loosely defined by some heuristic such as: keep closely related classes in the same package. UML's categories are a good example of this. I feel the need for a more rigorously defined notion based on the idea that the packages encapsulate (i.e. hide) their contents. Originally this concept was called a layer in SOMA, but it is now clear that this word should be reserved for the idea of client/server or architectural layers connected via API ports, as found in the OSI seven-layer model or the layers of the ROOM method (Selic *et al.*, 1994). Therefore, we now call the packaging units of SOMA **wrappers**. Wrappers encapsulate their components. No special notation is needed for wrappers because a wrapper is merely a composite object and we can fall back on the standard OML composition notation. We may also, as we saw in the last chapter, overload the term wrapper to mean also an object encapsulating a conventional system. This does no violence to our language because, after all, a plain vanilla object is nothing other than a simple conventional system consisting of functions and data.

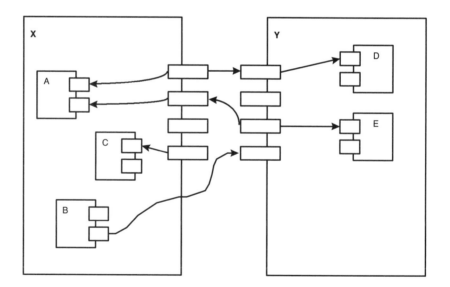

Figure 4.29 Wrappers and delegation

Wrappers delegate some or all of the responsibilities in their interfaces to the operations of their components. These delegations are referred to as implementedby links. They are as yet unsupported directly in *SOMATiK* but, pending this, one may readily annotate an operation with the syntax:

```
/* Implemented-by   Classname.operation_name */
```

Alternatively an operation in the scripting language can be used (see Chapter 8).

This notion corresponds to the idea that wrapper operations delegate some or all of their responsibilities to the operations of their components. Notationally, layers might also be shown using a 'Gradygram' notation as in Figure 4.29, which is sometimes preferable since it is easier to show implemented_by links in this way. Note that inbound messages cannot penetrate a wrapper but outbound ones can.

Wrappers encapsulate business functions and facilitate the use of existing components that are not necessarily object-oriented. A typical application is the application layer of a normal 3-tier architecture.

A viable alternative to the informal notation we have used here is OML's *cluster* notation (Firesmith *et al.,* 1997), which we do not present here because it would take us too far from our main theme. One could also use UML's *package* notation but it is unclear whether this enforces encapsulation properly. For an interesing comparison of the two notations in the context of wrappers see O'Callaghan (1997a).

This completes the exposition of the key concepts of object modelling that we will need for our discussion of requirements engineering in this book. We conclude this chapter with an important extension to these concepts that may be of use in some specialized business process modelling applications.

4.2.7 Fuzzy objects

Diversion

In SOMA an object may be a fuzzy object. A fuzzy object may be fuzzy in three senses: it may have attributes that take as values fuzzy sets, it may contain fuzzy rulesets and it may have superclasses from which it inherits only partially. A fuzzy object can be fuzzy in any one, two or all three of these senses. Fuzzy objects in an object model have particular value when defining fuzzy rule-based systems or when building business process models where fuzzy concepts are normal. The theory of fuzzy objects is described fully in the Appendix to Graham (1994) and in Chapter 6 of Graham (1995). It is only briefly summarized here.

Very briefly, a fuzzy set represents a linguistic variable such as *height* that takes imprecisely defined values such as *tall* or *short*. These fuzzy values can be represented by continuous membership functions such as those illustrated by the curves in Figure 4.30. A membership function shows how the 'truth' of a proposition that something like a *price* is *low* varies as the actual numerical value of the price varies. Thus, a fuzzy attribute such as price can take these functions as values: *low, medium, high*.

Fuzzy logic lets us perform logical inferences with linguistic variables. The logical operators of NOT, AND and OR are usually represented by simple computations as follows, although there are other possibilities for special applications:

$$f \text{ AND } g = \min(f,g)$$
$$f \text{ OR } g = \max(f,g)$$
$$\text{NOT } f = 1 - f$$

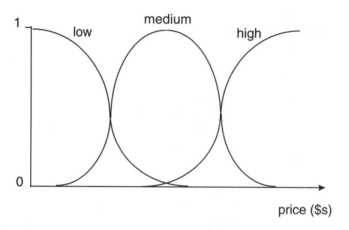

Figure 4.30 Some fuzzy sets

Implication is defined, in the usual way, by:

$$(f => g) = (\text{NOT } f) \text{ or } g = \max(1\text{-}f,g)$$

Given a 'term set' of permissible linguistic values, it is possible to extend it using the propositional operators and the fuzzy operations known as *hedges*. As examples the hedges 'very' and 'quite' are often defined by:

$$\text{VERY } f = f^2 ; \qquad \text{QUITE } f = \sqrt{f}$$

Thus, expressions such as 'very rich or not very poor' receive an interpretation as a fuzzy set.

Fuzzy single and multiple inheritance are well defined but we will not need to go into that level of detail in this text.

The existence of fuzzy variables leads to the possibility of fuzzy rules and rulesets in fuzzy objects. We can give an example of this using the policy adopted by the product manager of a fast moving consumer item such as washing powder. It is expressed particularly succinctly but represents a fairly accurate picture of how such prices are set in practice[1].

```
1.   OUR PRICE SHOULD BE LOW
2.   OUR PRICE SHOULD BE ABOUT 2*DIRECT.COSTS
3.   IF THE OPPOSITION.PRICE IS NOT VERY HIGH THEN OUR
     PRICE SHOULD BE NEAR THE OPPOSITION.PRICE
```

There are several things to note about this policy. First, it is expressed in vague terms and yet would be perfectly understandable to any other product manager as a basis for action. More remarkably perhaps, this is executable code in a language called REVEAL. This is possible because REVEAL uses fuzzy sets to implement the linguistic terms such as LOW. It is worth studying exactly how this code is implemented.

First, two fuzzy sets called LOW and HIGH are defined as vectors over the scale of relevant prices for washing powders. These are illustrated in Figure 4.31 (a) and (b). VERY is an operator that takes the square of every point of the curve representing the fuzzy set. The result VERY HIGH is shown in 4.31 (b) too. The words: OUR, SHOULD and THE are declared as noise words. BE is a synonym for IS and NEAR means the same as ABOUT.

Statement 1 in the policy means that the price should be as compatible as possible with LOW; i.e. the price ought to be exactly zero. This contradicts the assertion that it should be twice direct costs; a result of the need to turn a profit based on experience. The remarkable thing is that the fuzzy policy will automatically resolve this contradiction by taking that price that gives the maximum truth value for the intersection of the fuzzy sets. This is labelled X in Figure 4.31 (d). The peaked intersection now represents an elastic constraint, or feasible region, for price. Figure 4.31 (c) shows the fuzzy set ABOUT 2*DIRECT.COSTS.

The purpose of this example is to show how fuzzy rules, used to capture business policy, can be made to provide quite precise, although perhaps non-linear and complex, models of behaviour. In SOMA, rulesets are embedded in objects and can be inherited. Business policy can be modelled in this way and fuzzy rulesets are permitted. One may either create a special purpose 'policy' object to which all other objects refer or distribute the policy to the pertinent objects. Which is best will depend on the application.

---

[1] This intriguing example was originally developed by Peter Jones for the REVEAL user guide in the 1980s. The same example was used extensively by Cox (1994). REVEAL is discussed at length by Graham and Jones (1988).

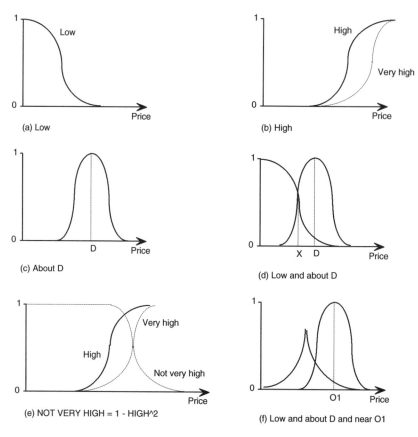

Figure 4.31 LOW, HIGH and some derived fuzzy sets

Rule 3 must now be interpreted. We take an actual value for opposition O and compute how true NOT VERY HIGH is for it. This truth value is T. The fuzzy inference rule is interpreted as truncating the output fuzzy set NEAR OPPOSITION at the level T. We now arrive at the result by taking the union of LOW AND ABOUT D with this truncated set. D stands for 2*DIRECT.COSTS here. Finally, if we want an actual value for PRICE rather than a fuzzy set, we must defuzzify. In this case we choose the mean of maxima method to do this. Figures 4.32 (b) and (c) illustrate that there are two cases. As the value of T exceeds the maximum truth in the feasible region there is a sudden jump in output from R2 to R1. This models exactly what happens in real life; decision output is discontinuous. In process control, smooth output is required and the centre of moments defuzzification rule would be used.

It is my belief and experience that fuzzy rules provide a very powerful modelling technique that helps, as do several other SOMA techniques, build a common, shared understanding between users and developers.

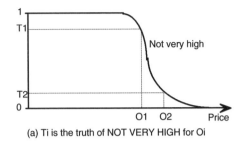

(a) Ti is the truth of NOT VERY HIGH for Oi

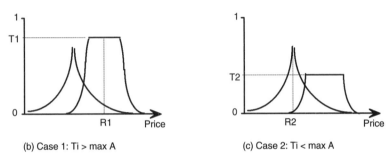

(b) Case 1: Ti > max A

(c) Case 2: Ti < max A

Figure 4.32 Fuzzy inference

⊟ 4.3 Bibliographical notes

Graham (1995) defined Version 1 of SOMA completely although several fragments of the method were to be found in various publications from as early as 1991. Fuzzy objects were introduced by Graham (1991) and were based on earlier work on fuzzy frames (Graham and Jones, 1988). Some examples in this chapter were taken from the *SOMATiK* Tutorial (Bezant, 1997).

Wirfs-Brock *et al.* (1990) is the most readily available source on responsibility-driven design.

5

Business process modelling

Tell me what you want, what you really, really, really want ...
Refrain from popular song

Business process re-engineering became a fashionable topic during the first half of the 1990s and received much attention. It was locally but not universally successful, and did help several businesses reorganize their operations and change their relationship to information technology radically and irreversibly. Typically this was also associated with a move to rapid application development and sometimes with the adoption of object technology.

Business process re-engineering cannot be accomplished without business process modelling and the object metaphor is ideally suited to modelling businesses. Conversely, rapid application development is nearly always an opportunity to re-engineer some aspect of the business. This chapter shows how a truly object-oriented approach to system modelling can be integrated with both rapid development and business process modelling. I show how starting with an object model of the business leads seamlessly to an object model of users' tasks that is clearly related to the objectives and mission of that business. Furthermore, I demonstrate that this task model can be linked seamlessly to an executable specification of the computer support system that we may want to build.

This chapter presents the core of the recommended requirements engineering technique. We will see how to apply the object modelling language developed in Chapter 4 to modelling businesses and to modelling users' tasks. Finally I show how a more conventional object model can be extracted from these earlier models and validated against both them and the business's objectives.

⊟5.1 De-scoping large problems – the mission grid

Our aim is to construct an object model of a business. For a small business this is straightforward but, unfortunately, building an object model of a corporation as large as AT&T, British Petroleum, Chase Manhattan or Dalgety is likely to produce a model of such complexity as to be virtually meaningless. Like earlier attempts to produce corporate data models, the exercise is likely to take so long that it would be out of date years before it was complete. Approaches based on Soft Systems' rich pictures or ORCA rôle models will not help a great deal with problems of this sort of scale. What then can be done to de-scope such a large problem to a scale where object modelling is apposite and effective? To answer this question, I propose a technique which I designate the MISSION GRID.

In analyzing any commercial enterprise, the first question we must ask is: 'who are the customers and other stakeholders in this business?'. Typical stakeholders might include – in addition to the ever-present customers – suppliers, regulatory bodies, trade associations, information providers and competitors. Once these are identified, we can define external goals that are shared with the customers and others. These are variously called shared goals or customer value propositions (CVPs) in the literature (e.g. Jacobson *et al.*, 1995). These statements sum up a state of affairs that both the customer and the enterprise would like to achieve on a regular basis, such as delivering a high quality product at a reasonable price while remaining profitable. This suits the customer who wants such a product but wants to buy from a reliable supplier who is going to stay in business and continue to improve the product. The mission grid technique mandates that we write these goals along one axis of a grid or spreadsheet. The external goals are insufficient to characterize the goals of a business; we must also define internal goals. Internal goals are those that the organization holds to for it own, private reasons and could be to do with cultural or ethical principles or more mundane issues such as keeping the managing director out of gaol. The latter consideration leads, for example, to the need to file proper accounts and tax returns. These goals are written against separate columns from the external goals on our spreadsheet, typically at the opposite edge of the page as in the example shown in Figure 5.1. The orientation of the grid is irrelevant. In this case the logical rôles are written along the top, the customer value propositions on the left and the internal goals on the right.

The next step in completing the grid is creative and challenging; it involves establishing what processes must be carried out in order to contribute to or accomplish the goals, internal and external. These processes must then be rearranged around yet to be identified 'logical rôles'. A logical rôle is a sort of abstract job description that unifies a coherent set of processes that could be accomplished using one basic set of skills, such as those likely to be within the capabilities of a single human agent or department. Assigning the processes to the rôles is quite a difficult thing to do well and the process is bound to be iterative and to involve a lot of interaction with domain experts and users within the business. In Figure 5.1 the rôles are the columns.

Often, two mission grids are developed: the first representing the existing situation and the second a vision of a re-engineered business. Ideally the AFTER grid is developed without reference to the BEFORE grid.

The mission grid has been found to be an excellent tool for communicating with business leaders about the nature of the business and its strategy in the large. These experts should always be asked to justify the CVPs and challenge every process: Is it necessary? Do we really want to be in that business? Will that goal be sustainable in forecast market conditions?

	Butcher	Master butcher	Cleaner	Accountant	
Make/offer product	Prepare product	Visit markets			
	Cutting	Define cuts	Clean workspace		
Inform public of products	Offer advice	Train butchers			
		Advertise & promote			
				VAT Analysis	**Produce VAT return**
	Take cash		Keep hands clean	Accounting	**Produce accounts**

Figure 5.1 A fragment of a mission grid for a butcher's shop

Certain rows or columns of the grid, or particular groups of cells (processes) may be candidates for outsourcing. The key desiderata in this respect are:

- Is the process a customer facing process?
- Is the process differentiating?

The phrase CUSTOMER FACING signifies that the process involves direct contact with the customer. It is usually unwise to outsource such processes to third parties. The many companies that outsourced their help desks in recent years are beginning to realize their error in relation to this principle. DIFFERENTIATING activities are those that your company does that actually characterize it in the eyes of its customers. For example, if you saw a hoarding advertising an organization that 'guarantees to take a percentage of your income every year while providing no direct service in return', then you could be pretty sure that the ad. referred to the Revenue. This statement differentiates that organization from all others. It is a capital error to outsource customer facing, differentiating processes. Processes that are neither customer facing nor differentiating are usually the most appropriate for outsourcing. Thus, the mission grid is a powerful tool for discussing business process re-engineering with the business. It is also the starting point for the implementation of the systems that must underpin such an enterprise and for object-oriented business modelling.

The processes in each cell of the grid can be thought of as mission statements for each process-oriented 'business area'. Each of these is likely to be: (a) small enough to make the construction of an object model of the business area feasible; and (in many cases) (b) suitable for enhancement with a fairly well focused computer support system.

5.2 Discovering business objectives and priorities

Having focused down to a particular process-oriented business area and defined its mission, we are now in a position to define the specific objectives of this process. Ideally, a workshop of the kind discussed in Chapter 3 will be the forum for this activity. In a workshop, the facilitator will ask other participants to call out and discuss objectives. These are written on a flip chart or other visible medium (e.g. text can be projected from a computer with which the requirements analyst or scribe records it). Experience has taught that there are usually about 13 objectives, either due to the fact that people run out of ideas after that much discussion, that 13 objectives comfortably fills two flip chart pages or, as a more remote possibility, reflecting some obscure law of nature yet to be articulated by rational Man.

As we saw in Chapter 2, in SOMA, no activity is allowed to produce a deliverable without it being tested. This principle is applied to the objectives by seeking a measure for each objective. For example, if our business is running an hotel and an objective is to provide a high quality service then the measure might be a star rating system as provided by many tourist boards or motoring organizations. Of course, there are cases where a precise measure is elusive. Discussing the measures is an important tool for clarifying, elucidating and completing the objectives shared and understood by the group. The discussion of measures helps a group think more clearly about the objectives and often leads to the discovery of additional ones or the modification of those already captured. Setting aside plenty of time for the discussion of the measures is seldom a waste of time.

The minimum requirement is that it must be possible to prioritize all the objectives. A formal preference grid can be elicited by asking that each pair of objectives be ranked against each other. In workshops, this is too time consuming and a quicker, more subjective technique is needed. One way to come quickly to the priorities is to allow participants to place votes against each objective. We usually permit each person a number of votes corresponding to about 60% of the number of objectives; e.g. 9 votes for 13 objectives. A good way to perform the voting is to give each eligible participant a number of small, sticky, coloured paper disks, of the sort that are sold in strips by most stationers.   Then the rules of voting are explained: 'You may place all your stickers on one objective or distribute them across several, evenly or unevenly according to the importance you place on the objective. You need not use all your votes; but you are not allowed to give – or sell – unused votes to other participants'.   Then everyone must come up to the flip charts all at once. No hanging back to see what others do is permitted. This helps inject a dynamic atmosphere into the proceedings and stops people waiting to see what the boss does before voting.

Sometimes   two   rounds   of   voting   should   be   done,   under   different interpretations, and the results added to reach a final priority score for each objective. Of course, two colours are then needed for the sticky disks. An example of two possible interpretations that can be combined is:

1. Vote from your point of view as an individual user.
2. Vote from a corporate viewpoint.

Another pair might be:

1. Vote from the supplier's viewpoint.
2. Vote from the customer's viewpoint.

The results often generate further useful discussion.

An objective that cannot be measured and/or prioritized must be rejected or, at least, consigned to a slightly modified mission statement. The priorities are a key tool for project management since they determine what must be implemented first from the point of view of the business sponsor. Technical dependencies must also be allowed for of course.   Often a discussion around these issues elicits new objectives, clarifies existing ones or leads to their recombination or even placement in the overall mission statement. Issues that cannot be resolved are recorded with the names of the people responsible for resolving them. Specific assumptions and exclusions should also be recorded.

We now have one mission grid for the whole organization, consisting of multiple processes, each expressed by a mission statement. Each mission statement is linked to several measurable and prioritized business objectives.

⊟ 5.3 Agents and conversations

Once the objectives are clearly stated with defined measures and priorities we can construct our first object model: an object model of the business area that we are dealing with. To do this we must understand what a business (area) actually is. Unlike many approaches to business process re-engineering and requirements engineering, SOMA offers a very definite perspective on this question, which I now present.

A key part of the SOMA approach to system development is the use of rapid application development (RAD) workshops for requirements capture and analysis. The RAD technique, of course, pre-dates object technology and I used it long before there were any methods for object-oriented analysis available. Running RAD workshops, I have found that data-centred or static modelling approaches to object modelling are not a good place to start with users. Obtaining an entity model or business object model takes quite a long time if attempted at the start of a workshop. Worse still, the developers in the group tend to dominate the procedure since they have more experience of modelling in this way. Quite often this leads to a neglect of the processes in favour of a static model. Many people with similar experience have observed that users respond better to a process oriented approach. However, if we want to extract an object-oriented model from the activity, constructing data flow diagrams is really worse than useless and likely to (a) be ignored by real object-oriented programmers and (b) lead to a horrid functional decomposition that poorer programmers can use as an excuse to write functionally oriented code – or 'flat C++' as we once saw it euphemistically described (Cox, 1994). My experience has shown that all these problems can be overcome by basing the requirements model on business processes using a modelling technique that is strictly object-oriented and is a generalization of both the data flow and the use case approaches. As a side effect of the approach, it turns out that if an entity model view is required for a conventional implementation, it can be extracted from the object model and agreed with users literally in a matter of moments.

BUSINESS PROCESSES

Both requirements engineering and business process re-engineering must start with a model of the communications and contracts among the participants in the business and the other stakeholders, customers, suppliers and so on. We should have already identified these 'external agents' as part of our mission grid construction. If not, doing so is a first step.

Consider some business or enterprise. It could be an entire small company, a division or department of a larger one or even a sole trader. A **business process** (or business area) is a network of communicating agents. Flores (1997) refers to this as a network of *commitments*. An **agent** is any entity in the world that can communicate; so it could represent a customer, regulator, employee, computer system or even a mechanical device of a certain type. Agents are autonomous and flexible. They respond to appropriate stimuli and they can be proactive and exhibit a social aspect; i.e. communicate. Typically agents exhibit some level of intelligence; human agents certainly so but mechanical agents insofar as they can initiate and respond to communication. This now begs the question of what it means for two agents to communicate.

This 'business' must communicate with the outside world to exist at all and, if it does so, it must use some convention of signs and signals thereto. These signals between agents are called **semiotic acts** and are *carried* by some material substratum. They involve a number of semiotic levels from data flows up to implicit social relationships[1]. For example, the substrate may consist of filled-in forms in a paper based office environment and the social context might be that one assumes that no practical jokes are to be played. If the substratum is verbal (or written) natural language then we can speak instead of **speech acts** or **conversations**. These are the speech acts of Austin (1962) and Searle (1969). Flores (1997) argues that business conversations have a constant recurrent structure based on only five primitive speech acts: assert, assess, declare, offer/promise and request.

Semiotic acts can be represented by messages, which are directed from the initiator (source) of the communication to its recipient (target). A typical such message is represented in Figure 5.2 where a typical external customer agent places an order with the business. This message includes the definition of the reply: {order accepted|out of stock|etc.}. By *abus de langage* we shall identify semiotic acts, or conversations, with their representation as messages from now on in this book although strictly they are different; the same semiotic act may be represented by many different messages[2]. This defines equivalence classes of messages and we can think of our actual message as a representative of its class; many contracts may express the same relationship so we choose one to represent its equivalence class.

A message implies that data flow, so that this approach generalizes data flow modelling. However, it also enriches it considerably. For one thing, data flow in both directions along message links (via the request and hand-over stages discussed below). This is why we have chosen to terminate message links at the recipient end with a filled rectangle rather than an arrowhead. The line segment is directed from the *initiator* of the communication, not from the origin of the data.

Figure 5.2 A message

We now begin to see that agents can be modelled as objects that pass messages to each other. Clearly agents can also be classified into different types as well. Therefore it seems well justified to refer to our business process model as the Agent Object Model (AOM). The question we face now is how to go about analyzing the

---

[1] Semiotics is the comparative study of sign systems and has been important in such diverse fields as mathematical logic, natural language processing, anthropology and literary criticism. It holds that signs can be analyzed at at least three levels: those of syntax, semantics and pragmatics.

[2] For a trivial example consider that the same conversation may be represented by a message in English, Chinese, German or Urdu.

messages. So far as I am aware, apart from the ORCA approach which overlaps my approach somewhat, there are only three candidate techniques:

1. Jackson System Development (JSD) (Jackson, 1983) can be used or some object-oriented variant of it such as KISS (Kristen, 1995). In my view this type of approach is far too close to system design to work well at the requirements elicitation stage.
2. Use cases (Jacobson *et al.,* 1992) are probably the most widely used alternative and are the recommended technique within UML. However, as we will see in Appendix B, recent work and experience have shown them to be both theoretically and practically flawed.
3. It therefore seems that an approach based on semiotics such as the one proposed here is all that is both available and realistic.

A semiotic or speech act is characterized at the semantic and pragmatic levels by a (possibly implicit) contract that both parties understand. The pragmatics of this contract represent a social relation just as a message represents a semiotic act.

We think of a business process as a network of related conversations between agents, represented by messages. The relationship between the messages can be encoded in a task ruleset or, better still as task associations as we will see later.

It is inconceivable in most businesses that the message initiator does not wish to change the state of the world in some way as a result of the communication. This desired state of the world is the **goal** of the message and every message has a goal even if it is often unstated: the contract representing the conditions of satisfaction of the conversation.

A goal is achieved by the performance of a **task**. The innovation here is twofold. Firstly, there is the realization that the tasks we perform can often be reduced to a few stereotypes: typical tasks that act as pattern matching templates against which real tasks can be evaluated and from which real tasks (or use cases) can be generated. This overcomes a possible objection that there could be an explosion in the number of use cases as I have often found. My experience indicates that there is no such explosion of tasks. For example, in a simple foreign exchange deal capture model there are only 11 tasks of which 8 are atomic (defined below). This structure is illustrated in Figure 5.20. Second comes the appreciation that tasks can be modelled as objects within a *bona fide* object model in the task domain as we shall see in the next section.

In business only serious conversations are relevant, and therefore we can argue that each message has a sixfold structure as follows:

1. A **trigger**: a world event that triggers the interaction.
2. A **goal**: a world state desired by the initiator.
3. An **offer** or **request**; which contains the data necessary for the recipient to evaluate the offer or request.
4. A **negotiation**; whereby the recipient determines whether the goals are shared and the conditions of acceptance leading to either a **contract** being

agreed or the offer rejected. The contract formalizes the goal and provides formal conditions for knowing when the goal has been achieved satisfactorily.

5. A **task** that must be performed by the recipient of a request to achieve the goal and satisfy the contract.

6. A **hand-over** of the product of the task and any associated data, which checks that the conditions of satisfaction of the goals have been met.

This structure accords generally with that of a *conversation for action* in the terminology of Winograd and Flores (Flores, 1997; Winograd and Flores, 1986), although we add the notion of a triggering event. We also note that there is a symmetry of offers and requests, so that we can replace every offer with an equivalent request by swapping the initiator with the recipient. In SOMA one always deals with messages in this **request canonical form**. Flores presents the theory, as shown in Figure 5.3, in terms of a customer (our initiator) and a performer (our recipient) who executes the primitive speech acts – shown in italics in what follows. The customer *assesses* her concerns and makes (*asserts*) a request of the performer (dually the performer makes an offer). A process of negotiation then ensues aimed at defining a contract that can be *promised* by the performer and accepted by the customer. This, and other stages in the conversation, may involve recursion whereby subsidiary conversations are engaged in. At the end of negotiation the contract defines the conditions of customer satisfaction and some task must be executed to fulfil their promise. Finally, the results of this work are *declared* complete and handed over to the customer who should *declare* satisfaction.

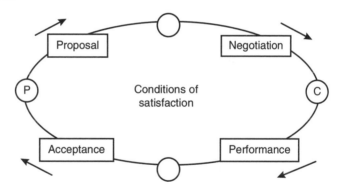

Figure 5.3 A Flores conversation for action

Figure 5.4 shows the structure of a SOMA conversation and illustrates that recursion can occur in each segment of the conversation and that either party may withdraw at each stage.

Consider the concrete example of buying a house. An initiator might say 'would you like to buy my house?' and the recipient would need to know, and would negotiate on, the price. This negotiation could well involve subsidiary conversations between her and a mortgage provider and a building surveyor. If everything is agreed then a contract will be agreed and signed (literally in this case). Now there is work to do; in England it is called conveyancing. The work involves searching local government records and land registry documents along with many – all fairly straightforward – tasks. So this is the place where we might rely on a standard task script, as exemplified for example by the words (or flowcharts) in a book on conveyancing. Finally, when this task completes satisfactorily we can hand over the keys and the contract is said to be *completed*.

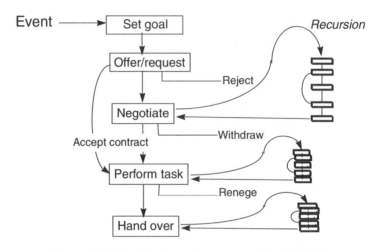

Figure 5.4 The structure of a conversation in SOMA

BUSINESS PROCESS RE-ENGINEERING Of course, in business process re-engineering, we are eager to capture not just the messages that cross the business boundary, such as order placement, but model the communications among our customers, suppliers, competitors, etc. This provides the opportunity to offer new services to these players, perhaps taking over their internal operations – for a fee of course.

Figures 5.5 and 5.6 show how this might be applied in the simple case of delivering medical supplies, based on what happened at Baxter Healthcare (Short and Venkatramen, 1992). Originally, Baxter took an order from the hospital's procurement department and delivered to its loading bay. Then the hospital was responsible for storing the goods and delivering them to the appropriate operating theatre (Figure 5.5). After re-engineering, goods such as surgical gloves are delivered direct by the supplier to the operating theatre where they are required (Figure 5.6). Of course, the message labelled OrderGloves has been modified. This gives an advantage over other suppliers in terms of service, reduces the hospital's inventory and logistics costs and means that a higher price can be charged by the supplier while remaining competitive. It also makes the hospital more dependent on the supplier.

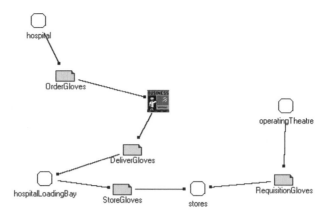

Figure 5.5 Re-engineering delivery logistics: before

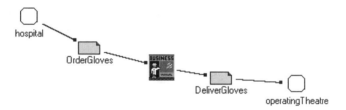

Figure 5.6 Re-engineering delivery logistics: after

MATCHING MODELS

Having analyzed the business process in terms of conversations, we now focus on the task performance segment of the conversation. Before doing so let us remind ourselves of the model sequence. We started with a mission grid leading to several processes. Each process has several objectives. Also there is now a network of conversations (messages). We should now ask two critically important questions:

- Does every message support the achievement of *at least one* objective?
- Is *every* objective supported by at least one message?

If the answer to either question is NO, then the model must be amended. Either we have missed some conversations or we are modelling conversations that do not contribute to the achievement of any stated business objective. Of course it is possible that we have missed an important objective and, in that case, the users should be consulted to see if the statement of objectives needs to be modified.

5.4 From conversations to tasks

Task modelling is a powerful, generic variant of use case modelling. It enables us to drill down into the agent model and model users' task performance in a very concise and thoroughly object-oriented manner. Our focus now moves chiefly to the task segment of the conversations. We now show that we can represent tasks as *bona fide* objects. Because of this we need no new notation and can rely entirely on the techniques presented in Chapter 4. This is in contradistinction to UML, which introduces a whole new set of notation to represent use cases and their interconnexions; principally using ellipses to represent use cases and various arrow icons to show how they are linked. We are in the happier position of being able to stick to the known representations for objects and the basic four structural links of classification, composition, usage and association[3]. The model is a model of a different subject matter but the modelling concepts are identical in structural terms. Remember that we are using the precepts of the object metaphor to model tasks. Generically, the classification relation allows us to group similar objects together into family trees. Thus too with tasks! *SOMATiK* can draw these structures automatically from the task cards of the model. As an alternative visualization of the classification tree, it can be presented as an indented list, as can all four structures.

Decomposing tasks into components is another important feature of the process for two reasons. Disaggregating tasks into components uncovers tasks which can feature as components in more than one high-level task; this supports reuse by containment. In addition, the count of 'atomic' tasks within a model, referred to as the *task point* count provides an important metric on the system's scope and complexity. This is discussed in more detail in Chapter 7. Each component task is a first class task in its own right, possessing its own task card where the full details of the task can be documented.

The operations of task objects are methods that invoke exception handling tasks. Exception tasks, or 'side-scripts', represent abnormal or unusual partial tasks which are executed in specific circumstances. We often find that exception tasks are reusable in the context of a variety of high level task scripts. As with other associations between tasks, there may be some level of iteration: there can be exceptions to exceptions. For example, in the course of our normal work we usually interrupt the normal course of activities by taking a vacation in the summer. But circumstances could arise where the task takes on an unusual urgency, such as the approach of an unexpected but important deadline. In such a case, we may well

---

[3] Interestingly Dan Rawsthorne of Dimensions Inc. (private communication) has developed a theory of use cases (with goals) that uses standard UML notation to connect them. His semantics coincide with a subset of ours. Alexander Cockburn (1997) also argues for adding goals to use cases.

suspend the holiday activities and rush in to the office to help deliver the required result.

Like all SOMA objects, tasks can encapsulate any number of rulesets. Because tasks are not executable entities, the rulesets may be written in any way helpful to the designer, though typically an informal If-then type of structure will be most helpful. Capturing business rules early in the analysis process, ensures that valuable information extracted during a workshop is not discarded, but recorded in an appropriately encapsulated way. Frequently this provides raw material for the development of more formal rulesets for inclusion in classes later in the development process.

Task objects may also have stereotypes such as the *Domain Object* stereotype. Like any object a task may be *Abstract* or *Concrete*. In addition, we can nominate whether it is performed manually or by the system.

We refer to the entire object model of users' tasks as the Task Object Model (TOM).

Although we model tasks as objects, a task is an aspect of the behaviour of an agent. It has parallels with the idea of an operation of a class. An operation of a class is invoked by the reception of an appropriate message: classically an object is defined by its identity and by its behaviour, and an operation is an aspect of its behaviour. Its behaviour is made visible on its published interface, and enabled by its published operations, by its internal attributes and by its private methods. Equally, a *task* in SOMA is a behaviour of some agent (an actor, an external entity or a system processing object) which is invoked by the arrival of a message for which the object is conditioned.

SCRIPT THEORY

Tasks can be described in several ways but it is most useful to describe a task using a **task script**. A task script represents a *stereotypical* task. It is a textual description of such a task (ideally a single sentence) with lists of nominated supertasks, component tasks and tasks that describe exceptions (side-scripts). This provides a notion of generalized exception handling that does not seem to be natural to users of the use case approach; where an exception (extends) path is often specific to the use case. Jacobson *et al.* (1992) define a use case as 'a behaviourally related sequence of transactions *in a dialogue with the system*' and 'a sequence of transactions *in a* system whose task is to yield a result of measurable value' (Jacobson *et al.*, 1995). My added emphasis indicates a slight conflict between these two definitions. I will take the view, shared by most users of the technique, that a use case describes a dialogue in the world and not in the system and that use cases are restricted to describing the system interface. Task scripts are part of a model of the world but differ in that they are not restricted to the interface. What is more important, task scripts describe *stereotyped* behaviour in the world.

As an example, consider a task script that describes the task of going to a restaurant. The idea is that one **always** does the same thing when visiting a restaurant. One **always**:

1. Enters the restaurant
2. Attracts the attention of a waiter
3. Takes one's seat
4. Reads the menu
5. Chooses a meal
6. Eats it
7. Pays
8. Leaves

This is certainly a good stereotype of the situations normally met with – at least in a US restaurant. However, no visit to any restaurant follows this script exactly. One may, for example:

1. Enter the restaurant
2. Attract the attention of a waiter
3. Go to takes one's seat
4. Slip on a banana skin ...

The script is broken and must be repaired before our culinary cravings can be assuaged. This is accomplished by permitting what we will call **side-scripts** that deal with stereotypical exceptions. **Side-scripts** are scripts for well known situations that may be invoked when an exception occurs in another script; we have the mental model of a script 'sending a message' to a side-script to ask for its help. In this particular case the side-script might proceed:

1. Get up
2. Brush oneself down
3. Look around to see who is laughing
4. Abuse them verbally or punch them
5. Return to the interrupted task

The point to note here is that the banana skin script does not just work in the context of the restaurant script. It will work anywhere: in the street, on the factory floor or in the office (if there are no carpets). In practice scripts can become complicated and have to allow for many exceptions; e.g. what happens when the bill arrives and you find you have lost your wallet? However, the script describes a well known and stereotypical situation: one that has been encountered many times before. To process such exceptions, task objects are able to send messages to each other. It turns out that task scripts can also be classified and (de)composed. For example the scripts for paying one's electricity, gas and water bills can be generalized into a 'pay bill' task script. In other words they can be regarded as objects within an object model. This Task Object Model is not the Business Object Model (BOM) that we will derive eventually. The Task Object Model is a model of the world and the Business Object Model is a model of a potentially implementable system.

The idea of task scripts has its theoretical roots in the AI script theory of Schank and Abelson (1977) and in the hierarchical task analysis popular in HCI work. Also, task scripts can be regarded as generic use cases. Use cases may be one sentence or an essay whereas atomic task scripts should consist of a single sentence. This means that measurement of process models based on task scripts is much easier than with use cases. Parenthetically, we should note that a side-script has exactly the same semantics as what Schank and Abelson called a 'subscript'. The renaming is necessary to avoid confusion with notions of specialization where the prefix 'sub' is commonly used.

So, tasks can be modelled as *bona fide* objects, where the attributes are the task script and various performance related items and the operations are exceptions to the script to be handled by other tasks. The most common approach to analyzing a task that arises from a conversation is to decompose the task into components and to keep doing this until the tasks are atomic. The scripts can be written using a task action grammar if desired; which we call SVDPI form because all sentences can be arranged into the form: Subject Verb Direct object Preposition Indirect object(s). It is always possible to keep on decomposing tasks ad infinitum, merely by adding more detail or descending to a lower level of Physics. We stop when words that are not in the vocabulary of the normal user would be introduced at the next stage of the decomposition. For example, in order capture the script 'the clerk moves the mouse to the Quantity field and enters ...' is not atomic because the word mouse is not part of the ontology of ordering. We should have stopped at 'the clerk enters the quantity ...'. In other words an **atomic** script is arrived at by decomposing task objects until:

1. the task script is a single sentence – ideally in SVDPI format;
2. further decomposition would introduce terms that are not in the domain ontology.

In Appendix B, I explain in detail the deficiencies of the unalloyed UML use case approach of Jacobson *et al.* (1992, 1995) and how the task object/task script approach overcomes these problems.

5.5 From the Task Object Model to the Business Object Model

In this section I explain how a Business Object Model can be elicited from a reading of the task scripts together with a good helping of creativity and design acumen.

Recall that external agents differ from internal agents in two senses: internal agents work within our business; and we know more about the tasks they are carrying out. External agents may conceal tasks we have no knowledge of, which will affect us because they lead to events that trigger messages or **triggering events**. In the case of messages initiated by actors or objects internal to the support system, we usually know the causes of these events, because they are the direct result of task execution. When the initiator is an external agent we nearly always lack this knowledge and the triggering event appears as a given. **Actors** are users of a system (adopting a rôle) and thus could be either internal or external agents but are normally internal. Therefore, we may routinely confuse internal agents with actors in practice. Messages always have triggering events, though for internal agents and system agents we will usually know the task that has led to the event.

AGENTS In the normal style of object-oriented development, external agents, such as
VERSUS customers, are usually represented in the Business Object Model by rather
BUSINESS unintelligent objects with few or no operations but typically several attributes. It is
OBJECTS important not to confuse these internal representations, which cannot do anything except store static data, with their real-world counterparts that do exhibit, often complex, behaviour. Such internal representations of external objects are nearly always persistent objects. There is a powerful alternative to this, more usual, object-oriented approach, which models intelligent customers and clerks as mere dumb data structures and the orders that are dumb pieces of paper in the real world as intelligent objects responsible for several operations, such as the validation of customer credit limits or checking stock levels. The alternative is to internalize part of the intelligence of entities in the world as *agents*.

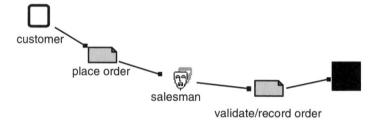

Figure 5.7 Order entry

In Figure 5.7 an internal agent (salesman) receives the customer's order and enters it into a business support system. The order is triggered by some unknown condition within the customer. Of course, this business support system is likely to be the computer system that we are trying to construct, but it could just as well be a card index or similar. Our task is to find the business objects. Referring to the above example, we evidently have a clerk, a customer, a product and, of course, an order. Usefully there is a rule too. Is the credit limit an attribute of customer or is it the responsibility of a credit manager agent? In banking systems it is often the latter because credit lines are handled by specialized systems; usually legacy systems. But now we come to the really fascinating question from the agent-oriented perspective: How intelligent is the order itself? Does the rule belong to the **Orders** class?

The knee-jerk reaction of the typical object-oriented designer is to place the rule and a good deal of the behaviour in **Orders**. But does this make sense to a typical user? I do not think so. In the world, customers and clerks are intelligent and exhibit behaviour. The order is a very dead, behaviour free piece of paper. But our systems push all the behaviour into the order and strip it away from customers and clerks who are usually represented in database tables which store details like name, address and login codes. The most these objects do is to calculate things like current debt, usually by collaborating with other classes such as **Orders**. In one way this is sensible; real customers can place orders with us, but we certainly do not want the system representation of customer to be able to do this. Business would become too easy – except that we probably either would not be paid or would be charged with fraud. However, in the case of the clerk it is less clear that this strategy is the right one.

The agent perspective allows us instead to visualize an agent in the system called **Clerk's Assistant**. This agent can take responsibility for all the order validation and confirmation behaviour that is needed and let us strip it away from **Orders**. This has three significant advantages:

1. If we are in a distributed system we can allow the assistant agent to be mobile with the attendant benefits of reducing network traffic and improving overall control structure.
2. Stripping the order of its behaviour may reduce the impedance mismatch between our new systems and legacy databases where orders are still stored, without behaviour usually.
3. The 'cognitive dissonance' between the system and the world is reduced. This means that discussions between users and developers are easier because they share a common model of the application. Smart clerks in the office are modelled as smart creatures in the computer (or partially so, because real intelligent computers don't and can't exist). Electronic orders are just as dumb as their paper counterparts.

Whether this approach is correct will depend entirely on the application and its circumstances. However, knowing that it is possible gives developers an extra tool of their trade. Next time you model a system consider the choice at least.

Earlier I referred to the coincidence that while the insertion of rulesets into objects in SOMA was not motivated by agent technology at all, this addition to object modelling seems to be pretty well all that is needed to model agents. I can reveal now that the original motivation was provided by a business process re-engineering project as long ago as 1989. Now it should be possible to see why precisely the same extension to object-oriented analysis needed to model business processes is needed to model system agents. The underlying metaphor is the same.

We can use internalizing agents to model the responsibilities of the sales clerk in this respect. In *SOMATiK* we can create a so-called agent class to do this automatically from the process model, although we must still enumerate and define its operations. Each agent class is equipped with an operation called *cAgentnameDæmon*. The purpose of the dæmon operation is to support time-based simulation. Dæmons awaken on every clock tick during a time-based simulation. The function performed by the dæmons is, of course, up to the modeller. Most often, modellers will include only representations for events that occur purely because of the passage of time. The agent stereotype can be thought of as internalizing within the system the real agents in the business world. With agents representing more of the business logic, the order is modelled as a data structure that will probably correspond far more closely to the representation that may exist in the legacy order database.

Nevertheless, for the purposes of the present exposition we will stay with the more usual approach of putting the intelligence into the order class. Let us examine the RecordOrder message in more detail. Figure 5.8 shows the detailed description of this message.

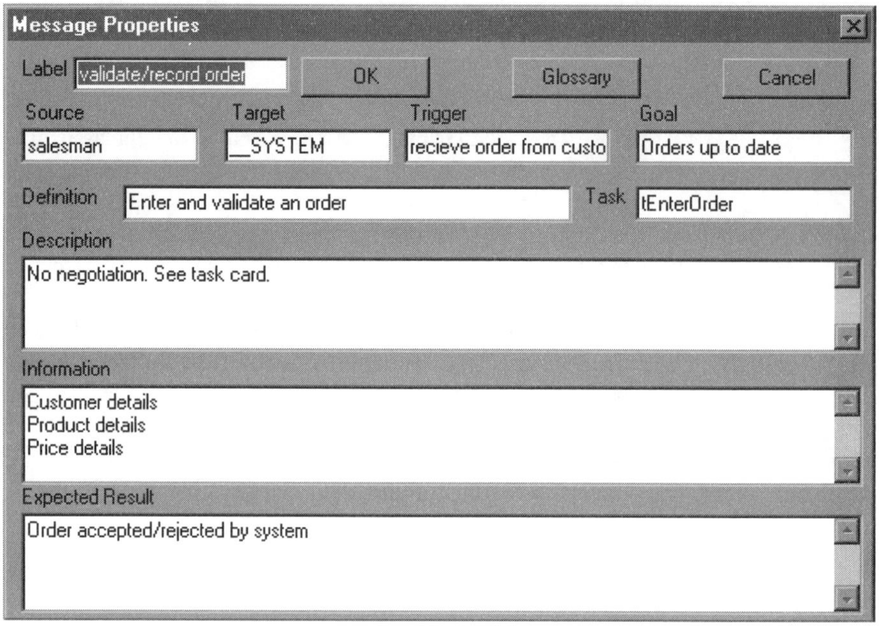

Figure 5.8 Message details

To relate Figure 5.8 to our description earlier in this section of the sixfold structure of a message or conversation, the Information field corresponds to the *request*, the Description field to *negotiation* and the Expected Result field to *handover*. The other field labels correspond directly and the software, *SOMATiK*, that produced this dialogue is currently being amended to make the correspondence more intuitive and consistent. A proposed dialogue layout is shown in Figure 5.9.

A message always has a goal, which is achieved by the performance of a task: the one named in the message definition (see Figures 5.8 and 5.9). This high level task can be decomposed into component tasks that, in *SOMATiK,* are entered using a structure known as a task card. The task card shown in Figure 5.10 is a summary of information contained on the five other hidden tab-cards. Each column corresponds to the tab directly above it and the graphics button directly below. The Task Script button gives access to the task's script. Only rulesets do not admit of a graphical view. Note that the Components column shows only the first level of decomposition of the top level task.

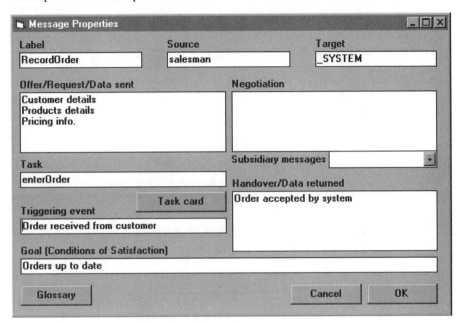

Figure 5.9 Improved message dialogue

The whole decomposition may then be displayed automatically in graphical form as shown in Figure 5.11. This is accomplished merely by clicking the button labelled ApO on the task card for the task. This graphical view is available for each of the four coupling structures: generalization/AKO (SuperTasks), composition/APO (Components), association (Associates) and usage (Exceptions). The views also act as model browsers: the pop-up menus for each task allow the user to navigate to its task card or other available structure views. The task card format emphasizes that tasks are to be regarded as objects (either classes or instances). Tasks may be classified and (de)composed. They may send messages to exception handling tasks and may be associated with other tasks; e.g. this task 'precedes' that task. Tasks have complexity and take time. This is usually only recorded for atomic tasks since it can often be inferred for the composite tasks; the time taken is assumed to be the sum of the times for the components at the next level and so on. This of course can be overridden. Complexities are also additive unless otherwise stated. An atomic task is illustrated in Figure 5.12.

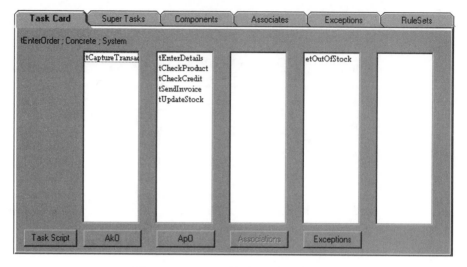

Figure 5.10 A task card in *SOMATiK*

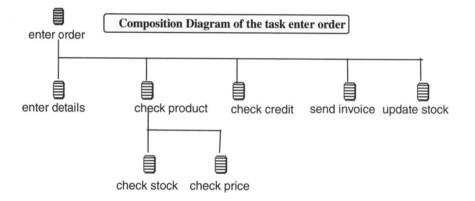

Figure 5.11 The task tree

Task associations can be used to allow the sequencing and co-ordination of tasks to be described. This effectively describes the way tasks combine to form complete business processes. However, in the situations most commonly found, it will be assumed that the sequence of task is read from left to right and that there is no concurrency. If the situation is more complex then the expressive power of task associations and rulesets together is sufficient to ensure than any level of complexity can be described. See Section 5.9 for more details.

There is also some complexity in the way that inheritance and composition structures interact, which again is rarely met in practice but which must be allowed for. The rules for handling this interaction were described in Chapter 4, Section

4.2.3 in relation to derived dependencies for business objects. Task objects are handled in exactly the same way.

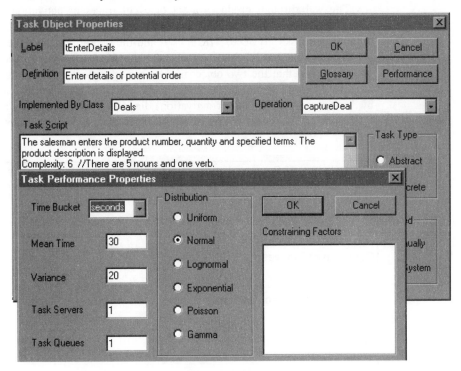

Figure 5.12 An atomic task script with performance facets

Once the analysis of the process models, business processes and messages is completed, we end up with a set of task cards representing decomposed tasks. It is assumed the decomposition continues to 'atomic' level where an atomic task is one that cannot be further decomposed without introducing terms foreign to the domain. Each atomic task is represented by a sentence – in a standard Subject/Verb/Objects (SVDPI) form where possible. The sentences in the Task Object Model are now analyzed (preferably, I find, by users during workshops) to discover the true business objects that will be the basis of the system model. The technique is basically a textual analysis where nouns indicate candidate objects and verbs candidate operations. Unfortunately this process is not seamless, violating one of the key benefits claimed for object-oriented methods; it is irreducibly creative. The next section explains how the seam can be mended. The classes so discovered can be printed by *SOMATiK* in the form of the class cards shown in Figure 5.13 for use in 'CRC' style walkthroughs. Alternatively, pre-printed class card forms can be completed in pencil. Note that the layout of on-screen class cards (Figure 4.5) matches that of task cards because the identical modelling metaphor is in use. This process creates the Business Object Model (BOM).

The walkthrough produces a set of event traces or activation diagrams that effectively describe the way business objects execute operations that support each of the business tasks. If *SOMATiK* is used and the operations have been expressed in the appropriate syntax, these traces take the form of system executions. This provides a test that the two object models are consistent and complete and usually leads to the model being 'debugged'. Otherwise, the walkthrough can be recorded by drawing an event trace (or activation) diagram by hand or using a conventional CASE tool. The event traces form the basis for system test scripts later in the project.

```
┌─────────────────────────────────────────────────────────────────────┐
│ Class Name    Product                              Concrete/Application │
│ Description: A product has a code, a name, a description, and a price   │
│                                                                         │
│ SuperClasses:                                                           │
│ Commodity                                                               │
│                                                                         │
│ Component Classes:                                                      │
│                                                                         │
│                                                                         │
│ Attributes and associations:                                           │
│ Product Name                                                            │
│ Product Description                                                     │
│ Product Price                                                           │
│ Product ID(Product, 1, 1)                                               │
│                                                                         │
│                                                                         │
│ Operations:                          Servers                            │
│ SetProductCode                       (Product - Create Product)         │
│   Establishes the product code and other                                │
│   details in the system database                                        │
│                                                                         │
│ ProductMargin                                                           │
│                                                                         │
│                                                                         │
│ Rulesets:                                                               │
│ ProductPricingPolicy                                                    │
│                                                                         │
│                                                                         │
└─────────────────────────────────────────────────────────────────────┘
```

Figure 5.13 A printed class card

▤ 5.6 Seamlessness

To further distinguish the SOMA task model approach from the use case approach
to business modelling, it is important to realize that – normally – in passing from a
business process model to a system model we are crossing the Rubicon, as it were.
There is no way back. Should we change our model of the system, as a result of a
coding improvement say, then we cannot detect the impact of the change on the
business model or objectives. In SOMA things are different if we realize that each
task tree corresponds to a plan for a business process. The root nodes of our task
trees are containers for the atomic tasks that constitute the detail of the plans. What
we must do is create a set of classes in the system model (BOM) that can help a user
execute this plan. Now, such an implementation must start somewhere. Therefore,
each 'root' task corresponds to **exactly one** system operation (and therefore *a
fortiori*) to exactly one class. This operation initiates the system process that
implements the plan. The identity of this class and operation are recorded as part of
the task properties and this enables *SOMATiK* to produce a complete set of event
traces, *proving* that the system can implement all business processes specified.
Thus, our task-oriented approach offers possibilities for seamlessness in the
transition from the business to the system model that seem to be unavailable in use
case oriented approaches. It also has implications for testing, as the event traces
can be regarded as test scripts.

There is some further work underway to explore the connexions between the
metrics based on counts of atomic task scripts (task points) and the measurement of
use case models.

I have introduced the reader to SOMA's twin object models: the Task Object
Model (TOM) and the Business Object Model (BOM) and suggested that they could
be linked using CRC-style walkthroughs with users and developers. I now want to
show how this linkage can be automated to provide a truly seamless link between a
system and its requirements. This link means that if the system changes we can
explore the impact on the business objectives and processes. It also offers the
possibility of a new notion of provable correctness: proving that the specification
meets the requirements.

SOMA uses a uniform object modelling technique to model several things. The
process life-cycle, for example, is modelled as a network of activity objects and
contracts between them. The Agent Object Model is a model of the business
process(es). The Task Object Model is a model of the tasks performed by users (and
other agents) as part of their business processes. The Business Object Model is a
model of the business objects that constitute a computer system specification. In
that sense we could call the TOM part: a model of the world or *world model*. The
BOM could be called a *system object model*. Sometimes there is a more refined
system model, built later on, called the Implementation Object Model.
Alternatively, one can produce an executable specification using the *SOMATiK* code

generation facilities. The general sequence of these models was illustrated in Figure 4.2.

While conventional methods offer different modelling techniques for almost every life-cycle activity, object-oriented methods introduce no such seams between analysis and logical design. There may be a 'seam' between logical and physical design when language dependent features are introduced, but using a language such as Eiffel effectively eliminates this seam too. Thus object-oriented development is claimed to be seamless. However, leaping from the requirements model to the system model, there remains more than a seam: a veritable abyss which, once leapt over, cannot be easily re-traversed.

Using *SOMATiK* there is a neat solution to this problem of the World/System seam which I will attempt to explain using a simple example.

AN EXAMPLE In the SOMA approach to object-oriented requirements capture for a business area, the first thing we do is establish the project mission and then drill down to a number of specific, measurable, prioritized objectives as previously described. Next, we build a business process or context model showing: external agents (the stakeholders in our business area), internal agents and support agents (systems). Messages representing conversations between these agents are then introduced. Figure 5.14 shows how this might be applied to a system designed to capture foreign exchange trades. In this figure, the external agent c/party[4] sends a message to an internal agent (dealer) inviting him to strike a foreign exchange bargain. The dealer then must negotiate the terms, validate the trade and enter it into the system. This is represented by the message enter_deal.

We must find a goal for each such message and its associated task. This is called the root task because it is at the root of a composition tree. The tree for enter_deal is shown in Figure 5.15. We analyze and decompose the tasks for each goal in this way, ending at the atomic tasks; which are the leaf nodes of this tree. Next we write task scripts for the atomic tasks.

Figure 5.16 shows the script for the task Enter Details. It is easy to see from this script that a number of classes are mentioned; e.g. Instruments, Counterparties and (implicitly) Deals. Also there are some obvious attributes, such as Buy/Sell. Finally the operation enter is mentioned. After a preliminary analysis of this and all the other scripts and a walk through the system design, we realize that the task enter_deal at the root of the tree corresponds to a responsibility of the class Deals: captureDeal in this case.

As suggested in Figure 5.12, the ImplementedBy operation field of the root task object enter deal contains the text: 'captureDeal', an operation of the Deals class. This makes a permanent link between the process plan represented by the root task and the software that will help the user execute this plan. Because of this link we can animate the specification.

---

[4] A bank's trading customer is often referred to as its counterparty.

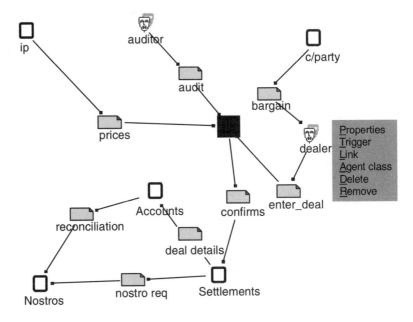

Figure 5.14 Business process (or context) model for trade capture

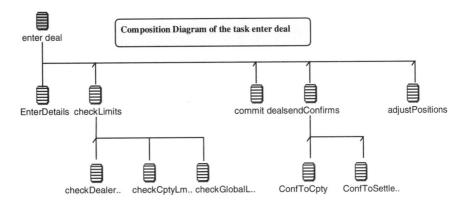

Figure 5.15 Task tree for enter deal

The dealer enters the following data:
counterparty, instrument, amount, rate, buy or sell,
special settlement conditions

Figure 5.16 Task script for EnterDetails

Selecting the Trigger option on the menu shown in Figure 5.14 will display a list of events that are relevant to the dealer actor. Selecting the event **deal done** will trigger the task **enter deal**. This, in turn, triggers its initiating operation: captureDeal. Any operation scripts and windows that the developer has created are executed and displayed for interaction now, and any calculations specified performed. While this is happening *SOMATiK* records a trace of the entire interaction in script form, which can be saved, replayed and displayed graphically in the form shown in Figure 5.17.

Should the execution crash, some flames appear in this diagram directly underneath the operation that failed. The analyst can click on the operation, amend it and re-run the trace. The code is written in a high level scripting language that can be learnt in a day or less. *SOMATiK* thus produces a prototype that can be executed and tested.

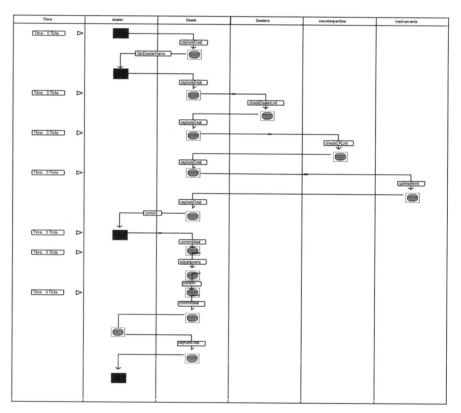

Figure 5.17 The active event trace of deal capture produced by *SOMATiK*

**LINKING
TASKS TO
CLASSES**
Another way of looking at the seamless nature of the specification process that we have described by way of this example is illustrated schematically in Figure 5.18. This shows the mission statement of a project fanning out to its various objectives. Each objective relates to a number of communication acts (messages) in the model. Each message has exactly one goal and exactly one root task. The root tasks correspond to one or more atomic tasks. So far, all these links are totally traceable; at least in principle. For that reason, it is easy to arrive at the TOM in an iterative fashion.

Now we take the leap from the world to the system. We identify the business objects partly based on the nouns discovered in the scripts. We define classification, composition and association structures. For each class we find responsibilities and rules, partly based on the verbs found in the scripts. This is a creative process that cannot be automated. We have lost traceability; we have crossed the Rubicon.

However, we can at least validate the mutual consistency of the two models using a group of users and developers. They walk through with class cards (rôle playing the classes) to prove that all tasks are correctly supported and that there are no processing or storage absurdities. The automatic linking of the two models described above amounts to finding a means to record and replay this dynamic scenario interaction.

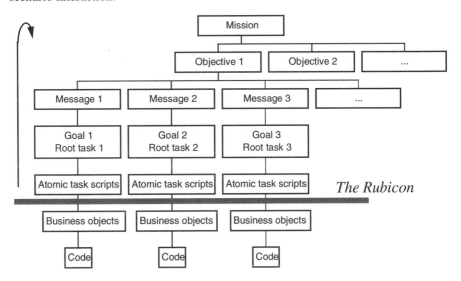

Figure 5.18 A seamless process

How did we make the leap from world model to the system model seamless? The trick is to notice that the task trees constitute 'plans' for interaction during task performance and, thus, for system execution. Each root task corresponds to **exactly one** system operation: in the class that initiates the plan. Making this link means that we can generate event traces automatically. Now we have a seamless link from mission down to the code – **and back**! Because we can refine the business object model and generate working code, we can trace changes to the code back to their effects on the task models and even the mission.

We saw earlier in Figure 5.12 that there was an attribute of a task called *Implemented By* which allows the class implementation of a task to be described. Of course, since the two domains are not in any sense a one-to-one mapping, this implemented by link simply acts as the gateway from one domain to another. The *Operation* field allows us to specify the operation of the implementation class that begins the system's support for the task. When first documenting a task, these data will not be known. Only after the Business Object Model has been constructed can we return to the task property descriptions and fill in these data. This closing of the loop is of great importance to the overall process. It is the means by which task simulations can be set up for execution and validation of the model.

The implications of this approach to software engineering for quality and testing are, I hope, obvious:

1. The stored event traces constitute acceptance test scripts for later verification of the system built.
2. The involvement of users in the creation of these traces (during the walkthrough) proves that the Business Object Model supports the Task Object Model accurately and completely.

The second point is that we have a technique for proving the correctness of system specifications against the requirements model. Normally, the notion of correctness is only applied to proving that the implementation meets its specification. This suggests an approach that glues the two technologies together; but the demand for a Z code generator for *SOMATiK* is, at present, quite limited I suspect.

Strictly speaking, the technique that we have described *validates* the Business Object Model rather than *proves* that it is correct in the mathematical sense. But this is in accordance with our desire to build shared understanding between users and developers. The slogan is: 'Don't prove that it works; convince me'. Validation against task scripts and, ultimately, scenarios approaches proof in the limiting case, when we can be sure that we have exercised every scenario. Therefore we now turn to current research into how to ensure that this is the case, or at least maximize the completeness of the set of scenarios.

5.7 Ensuring the completeness of scenarios

As we saw in the previous chapter, engineering can be split into requirements elicitation and requirements analysis. The former finds out what people want and need, expressing it as an agent communication and task model, and the latter builds a model that can execute to support the needs defined in the earlier models. We have now seen that this process can be made seamless in the sense that we can prove that the Business Object Model will actually support the task in the Task Object Model and *a fortiori* the business objectives and the conversations of the Agent Object Model. This is a step forward from proving that the implementation model meets its specification; which is the territory of traditional formal methods and 'proofs of correctness'. What is not, however, guaranteed is that the requirements expressed in the agent and task models are in any sense complete with respect to human frailties.

Recently there has been some interest in this question in Academe and results are just beginning to emerge from research. One of the most interesting developments is the SAVRE system (Scenarios for Acquisition and Validation in Requirements Engineering), developed as part of the European Union funded CREWS (Co-operative Requirements Engineering With Scenarios) project. The CREWS-SAVRE project (Maiden *et al.,* 1997) sets out to achieve systematic scenario use and generate useful scenarios, taking into account problem specific patterns of normative behaviour and the insights of human error theory (Reason, 1990), cognitive science and software engineering. As Pohl *et al.* (1997) have pointed out, current methods and tools such as Objectory provide little support or guidance in this area. The CREWS project aims to make scenario generation and walkthrough more systematic, useful and cost-effective.

The SAVRE tool generates scenarios to acquire and validate user requirements in a semi-automatic fashion based on parameters set by its user. A wizard then supports a systematic walkthrough of the generated scenarios, ensuring that all paths are explored and all requirements are validated. In the course of this, the tool suggests generic requirements statements that the user can add to the specification. Each scenario consists of hypothetical situations in the target environment, acting as a sort of test script. CREWS has developed theories of standard and alternate courses based on normative behaviour specific to certain problem classes and non-normative events and states for general situations (*cf.* Maiden and Sutcliffe, 1994). The user can either retrieve reusable use cases (task scripts) or choose NATURE object system models (normative behaviour for pre-defined problem domains) from which to generate them. NATURE (Maiden and Sutcliffe, 1994) is a set of object models for specific domains developed as part of another ESPRIT project. The current tool has about 250 types of problem in its database. Task scripts are viewed as having one initial event and at least one each of the following: end events, agents, sub-actions and objects. The states of the object may change as a result of the task execution. The tasks are linked using preconditions on the actions defined in the object model. The wizard now guides the user through scenario generation based on the following five selection types of alternative courses:

- Agent Interaction Patterns.
- Generic Exceptions (e.g. actions that start but never end).
- Permutation Exceptions (e.g. combining two events that occur concurrently).
- Permutation Options (e.g. temporal links between events and actions).

■ Problem Exceptions (e.g. HCI handshake failure).

For example, in a command and control system the normal course script might be presented as 'crew reads mobilization instruction'. The system then asks a series of questions such as: 'What happens if the event does not occur?' or 'What happens if this event occurs twice?' The user must then add a note to the specification.

Ensuring that scenario sets are complete is important if we want to argue, as in the last section, that SOMA proves the correctness of the object model against the requirements as expressed in the agent and task models. The ability to check requirements model exhaustively in this way may be critical for certain applications. Furthermore, the classification of problem exception classes and the work on the temporal logic of task sequencing will be of lasting value. However, keeping the requirements document as a piece of text rather than in the form of task objects is a limitation. In SOMA we recommend that the task scripts (and indeed the agent model) be the final and only repository of the requirements. At the time of writing we are still working towards integrating the ideas from the CREWS project into SOMA. Task sequencing and decomposition are already well handled in SOMA using composition structures and task associations.

5.8 Model animation and simulation

Diversion

SOMATiK extends the original definition of SOMA by providing techniques for animation and time-based and event-based simulation. The reader who has neither an interest in *SOMATiK* nor in the potential animation of models may skip directly to Section 5.9. We begin by presenting an abbreviated description of the *SOMATiK* scripting language following closely the presentation of Bezant (1997).

5.8.1 Executable specifications

A central idea of SOMA and some other methods such as ROOM (Selic *et al.*, 1994) is that of being able, with suitable tool support, to *execute specifications*. People can experience considerable difficulty in understanding the dynamic behaviour of a system when provided only with static representations of it. With this in mind, *SOMATiK* provides for the definition of operations in a high level scripting language which allows the class collaborations to be viewed dynamically. This allows each relevant task identified in the earlier phases of business process modelling and analysis to be tested against the system as designed. It also tests the classes and operations that have been agreed upon during the process. An operation is defined by its script, which serves as a precise definition of the operation's specification and as a method implementing that operation, thus enabling validation of the specification as we saw in Section 5.6.

The *SOMATiK* scripting language acts as a specification language. It supports fairly realistic simulations of the dynamic behaviour of every properly defined operation. Perhaps more importantly, it is easy enough to learn in a day or less and sufficiently robust in use to allow prototypes of operations to be built much more rapidly than in any other candidate prototyping tool such as Delphi, Smalltalk, Visual Basic or a Java environment. The language is thus characterizable as a *scripting* rather than *programming* language. This removes the responsibility from the designer of grappling with the syntax of complex language. Programming is accomplished solely using a point-and-click metaphor; the structure of every statement is determined by *SOMATiK* based on the user's selections from the menus it offers. All the designer needs to think about is the semantics of the operation being specified. The scripting language is block-structured, with blocks being created top down. This means that, for example, to create a window block you first select *Window* from a dialogue box, which generates the BeginWindow/EndWindow pair of lines as shown in Figure 5.19. Next position the line selection cursor over EndWindow and click the Insert button, which is always displayed. Since you are inside a window block, only relevant commands such as *OnOK* or *OnEnter* are selectable. Selecting *OnChange* causes *SOMATiK* to ask which of the attributes of the chosen window you wish to respond to changes of. You must define such a window if you have not already done so. We have chosen the attribute orderNo. Thereupon *SOMATiK* inserts the two lines of an event notification block inside the window block. A similar process is then used to insert an event handler into the event notification block. In this case its function is to retrieve an instance of Orders based on the entered value of orderNo.

```
/* example operation script for Orders.order */

BeginWindow ('Order Dialogue')
        OnChange 'orderNo'
                GetInstance ('Orders','orderNo')
        EndHandler
EndWindow
Operation: 'sendInvoice' of Class 'AccountsWrapper'
       Send: ;
    Receive: ;
Operation: 'deliver' of Class 'DispatchAgents'
       Send: ;
    Receive: ;
```

Figure 5.19 A simple operation script

To complete the script in Figure 5.19, click the Append button and select the Operation radio button. You will be asked to pick the class and then one of its operations from the drop-down lists displayed, as illustrated in Figure 5.20. Of course, for this example, this must be done twice.

An event handler can be any valid statement of the language. We could extend the example and have the operation call rulesets to carry out either computation or run some inference process.

SENDING
MESSAGES
As is normal in object technology, class collaboration is implemented by message passing. This means the sending of messages to operations of either the current or a different class. Operations are inserted into the script from the dialogue shown in Figure 5.20 as discussed above. Messages are either *class messages* or *instance messages*. In the case of instance messages, the attribute that determines the intended instance is selected from the second drop-down list. The message is completed by adding any parameters that must be passed with the message or returned with the response to it. The parameter list is built by choosing from lists of attributes provided in the drop-down boxes as shown in the figure.

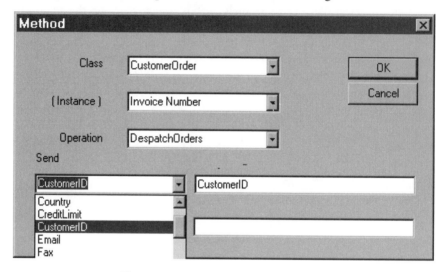

Figure 5.20 Creating a message send

To call a ruleset from an operation select the Ruleset radio button and choose your ruleset using the dialogue box that will then offer a list of available rulesets. You may create a new ruleset at this point is required. Private rulesets are similar to private methods in C++, in that they are not visible on the published interface to a class. Only rulesets encapsulated by the current class may be invoked from its operation scripts. Public rulesets, as described in Chapter 4, are not implemented in *SOMATiK*.

Logical attributes, which can only take the values TRUE and FALSE, are used within If/then statement blocks to govern the flow of control. If/then blocks are created in a manner similar to the window blocks described above. However, logical attributes must have their values set by the execution of rulesets. Setting the values of these attributes in a simulation run can be used as the equivalent of putting buttons in the user dialogue windows of a final system with a more refined user interface.

5.8.2 Running simulations from the Agent Object Model

Recall that a message in the Agent Object Model represents a conversation and that a task script defines the work performance aspect implied by the contract implicit in the conversation. When a task is to be supported during a simulation run, as a result of an event occurring in the Agent Object Model, we move sequentially from the Agent Object Model to the Task Object Model and then to the Business Object Model. It is important to understand the meaning of these transitions clearly. The AOM and the TOM are in the world of the users and their business processes: part of what Cook and Daniels (1994) call the *essential* model. These models are concerned with the activities that must be carried out if the proposed system is to be of use to a business. The BOM lies in the systems world: Cook and Daniels' *specification* model. It specifies the classes that must be created if the system is to be made operational; or at least one possible design of such classes – there may be many alternative decompositions that could be imposed at design time due to architectural and other considerations. The purpose of an animation and simulation however is to confirm that the BOM classes actually do support the user tasks which our analysis has determined must be supported for a valid business process.

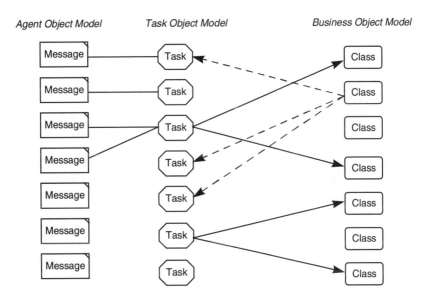

Figure 5.21 Connexions between messages, tasks and classes

With *SOMATiK* to hand we can validate a particular class design by linking these three models together by a simulation of the class model's support for the tasks of agents. Clicking on the icon for an agent in the Agent Object Model displays a pop-up menu from which the user can select one of the events that the agent knows about. Selecting an event/message pair then causes *SOMATiK* to simulate the passing of that message to the appropriate agent. This in turn invokes of the root task object of the message. Each step that *SOMATiK* performs is logged in an event trace, which can be represented either as text or diagrammatically.

Messages always have exactly one root task but may have several component tasks. Furthermore, the same task may be (re)used by several conversations; or rather by one of the agents involved in them to be precise. Task objects and classes (i.e. business objects in the BOM) do not correspond to each other in a one-to-one fashion: the mapping can be more complex. Figure 5.21 illustrates this, showing that a task can be implemented by several classes and that a class may support several tasks. However, it is equally important to remember that there is only one initiating class supporting each root task, as we have already seen in Section 5.6. Although several classes may collaborate to achieve the apotheosis of a particular task, it is also true that there is only *one* class which is the instigator of the Business Object Model's support for this task. Execution always begins with the execution of a unique operation. This initiation point is recorded in the Properties section of a task. It is the link to the class domain from the task domain: the *Implemented By* class and operation.

As a set of several event traces is created each one may be stored. They can be processed by *SOMATiK*'s Event Trace Cross-Reference Manager. This checks that each of the root tasks in the task model has been exercised and reports on any classes, or operations of classes, which were not referenced in any trace. To the extent that unreferenced classes or operations are found, this signals possibly redundant classes or operations in the model. Of course, these may have been included because it is know that a further development of the model yet to be constructed will need them; but it is also in the nature of iterative development that classes and operations may be proposed and subsequently discarded and the completeness check is a valuable aid. It prevents superfluous classes from being included in the actual development work downstream from the requirements engineering. Redundant operations and classes can be deleted if they are confirmed as surplus to requirements given the latest state of the model(s) and the development team's understanding.

Once the principal parts of the business process have been modelled correctly, we could use the event trace facilities described above to create regression tests which can be re-executed at appropriate points in the development to ensure that modifications to the business object model have not corrupted our understanding of the problem or diverged too far from our mission. This is the purpose of the animation script facilities. An Animation Script is comprised of a temporally ordered list of tasks. It can be invoked as a unit from the Run menu. The resultant event trace can be used to confirm of the class design and for regression testing purposes as discussed above.

5.8.3 Discrete event and time-based simulation

Simulation was at the very root of object technology from the early days of object-oriented programming and the Simula language. Simula came out of work on discrete event simulation and operational research dating back to 1949, with the motivating problem being the design of nuclear reactors. The differential equations involved in such problems were too hard for even numerical solution, so alternative techniques had to be developed from first principles. A successful technique is to simulate a world which moves (transforms its state) in discrete steps corresponding to time intervals. With such simulations, which can be run and re-run on a computer, the effects of different parameters can be observed rather than calculated. This is analogous to the use of spreadsheets for 'what if' analysis. However, the languages available in the Sixties were not particularly suited for simulation. Whereas the abstractions of conventional languages like FORTRAN attempted to describe processes in the computer, Simula, with its abstractions, essayed to describe real-world processes.

The seminal simulation problem involved objects which were neutrons and absorbent rods in a nuclear reactor. A more readily understandable example is the simulation of traffic passing through a complex intersection which involves random arrival rates, saturation flow rates, traffic light settings and queuing. The vehicles are generated and tracked through the system as it passes through discrete time steps, rather like time-lapse photography, and the behaviour can be observed, at each time step, in terms of queue lengths, delay times, junction locking and similar features. It is also possible to observe global phenomena such as stability or convergence to a stable state. A simulation of a system, once constructed, can be tested under different assumptions on such variables as volume, signal linking or cycle times.

The sort of simulation discussed so far in this section is based on events triggering messages between agents, which in turn imply the execution of tasks that cause operations of business objects to be invoked, but not with respect to any particular flow of elapsed time. The authors of *SOMATiK* call this 'event-based simulation', although as we have seen above the term DISCRETE EVENT SIMULATION is traditionally held to involve the simulation of discrete time steps. Since one can store sequences of such event simulations as scripts (not task scripts, but the animation scripts of the previous paragraph), they also refer to script-based simulation. It is also possible to base simulations on the passing of simulated time in *SOMATiK* in which case the term 'time-based simulation' is used.

The task performance properties of a task object state the constraints placed on the performance of a system. Figure 5.22 shows an example in which a task must complete in under two seconds, which is thus a constraint on the final design and implementation of the system and upon its target hardware and environment. At any given point during model construction, only the available, necessary and relevant information need be entered of course. There is no need whatsoever for all these data to be put in unless a time-based simulation is envisaged.

The task performance properties include the mean and variance of the task latency for a given time bucket: seconds, minutes, days, or even decades, as appropriate. If it is known, a probability distribution for the task occurrences can be chosen from the radio buttons shown. A textual comment detailing any further constraints is also catered for. For example, if the model is of things arriving in a queue at random then the Poisson distribution is normally chosen. A very familiar example of a Poisson process is given by vehicles arriving at a set of traffic signals. If the model is of the time taken to perform some manual task, such as completing a tax return, the normal distribution is more appropriate.

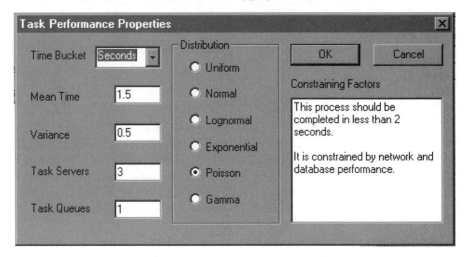

Figure 5.22 Task performance properties

The task performance specification shown in Figure 5.22 also includes the number of task servers and the number of task queues to be set up in the system. An airline check-in area, for example, often has a number of desks (servers) and a separate queue for each. Post offices on the other hand have multiple servers but only one queue. This arrangement was adopted as a result of one of the very earliest Operational Research projects in the 1950s.

Time-based simulation enables designers to observe the apparent development of a system in time, but where time is modelled rather unrealistically as a sequence of discrete evenly spaced points or *ticks*. Time-based simulation in *SOMATiK* simply sets an internal pseudo-clock running, for the desired simulation interval. It then fires each of the agent dæmons at each tick.

MULTIPLE THREADS

In real businesses there will usually be multiple independent paths (or threads) of execution for at least some important business processes. This increases the complexity that modellers must deal with when it occurs. The threads may also need to be synchronized at various points, making life more complicated still.

SOMATiK provides support for modelling multiple parallel threads through the *BeginParallel* directive of its scripting language. Inter-process synchronization is provided through a semaphore model. Concurrent executing processes can be spawned from any operation of any class by invoking a *BeginParallel* command. All operations specified inside the scope of a *BeginParallel/EndParallel* program block are fired ostensibly at once and in parallel. Of course, the simulation is actually being carried out on a normal sequential (i.e. Single Instruction stream, Single Data stream or SISD) machine. This means that the processes are not really processed in parallel; it only appears to be so. The order in which processes fire is just the order in which the processes are listed within the parallel program block. The *Semaphore* class is provided as part of the system. An instance of this class has as attributes its identity (or name) and its state, which is one of **Set** or **Cleared**. The public interface of the class contains responsibilities called **Set** and **Clear**, which set this state variable in the obvious manner, and one that will respond to other process instances that request notification of state changes. These messages can originate from any operation of any class that has the appropriate directives included in its operation scripts. Semaphores can be set and cleared using the **Set** and **Clear** operation script directives.

```
Notify ("Waiting for event 1")
Dwell Until: 'event1' ;
/* reactivate when another thread sets the
        inter-process semaphore event1 */
Notify ("Event 1 has now occurred"
```

Figure 5.23 Synchronizing execution threads in the scripting language

The *Dwell* directive can be used to suspend the execution of a process. The period (in ticks) during which a process is suspended can be set either as a fixed number of ticks or as a calculated, variable number of ticks. Alternatively, the process can be suspended until one or more semaphores are set.

Figure 5.23 shows a part of an example wherein a script suspends execution of the thread in which it has been invoked until some other currently executing thread asserts the semaphore *event1*, at which point the original thread is resumed.

5.8.4 Combining script and time-based simulation

I understand that one of the primary motivations behind the provision of the time-based simulation features of *SOMATiK* was to create a background against which discrete event simulation of interactions among classes could be studied. This is accomplished by overlaying an animation script on top of a time-based simulation.

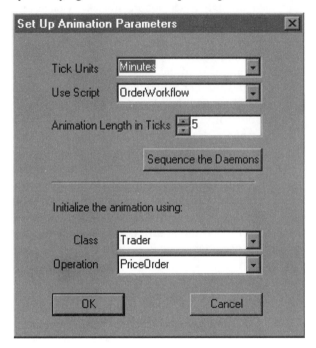

Figure 5.24 Setting up a simulation script

The animation parameters are set using the dialogue box illustrated in Figure 5.24. The modeller must state the time bucket units used for the pseudo-clock ticks to determine a time-base for the simulation. At each tick every agent dæmon is polled to see if there is a reason to fire an activity. A nominated animation script is selected using the *Use Script* combo box and the duration of the simulation in ticks is established. Sometimes one may want to modify the sequence in which the dæmons fire and this is allowed for. Conceptually, they fire in parallel at each new tick. In reality however, on an SISD machine, however, they will execute serially as already pointed out, and this can affect the results of the simulation. Usually there is no effect, but the facility is provided to override the default sequence (in fact the sequence in which the dæmons were created) just in case. In case there is a need for some special processing at the start of the simulation, an operation of a nominated class can be specified. This operation will be executed at tick zero.

⊟ 5.9 Task associations and sequence diagrams

When faced with a number of users' tasks it is intuitively clear that there must be relationships among these tasks. For instance, a library loan cannot be recorded until an access record for the book concerned has been located in the library database. We can conclude from this that the task of setting up a record for a book *enables* the task of issuing the book on loan. We cannot lend a book before buying a copy of it; so that the purchasing task *precedes* the lending task. A delinquent lender who fails to return overdue books will normally be placed on a suspended list. In this case, suspending the lender *disables* lending to that person. A librarian may be talking with a researcher while recording a loan for someone else at the same time: the give advice task *parallels* the lend book task.

All these relationships are modelled in *SOMATiK* using task associations and task association sets. A **task association** is a named, directed relationship between two tasks (strictly, between two instances of tasks). In *SOMATiK*, the relationship is classified into one of the following types: Succeeds, Precedes, Enables, Disables or Parallels.

As we have seen, tasks are operations of agent objects, and so a task association written *Assoc01(AgentX.A,AgentB.Y)* might represent a message transmitted from AgentX in the course of executing its task A to AgentY invoking the execution of task B. The agents can be internal, external or system agents. A **task association set** is a named collection of task associations. It represents a time-ordered, possibly parallel collection of tasks, and is an object in its own right. It is a directed graph whose nodes are tasks and whose arcs are task associations. It represents a related, coherent set of tasks that support a business goal. A task association set is equivalent to one or more sequence diagrams. SOMA sequence diagrams can support the ideas of branching and concurrency, as we will see shortly. A simple linear association set will have only one realization as a sequence diagram, whereas branching association sets have a unique sequence diagram for every path through the network represented by the association set. Therefore a UML sequence diagram, which cannot show these aspects of a model, represents a strict subset of an association set, not expressing the complete situation.

Task associations, like any other objects, can be linked by any of the four object structures, notably that of composition. Large task association sets can be desegregated into components, and so a hierarchical set of views of tasks can be generated. For example, an association set called 'Process Order' could contain the tasks concerned with validating the external system that issued the order, checking to see whether the order violated any legal or compliance constraints, deciding whether the order should be priced manually or automatically and so on.

Other processes represented as task association sets can be re-usable in many contexts within an organization – a good example being transaction capture which is structurally identical whether pencils or zlotys are being purchased, even though the subject matter is quite different: stationery *versus* foreign exchange. Task reuse of this kind can simplify the diagrammatic representation of large scale processes enormously. The capability for drilling down through different diagrammatic levels is also supported, as we shall see.

The reader should note carefully the difference between an association set of tasks and a task decomposition: all component tasks in a task composition structure are carried out by the same agent; tasks within a task association set will be carried out co-operatively by a set of agents. In this sense, therefore, a task association set corresponds more closely to a use case in the sense of Jacobson *et al.* (1992) than does a unitary task. See Appendix B for more information on the relationship between tasks and use cases.

5.9.1 Sequence diagrams

Recall from Section 5.3 that a conversation between agents has a sixfold structure. We can use sequence diagrams based on task association sets to represent the recursion in conversations illustrated previously in Figure 5.4. To illustrate the general idea of this consider the simple process of buying a cup of coffee. The Agent Object Model visualization of the conversation is shown in Figure 5.25.

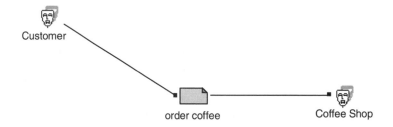

Figure 5.25 Getting some caffeine into the bloodstream

A sequence diagram representing this conversation is shown in Figure 5.26. The task association set behind this diagram covers the four stages of *request, negotiate, perform* and *handover*. A 'thirst' event causes the customer to initiate the process by asking for the price of a cup of coffee (the *request* or *preparation* stage of the transaction). The seller proposes a price, which the customer ponders (*negotiation*) and accepts in this case. If the price is tolerable, the vendor makes and delivers the coffee (*task execution* or *performance*). If the coffee is hot and strong enough, the customer takes and pays for it (*handover*).

One of the strengths of this way of grounding sequence diagram in a model of task associations is that the various failure branches that could occur can be added, and we can auto-generate sequence diagrams covering all the possibilities for discussion by the development team and the users.

Figure 5.26 A sequence diagram representing a conversation

The process could fail at the proposal stage, perhaps because the shop is about to close or has run out of the basic ingredients of coffee making. The negotiation could collapse because the customer thinks the price is too high. Failure at the perform stage could occur because the espresso machine breaks down. At the acceptance stage the customer might abort the process because the coffee is too weak (no reference to Java is intended here). We could add task associations at each of these failure points. In Figure 5.28 the diagram now appears with 'tensor multiplication' symbols ⊗ showing tasks that have alternate (disjunctive) outbound associations. These act as an aid to navigation, helping us to visualize the possible paths.

The union of all possible paths can be summarized as a task association set and vizualized as shown in Figure 5.27, the equivalent sequence diagram of which is shown in Figure 5.28. The tensor multiplication symbols indicate the existence of branching points in the conversation. This is how the recursion in conversations illustrated schematically earlier (Figure 5.4) is represented in *SOMATiK*. A 'tensor addition' symbol ⊕ can be used on the shoulders of the task boxes to represent the alternative, concurrent situation: indicating that there is more than a single branch out of the task. These other paths can be drawn separately. The basic sequence diagram for this set is similar to the one in Figure 5.26 but the disjunctive 'tensor multiplication' symbols represent the failure points shown in the association tree. We can examine each path individually, as shown by way of example in Figure 5.29.

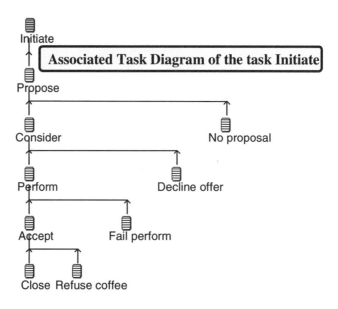

Figure 5.27 A task association structure diagram (all associations are 'succeeds')

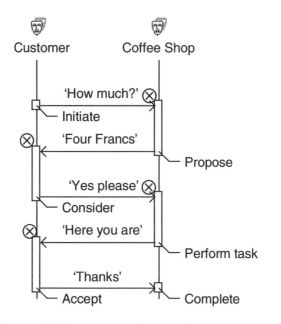

Figure 5.28 A sequence diagram with concurrency

One important aspect of the approach of Flores, which has influenced both SOMA and *SOMATiK*'s treatment of conversations is the idea of *nesting* conversations. Any stage of a conversation may involve recurrence to a further level. The association set approach uses nested association sets to partition the resultant complexity.

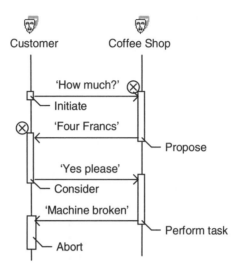

Figure 5.29 Sequence diagram showing a failure point in a negotiation

The approach taken by Flores is exemplified quite differently in the tool produced by his company Action Technologies Inc. (ATI). Their Action Technologies Workbench enables modellers to draw conversations, using a notation based on that shown in Figure 5.3 and generate workflow applications in products such as Lotus Notes. As a result of this approach the work of Winograd and Flores has been criticized in the requirements engineering literature as leading to rigid, inflexible régimes disliked by users who have to follow the workflow system's laid down rules. I feel that this does not detract from the basic theory though and anyway, our purpose is not to build workflow models but to provide a starting point for object-oriented analysis.

SEQUENCE DIAGRAMS AND UML UML sequence diagrams describe phenomena that occur in a specified sequence, but nothing in the semantics of UML sequence diagrams shows causality. It is important to understand the implications of this. The arrows on a UML sequence diagram represent the steps in a sequential process – and nothing more than that. The following sequence of events:

1. The sun rises.
2. The birds begin to sing.
3. The rush hour traffic grinds to a halt.

can of course be easily represented in UML by a sequence diagram. Common sense dictates that the first and second phenomena are causally linked. (In a certain sense, the sun sends an electromagnetic message to the birds, which causes them to sing.) The causal links between the first two steps and the third are less clear. Of course, singing birds do nothing to alter traffic conditions. The sun rising has equally little direct effect. Although most of us have electric light nowadays, we nevertheless tend to go to work during daylight, and in this sense the rising of the sun will presage a traffic jam. However, to explain this synchronicity, we would have to expand our model to include some representation of people, land use, traffic patterns and transport modes. This is both a strength and a weakness of the UML version of sequence diagrams. Hidden and essentially irrelevant stages in linked sets of actions can be eliminated, thus simplifying the diagrams. On the other hand, viewing an incomplete diagram that takes advantage of this simplification can lead to erroneous assumptions about causality between the arrows of the diagram. This becomes especially significant when an analyst hands over a specification to a developer. Eventually, a program must be written, and it must be complete and without discontinuities in its control flow. Without clear guidance, the developer may just make assumptions about the sequence of control. To deny this is to ignore the time and budget pressures that exist in real organizations. Gaps in design turn up not as discontinuities in program control flow, but as *ad hoc* conceptual leaps. These can materialize as bugs, which are fixed only at great cost – particularly since this kind of error cannot be traced back to the specification. This is one manifestation of a well-known process model relationship: time saved during analysis leads to extra costs in maintenance.

AN EXAMPLE In the training material supplied with the UML version of Rational *Rose* we find the advice that sequence diagrams can be used early on in the analysis of requirements. An example is given concerning simple order processing, whereby one constructs a sequence diagram based on the idea that a customer asks a clerk to place an order. Naturally, the customer and the clerk appear on the sequence diagram. The clerk needs to know the stock availability and the price, so he looks these up on a price list and a stock record. Here the temptations of the devil begin and we can posit instances called stock_record and price_list_item. *Rose* adds to the temptation by making it easy to convert these instances into classes: StockRecords and PriceList. Now, to any seasoned object designer this is patently the wrong thing to do. It would be obvious to such a person that the Products class should know (or be able to obtain) the stock and price for any of its instances, or indeed the averages of these numbers. Creating the sequence diagram before the basic class model is therefore very dangerous for any but the most experienced object designer.

Thus, the *Rose* approach can lead to an absurdly bad design from the viewpoint of object-orientation. I recommend a completely different approach whereby the Business Object Model is built from the Task Object Model and the designers are encouraged to see that the Products class should have features corresponding to product price and stock level long before any sequence diagrams are drawn. The latter should be used to document and validate complex business processes only after the first cut object model has been built.

Another problem with UML sequence diagrams is that they are interpreted as instances of system classes, the operations of which send messages to each other represented by horizontal arrows. The vertical boxes on such charts, similar to the ones of Figure 5.26, represent operations. In our approach the instances are thought of as real world agents and the boxes represent their tasks. The horizontal arrows represent task associations such as *precedes*. I think this is a better approach because, rather than think of the unwinding of the operation stack frame, we situate our model firmly in the world of the user. This leads to a more fruitful dialogue between users and developers during requirements analysis and an improved chance of a shared understanding of the problem at hand.

5.9.2 Conjunctive, disjunctive and nested association sets

As we have seen, task association sets can include parallel paths. As an example, consider this time the process of making a cup of *instant* coffee. The process involves filling a kettle with water and putting it on to boil. While the kettle is heating, the cups and (optionally) milk and sugar are located. Next the coffee granules must be dissolved using the hot water, after the kettle has boiled. These tasks and their relationships can be shown in a task association structure diagram as in Figure 5.30, which illustrates the parallelism between the two main activities clearly. This can also be realized in sequence diagram form as shown in Figure 5.31. Note the $\oplus$ symbol on the shoulder of the task *Fill Kettle*. This 'tensor addition' notation (a plus sign inside a circle) has the semantics of AND (or conjunction). It indicates that there are multiple associations arising from the task that it annotates, and that all task sequences arising from this task are included on the diagram.

Concurrent branches can, of course, be represented one at a time on separate sequence diagrams. For example, in Figures 5.32 and 5.33 the two concurrent branches from Figure 5.31 are displayed separately. Note that the tensor multiplication symbol on the shoulder of the *Fill Kettle* task indicates that there is more than one branch out of the task, and that only one branch is being displayed on the diagram.

On occasion, task association sets and their realizations as sequence diagrams may become rather large. Figure 5.34 shows part of such a diagram. In such a case we can decompose an association set into smaller sets to help us apprehend the structure more clearly. Thus in *SOMATiK* we often substitute a single composite task for an entire association set, thereby imposing a nested structure. A composite association set is shown by shading its task box on the sequence diagram. In Figure 5.34, the association *assoc1* links the task *task1* to a complete association set *TASet1*. The association can be thought of as precedes for the purposes of the example. Similarly *assoc2* and *assoc3* both link task3 to entire association sets. Expanding either of these association sets (by clicking their icons) will reveal a diagram of the whole nested association set, This is depicted in Figure 5.35 for the case of the association set *assoc3*.

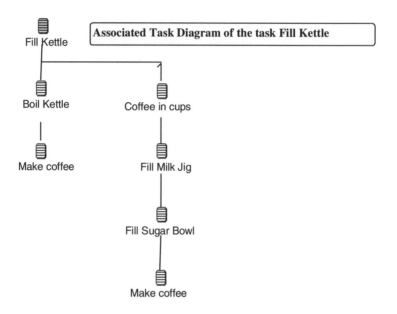

Figure 5.30 Task Association diagram

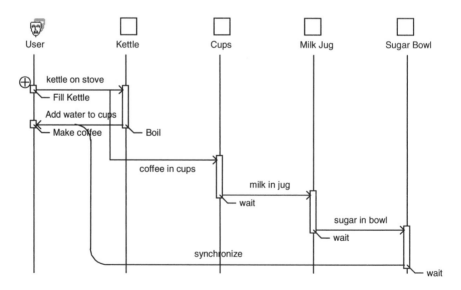

Figure 5.31 Parallel (conjunctive) sequence diagram

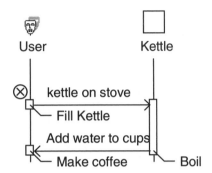

Figure 5.32 One branch of a concurrent sequence diagram

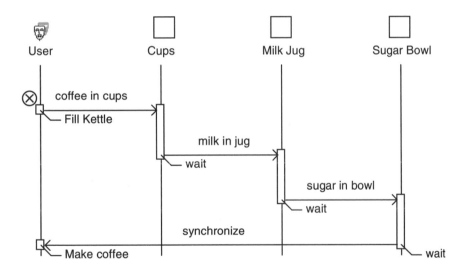

Figure 5.33 The alternative branch of the diagram

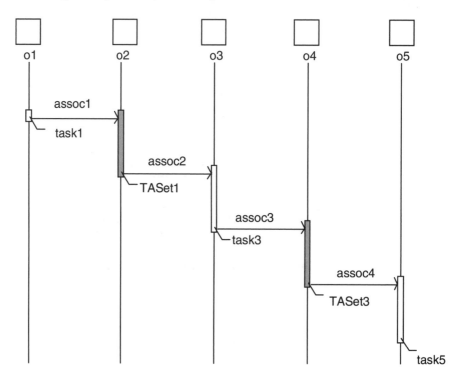

Figure 5.34 Nested association sets

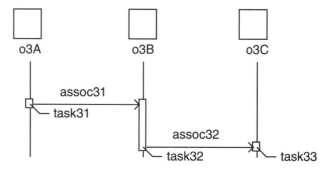

Figure 5.35 A component association set

COMPOSING
ASSOCIATION
SETS

Association sets are themselves *bona fide* objects, and as such can be linked by all four SOMA structural relationships between objects, including composition. In the example just given, *TASet1* and *TASet3* are nested in (i.e. are components of) an association set called *Main*. Clicking on the icon for *Main* allows us to examine the summary composition tree as shown in Figure 5.36(a) in OML notation. This shows the components *TASet1* and *TASet3* of which we were already aware, but also that *TASet1* in turn has a, previously hidden, component *TASet2*.

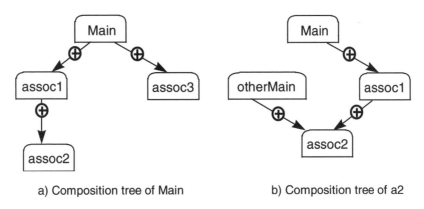

a) Composition tree of Main   b) Composition tree of a2

Figure 5.36 Association set composition structures

Clicking on *TASet2* (if we are using *SOMATiK* at any rate) expands the tree from the perspective of *TASet2*, which shows us that *TASe2* is in turn a component of another erstwhile hidden association set called *otherMain*. Note that the idea of specification re-use is once more central to the approach.

5.10 Bibliographical notes

The theory of business process modelling presented in this chapter is largely original, although I have been motivated by the work of many others; notably Jacobson, Flores and Winograd. Some of the material in Section 5.5 and 5.6 was first presented in a series of articles in the SIGS journal *Object Expert*.

Although SOMA always allowed for associations between tasks, Peter Jones first elaborated the theory of task association sets and their equivalence with sequence diagrams. He also developed the ideas concerning time and event based simulation presented in the digression of Section 5.8. I am also indebted to Peter for several of the examples used in Sections 5.8 to 5.9. The presentation in Sections 5.8 and 5.9, follows the *SOMATiK* user documentation and Peter's notes closely on these topics (Bezant, 1997 and private communications). Further elaboration of these theories and their practical application, with many fascinating examples, will be found in Jones (1999) which is hereby commended to the reader.

6

Modelling intelligent agents

... his intellect is improperly exposed

Sydney Smith (Lady Holland)

W e need to understand how to model intelligent agents for two quite distinct reasons. First, to see how business processes can be modelled using objects that represent agents – as in Chapter 5 – and, second, to understand how object-oriented models can be used to describe the agent-based computer systems that are becoming increasingly important.

The purpose of this chapter is to introduce and discuss agent technology: its nature, importance and applications. To set the scene, I attempt to situate this, perhaps unfamiliar, technology in the context of modern information technology.

6.1 The rôle of intelligent agents

Increasing complexity of business problems is starting to generate market demand for 'smart' software systems that co-operate with end users by being able to reason about the tasks they perform: intelligent agents. Some problems are harder to solve with other technologies (e.g. searching the Internet). Agent technology also provides an effective metaphor for domain analysis, systems design and implementation. It facilitates 're-use' at the knowledge level.

Adding rules to the interfaces of objects has the useful side effect of enabling us to model intelligent agents and multi-agent systems without any special purpose agent-based modelling machinery. Agents are autonomous, flexible software objects that can respond to changes in their environment or context, engage in 'social' acts via a common agent communication language and be proactive in the manner of the Intellisense agents in MS Office for example.

6.1.1 Agents, objects and modern information technology

Modernity, in computing circles today, seems to be characterized by just a few fashionable technologies:

- Rapid Application Development (RAD);
- Business process modelling and re-engineering;
- Object Technology, including object-oriented languages, tools, databases and methods;
- Java and network computing; and now
- Agents.

Of course, more fundamental than all these is the presence of constant change and it is this that leads to the perpetual striving of both technologists and managers for new technical solutions.

RAD has two connotations. It is often taken to mean the sort of 'rabid' application development advocated by the salesman for some 4GL or other. Such a person will claim that development is so simple with this tool that you can build the application in front of the users, possibly in a workshop setting. He may even claim that the users can learn to build their own applications. Anyone with a few years in the industry knows from painful experience what utter hogwash this is – and dangerous hogwash at that. The more sensible connotation is that developers and users work together to establish requirements and prototypes are used to assist in this process. The prototypes are then thrown away when serious developments begin, although the developers and users stay in close contact throughout the project. For this reason the approach is often known as JAD: Joint Application Development. All the two approaches share is a commitment to the workshop format. My understanding of RAD is definitely the latter. One way to ensure that prototypes are thrown away is to use a PC based tool prior to migrating to a live UNIX environment but, with the advent of p-code based languages such as Java, it may be necessary to select a tool with deliberately restricted user interface features. This will help manage expectations.

If you are convinced that both RAD and OT are needed then the outstanding questions are whether and how they can be combined. We have seen how this can be accomplished in Chapter 5. We should also ask why agent computing contributes to the goals of the modern software engineer. One of the major reasons that corporations are adopting object technology is the move to client/server architecture. Even 3-tier architectures are often beset with severe network bandwidth problems. Using mobile agents can reduce the amount of network traffic. The mobility of agents means that, when it is more efficient, we can send the program across the network rather than a request to retrieve unfiltered data. Smart agents can be used to personalize systems for individual needs and skills, which has the effect of reducing the cognitive and learning burden on these users.

Agents that can learn, adapt and exchange goals and data can be used to speed up information searches, especially across networks or the Internet.

Another area where agent computing is becoming influential, at least as a modelling metaphor, is in business process modelling and re-engineering. The term 'business process re-engineering' was introduced and popularized at the beginning of the 1990s by *inter alia* Hammer (1990) and Davenport and Short (1990). However, the activity was not then entirely unprecedented in the work of systems and business analysts (see e.g. Checkland, 1981). The introduction of such comprehensive changes to the way an organization organizes and executes its work is characterized by the need for radical surgery; that is the company must be aware of some serious threat or inefficiency that jeopardizes its very existence to invest in a BPR project. It is also dependent on the use of IT – a fact acknowledged by all the management gurus who have written on the subject but seldom explicated[1]. Typically, re-engineered companies replace their hierarchical management structures with flat ones. This places responsibility at the point where effective action can take place, rather than requiring long chains of permissions before a simple problem can be rectified. The focus in most work on BPR is on process and this is as it should be. However, as Taylor (1995) has pointed out, an exclusive obsession with process can be dangerous because business depends on the management of resources and the structure of the organization as well as on effective processes. Thus, any approach to business process modelling needs to be able to model all three aspects: resources, organization and processes. It turns out that the agent metaphor when combined with an object-oriented perspective on systems analysis provides an effective solution to this modelling problem. Furthermore, modelling a user's responsibilities with an intelligent agent can often reduce the cognitive dissonance between the user's mental model of a system and its actual structure.

6.2 What is an agent?

Agent technology has its roots in the study of distributed artificial intelligence (DAI), although the popularity of the approach has had to wait for more mundane applications in mobile computing, mail filtering and network search.

User and supplier organizations that are actively pursuing agent technology include Alcatel, Apple Computer, ARPA, AT&T, Banco Popolare di Sondrio, BT, DEC, HP, IBM, Logica, Lotus, Microsoft, SBC Warburg and Xerox PARC. An agent system handles malfunctions aboard the space shuttle. The White House uses e-mail agents to filter thousands of requests for information. MIT has built agents to schedule meetings. Ovum predicts a market for agent technology of $4,000m by

---

[1] An exception is the book by Halé (1996) which does offer a notation and a definite approach to the process.

the year 2000. Researchers from the fields of robotics, entertainment, knowledge based systems, human computer interaction, databases, distributed systems, communications networks, cognitive science, psychology and virtual reality have all shown a keen interest.

Sample applications of agent technology to date include data filtering and analysis, brokering, process monitoring and alarm generation, business process and workflow control, data/document retrieval and storage management, personal digital assistants, Computer Supported Co-operative Working (CSCW), simulation modelling and gaming.

Agents in current systems perform information filtering, task automation, pattern recognition and completion, user modelling, decision making, information retrieval, resource optimization based on negotiation (e.g. in air traffic control), routing, simulation and planning.

Other current applications include:

- User interface agents (such as Microsoft's Intellisense)
- Battlefield command and control
- Process monitoring (of networks and of business processes)

Along with the plethora of new applications there is a great deal of very confusing terminology facing anyone attempting to understand the technology of intelligent agent computing. We read many conflicting and overlapping terms such as Intelligent Agents, Knowbots, Softbots, Taskbots, Personal assistants and Wizards. Also we may often encounter writings on network agents which are not true agents in the sense of most of the above terms. Furthermore there are several competing definitions of an intelligent agent in the literature. For example we find:

- 'An object that thinks!'
- 'An object with a head!'
- 'A smart computer program'

Russell and Norvig (1995) characterize an agent as 'anything that can be viewed as perceiving its environment through sensors and acting upon that environment through effectors. A rational agent is one that does the right thing'.

A report from Ovum (Guilfoyle and Warner 1994) tightens this slightly: 'An agent is a self-contained software element responsible for executing part of a programmatic process, usually in a distributed environment. An intelligent agent makes use of non-procedural process information – knowledge – defined in and accessed from a knowledge base, by means of inference mechanisms.'

But a more compelling definition comes from Genesereth and Ketchpel (Riecken, 1994): 'An entity is a software agent if and only if it communicates correctly with its peers by exchanging messages in an *agent communication language*.' This is a most important point if agents from different manufacturers are to meet and co-operate. Kendall *et al.*, (1997) say that agents are objects 'that proactively carry out autonomous behaviour and co-operate with each other through negotiation', which further supports this view.

Agent communication languages (ACLs) perform a very similar rôle to object request brokers and may be implemented on top of them. ACLs are necessary so that agents can be regarded as distributed objects that need not know of each other's existence when created. There are two kinds of ACL, procedural ones such as General Magic's Telescript, and declarative languages such as the European Space Agency's KQML/KIF.

One might add that an agent is an entity that can sense, make decisions, act, communicate with other entities, relocate, maintain beliefs and learn. Not all agents will have all these features but we should at least allow for them. One way to do this is to classify agents according to the level of features they exhibit. We will consider four levels in order of increasing complexity and power:

- Basic software 'agents'
- Reactive intelligent agents
- Deliberative Intelligent Agents
- Hybrid Intelligent Agents

BASIC SOFTWARE AGENTS

It is common to apply the description AGENT to quite ordinary code modules that perform pre-defined tasks. This is an especially common usage in relation to macros attached to spreadsheets or database system triggers and stored procedures. Such 'agents' are usually standalone and have no learning capability, no adaptability, no social behaviour and a lack of explicit control. The term is also applied to simple mail agents or Web macros written in PERL (Practical Extraction and Report Language) or Tcl (Tool command language) (Ousterhout, 1994). The PC automation scripts to be found in HP's NewWave environment were an even simpler example.

While Ovum thinks that this simple type of agent will take on the features of the more sophisticated types of agent, that use DAI techniques, Goodall (1994) argues that basic software agents will not be thus influenced: they will meet '99.9% of users' [requirements] without the need for any "intelligent" technologies'

REACTIVE INTELLIGENT AGENTS

Reactive intelligent agents represent the simplest category of agent where the term is properly applied. These are data driven programs; meaning that they react to stimuli and are not goal oriented. They perform pre-defined tasks but may perform symbolic reasoning, often being rule-based. They are sometimes able to communicate with other agents. They may have learning capability and emergent intelligence. At a macro level they may sometimes exhibit explicit control but there is no explicit micro-level control. They cannot reason about organization. Homogeneous groupings of such agents are common.

Examples of reactive intelligent agents include monitor/alert agents encoded as a set of knowledge-sources or rules with a global control strategy.

DELIBERATIVE
INTELLIGENT
AGENTS

Deliberative intelligent agents are mainly goal driven programs. They can have the ability to set and follow new goals. They typically use symbolic representation and reasoning; typically using a production rule approach. They typically maintain a model of their beliefs about their environment and goal seeking status. They may be mobile and able to communicate and exchange data (or even goals) with other agents that they encounter.

Deliberative agents may have learning capability. They can reason about organization and are able to perform complex reasoning. Their intelligence is programmed at the micro level at which there is explicit control. Heterogeneous grouping of these agents is possible. Data retrieval agents that will fetch and filter data from a database or the Internet are typical examples of this kind of agent.

According to some authorities (Kendall *et al.*, 1997) this is the weakest permissible use of the term AGENT. **Weak agents** on this view are autonomous, mobile, reactive to events, able to influence their environments and able to interact with other agents. **Strong agents** have the additional properties of storing beliefs, goals and plans of action, learning and veracity; although there is some dispute over the meaning of the latter property.

HYBRID
INTELLIGENT
AGENTS

Hybrid intelligent agents are a combination of deliberative and reactive agents. Such agents can be mobile and may try actively and dynamically to co-operate with other agents. If they can also learn, they are **strong hybrid intelligent agents**. Such agents usually contain (or may access) a knowledge base of rules and assertions (beliefs) and a plan library. An interpreter enables the agent to select a plan according to its current goals and state. When an event occurs a plan is selected (instantiated) to represent the agent's current intention.

6.2.1 Current trends and pitfalls

Although the potential benefits are enormous, there are still many open issues in intelligent agent technology. The theories of agents are still largely incomplete. There has been a complete absence of methodological guidelines hitherto. There is still a limited choice of development tools as discussed above. The underlying technology is potentially very complex. Finally, we have yet to accumulate large amounts of experience and expertise based on 'real-life', large-scale applications

Agent design remains something of a black art because there are no published guidelines on how to select appropriate agent architectures for different classes of problem-solving. A designer must also struggle to answer the questions of how an agent acquires its knowledge and how that knowledge should be represented. One must decide how a complex task should be decomposed and allocated to different agents. The question of the 'agent communication language' must be addressed too: how should heterogeneous agents co-operate and communicate with each other? Finally, there are new problems of a legal and ethical nature, such as whether an intelligent agent can ever be trusted. People might think that their jobs are threatened and this too could be a barrier to acceptance.

We have seen that there is a plethora of agent definitions and approaches – many of which seem dubious. The current trend towards endowing computers with more intelligence is expected to grow, but may be slowed down by a shortage of skilled resources. Further proliferation of agent-based software into mobile and WAN-based computing is likely to be the most visible symptom in the short term. Many challenges remain, both theoretical and practical. We can expect to see increasing use of OO methods and tools to model and deliver agent-based systems. It is clear that there will be increasing utilization of distributed object-oriented technologies such as CORBA with no use of agents. On the other hand, intelligent agents show great promise as an enabling technology to help realize large-scale OO developments. The emergence of standard agent-based architectures and ACLs may lead to a market in tradable agents.

6.2.2 The architecture of agents

Intelligent agents are intelligent in the sense that they embody some kind of expertise or the ability to learn. This expertise may be encoded as production rules, in which case the agent must be equipped with an inference engine to process them. Learning algorithms are usually, of course, procedural in nature and may be based on decision branching (e.g. ID3), neural nets or genetic algorithms. Agents need to communicate with users and with each other. As I have mentioned, the best way to do this is via a standard agent communication language. Unfortunately, such a universal standard is not yet agreed so that designers are often forced to create one or work within a proprietary environment.

We can generalize about the basic architecture that most agent system share. Figure 6.1 shows a typical architecture. Each agent has a controller that stores or can access its inference engine and problem solving strategy. The agent encapsulates two kinds of knowledge in its knowledge base: persistent and transient. The persistent knowledge often takes the form of attributes and methods that represent its skills in an object-oriented implementation, but the methods may be coded non-procedurally; Prolog is a common implementation language. The agent may also store knowledge about the rôles that it plays in the overall agent organization and about its plans. Plans, which are fixed, are to be distinguished from those that vary during execution, the latter being part of the agent's transient knowledge base along with its current assumptions, beliefs, acquaintances and short term goals. Agents communicate via a message queue and deliver messages to 'post offices' on the network which deliver to other agents, systems or users. The reader will note the resonance of this communication architecture with that of object request brokers and the latter can be used to implement agent-oriented systems. Actual agent-based systems vary considerably but share this basic approach in outline at least.

One of the chief problems with current client/server systems is the amount of network traffic generated. Even on high speed LANs this can lead to unpredictable performance levels: which is worse than predictably slow performance for most people. Many companies have tried to address the problem by moving away from their first generation 2-tier systems, with all the additional problems of stored procedure calls, to 3-tier systems based on the use of remote procedure calls (RPCs). In a 3-tier system much of the processing logic is moved to an intermediate 'application server' that is access by clients needing an application's services, often nowadays via an ORB. The calls to the database are now mostly pure SQL data retrieval. The architecture of a typical such system is shown in Figure 6.2. Note how busy the network may become. This is largely because applications retrieve tables that contain many data irrelevant to the user's purpose. Note also the need to use what Jacobson *et al.* (1992) call 'controller objects'. These dangerous beasties are objects that can control multiple execution threads and, because of this, may need access to the implementations of several other objects or have to maintain complex knowledge about them at the very least. There is thus a danger that this violation of encapsulation could throw away all the maintenance advantages of object-orientation.

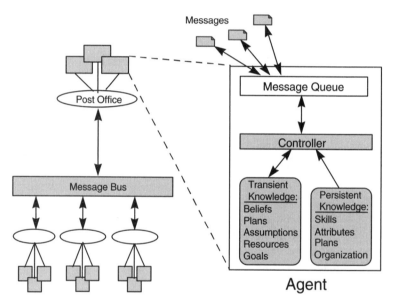

Figure 6.1 A typical architecture for an agent

Agents come to the rescue. With agents it is possible to send a program across the network rather than an RPC or SQL statement. As illustrated in Figure 6.3, this mobile (or missionary) agent takes over the responsibilities of the controller objects, and can do so without the heinous violation of encapsulation (because agents can be represented as *bona fide* objects). Since the agents can contain logic they can filter the data they retrieve and return to the client with a packet of relevant data only. In this way data traffic is reduced for a whole class of applications where searches are based on complex criteria.

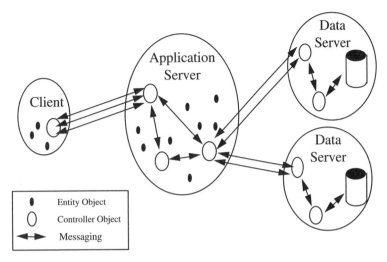

Figure 6.2 3-tier client/server: RPC approach

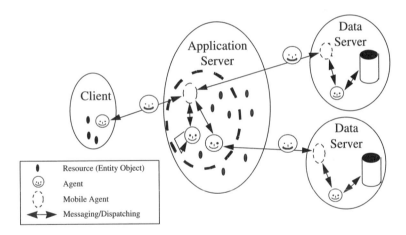

Figure 6.3 3-tier client/server using agents

The agent model is a model of distributed problem solving. There are several approaches to the co-ordination of distributed co-operating agents. These include centralized control, contracting models (as found in object-oriented approach or for example in Smith's Contract Net), hierarchical control via organizational units, multi-agent planning systems and negotiation models. These are not discussed further here, but one type of strategy is especially important for systems involving multiple, co-operating agents that each apply specialized knowledge to help solve a common problem. A common architecture for such applications in the past is known as the 'implicit invocation' architecture. Implicit invocation systems are also commonly referred to as **blackboard systems**.

Blackboard systems have been applied to speech understanding and to military systems where, for example, a fighter pilot has to process a vast amount of incoming data in order to select from a limited range of actions. The model is one of several independent knowledge based systems monitoring the input and advising the pilot when something interesting occurs; e.g. when a real target or threat is identified among many dummy targets or threats. The financial trader is in a similar position, being the recipient of a vast amount of data from several information feeds; all of them in need of analysis to determine (a) if anything interesting has occurred requiring further analysis, and (b) what the appropriate action should be.

A blackboard system is so called because it imitates a group of highly specialized experts sitting around a blackboard in order to solve a problem as illustrated in Figure 6.4. As new information arrives it is written up on the blackboard where all the experts can look. When an expert sees that s/he can contribute a new fact based on specialist knowledge, s/he raises a hand. This might be to confirm or refute an hypothesis already on the board or to add a new one. The new evidence will now be available to the other experts who may in turn be prompted to contribute to the discussion. The chairman of the group monitors the experts and selects their contributions in order, according to an agenda visible on the board. Common storage is the blackboard, and the agenda is under the control of a specialized inference program. In the trading context, our experts might be represented by a technical analysis expert system, a fundamental analysis system, an option strategy adviser, and so on. If, for example, new price information arrives from the wire, the chartist might detect a possible reversal but need to await confirmation before a sell signal is issued. However, the fundamental analyst only needed this small piece of confirmatory evidence to suggest a flagging in the security's fortunes. The combined evidence may be enough to generate a valid signal and thus, incidentally, beat all the pure chartists to the winning post. Perhaps also this action of selling the security will attract the attention of the option strategist who now sees a need to modify positions to maintain a risk free hedge or to avoid an otherwise unexpected exercise in now unfavourable market conditions.

The usual blackboard model requires that we think of the blackboard as 'broadcasting' its contents. An object-oriented model of a system does not permit such a metaphor but there is a simple remedy. We ask every agent (or other object) to register interest in the contents of particular pigeonholes. When the contents of a pigeonhole change the agent is sent a message either with the new data or merely a 'has changed' flag. If the latter, the agent must decide whether to send a retrieval message to the blackboard object. The agent may notify the blackboard of any significant changes in its state: its 'opinions'. The architecture of the blackboard is shown in Figure 6.5. This notion is now widely recognized as an example of an 'architectural pattern'. Chapter 7 returns to blackboard systems from this point of view. Here we merely point out the importance of this architecture for systems where intelligent agents need to co-operate in achieving shared goals or during collaborative problem solving.

Figure 6.4 Blackboard systems

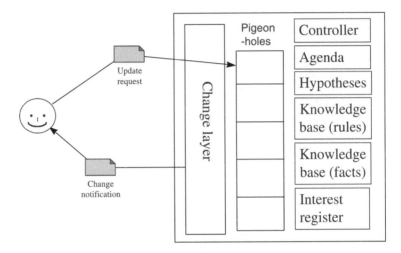

Figure 6.5 Blackboard architecture

⊟ 6.3 Modelling agent systems with objects

We now turn to a discussion of the relationship between agents and objects and show how suitably extended object-oriented methods can be used to model agents. This leads naturally to a discussion of how to use the agent metaphor to model business processes.

Developers designing agent systems need a modelling technique and it is natural to want to use the metaphors of object technology because agents, like objects, obviously encapsulate both state and behaviour. Certainly, object-oriented languages, such as Java, CLOS, and so on, can be used to build agent-based systems but most object-oriented methods find it *very* hard indeed to represent intelligent agents that encapsulate reasoning capability. Indeed most agent-based implementations use a mixture of procedural and non-procedural languages, such as C with Prolog. The difficulty with modelling is that most of these methods do not allow for objects to encapsulate second order information about themselves: how attributes and operations are related to each other. Methods that support class invariants, such as BON (Waldén and Nerson, 1995) go some way to solve the problem but still find it difficult to represent the inferencing capability of intelligent agents. BON invariants must be converted into procedural code in Eiffel, losing the non-procedural character of production rules in the process. Such methods fail to realize the need to chain rules together and perform inference (search) across them. The only method, to my knowledge, that encapsulates rulesets within objects is SOMA, although the OPEN framework admits this possibility by incorporating the SOMA approach.

Table 6.1 Comparison of the features of first generation OO methods with the requirements of agent technology

Agent technology	*First generation OO methods*
Agents perform tasks using resources	Jacobson's controller objects perform operations with his 'entity' objects [*sic*]
Within organizations (FUNs), agents play rôles with associated responsibilities and co-operate to provide services	Wirfs-Brock's classes collaborate with given responsibilities
Agents and FUNs provide well-defined services to clients	Wirfs-Brock contracts
Agents need to monitor events in databases and trigger operations when they change	No explicit support
Heterogeneous agents need ontologies to co-operate	No support
Intelligent agents contain rules and can reason	No support
Agents manage their own threads of control	Scant support (except Actor models)
Some intelligent agents need to reason in the presence of uncertainty	No support

Any attempt to cobble together a method for agent-based systems from the first generation OO methods is therefore doomed to failure. I have encountered several attempts to use a goulash of techniques from OMT, Objectory, RDD and so on. All of them had problems. Table 6.1 highlights some of the deficiencies and mismatches of the early OO methods in this respect.

Other difficulties include modelling agent co-ordination, task allocation, knowledge sharing and interacting goals where agents might need to reason about the beliefs or co-ordination strategies of other agents. Notice that several requirements for modelling agent systems are entirely unsupported or only receive support in non-standard approaches that use delegation and active objects, as with methods that have tools to model actor systems. Where there is some support, we must ask: Is the support adequate for agents and does it conform to object-oriented principles? We might, for example, note that Jacobson's 'controller objects' are introduced to manage threads of control that pass through several other objects. Implementers are frequently tempted to allow controllers to violate the encapsulation of the controlled objects. Encapsulation must be preserved when we design agents to take on this control function. This is easier in the approach advocated here because agents only communicate with the interfaces of other objects and other agents (using an agent communication language preferably). This militates against the danger of very severe maintenance problems when 'control' objects violate encapsulation.

FUNCTIONAL UNIT (FUN) is a term introduced by Farhoodi (1994) to capture the idea of a composite agent: a set of agents organized into a group of co-operating agents within a defined organizational structure and encapsulated by a single interface. The interface intercepts all messages and delegates them to appropriate staff agents. This concept is called a WRAPPER in SOMA when applied to vanilla flavoured objects. Here only methods that support the concept of layers as containing objects, or in other words wrappers, provide the sort of support needed. Vague notions of subsystems, packages, class categories or clusters based on arguments about cohesion are not normally useful. Wirfs-Brock's contracts (that cluster services) are also needed in a sufficiently powerful approach.

Another, more specialized, use of FUNs in agent modelling involves modelling the rôles that an agent can adopt. Functional context can change expectations about an agent's behaviour and reduce communication thereby. Individual agents perform tasks that may be represented as operations in their interfaces. These tasks can be abstracted away from the class the agent belongs to and stored within rôles. Rôles are like classes except that their instances can migrate to other rôles (dynamic classification). In effect, agents are responsible for the tasks stored by a rôle. Also the agent can be designated as a component of a FUN that stores rôles and can provide substitutes when the agent fails.

A purist view of object modelling – i.e. one based on the semantics of most object-oriented programming languages – does not support the concept of broadcasting: messages must be directed to a specific address. The solution to this problem is reasonably straightforward. We must create a blackboard object and allow agents to register interest in some or all of its contents. Implicit invocation (blackboard) architectures are common in agent systems and were discussed above.

As it turns out, most of the problems referred to above are overcome by SOMA, even though its innovations were not designed for this purpose but to extend object modelling to business process modelling problems. I will try to explain this rather remarkable coincidence.

SOMA objects can be classes or instances and are just like those found in all other methods except that they can contain structures called RULESETS. Rulesets are encapsulated by objects and may be inherited, like any other of the object's features. They permit objects to perform reasoning. Recall that rulesets can be viewed as sets of chainable class invariants and, in that sense, are an obvious generalization of the latter.

It should be apparent that rulesets, thus defined, are all that is necessary to make objects into agents. Forward chaining (data-driven) rulesets enable reactive agents and backward chaining (goal driven) régimes support deliberative agents. Because each object can contain more than one ruleset and each ruleset may have a specified régime, hybrid agents can also be described. Note that learning abilities would not normally be represented as rulesets but, more likely, by operations – or a mixture of the two.

Repositories of SOMA business objects become, effectively, the domain ontology. This object-oriented ontology extends the concept of a data dictionary, not only by including behaviour in the form of operations but by encapsulating business rules in an explicit form.

Intelligent agents may have to operate in the presence of uncertainty and uncertainty comes in many guises: probability, possibility and many more. Modelling systems that restrict the logic in which rules or class invariants are expressed to standard predicate logic or first order predicate calculus (FOPC) are too restrictive. SOMA allows the designer to pick the logic used for reasoning: FOPC, temporal logic, fuzzy logic, deontic logic (the logic of obligation or duty), etc. Just as a ruleset has an inference régime, it has a logic. In fact the régime and the logic are intimately related. For example, standard fuzzy logic implies (usually) a one-shot forward chaining strategy that treats the rules as if they all fire in parallel. In SOMA support for fuzzy reasoning is particularly strong: fuzzy objects with fuzzy valued attributes are possible and partial (fuzzy) inheritance is clearly defined. I understand that in future *SOMATiK* will support these techniques using fuzzy compiler technology from Bezant Limited. Support for other logics will depend on suitable applications arising in practice, but none are ruled out in the method itself.

Objects with rulesets support the modelling and design of intelligent agents and systems but agents are also the key to modelling business processes and reducing the cognitive dissonance between models of the world and system designs.

6.3.1 Modelling business processes with agents

Up to now I have been writing about the technology of intelligent agents and the way object-oriented analysis methods can model agent-based systems: in particular, about the SOMA approach. The assumption has been that someone who wants to develop a computer system using mobile intelligent agents can use SOMA to model the requirements before and during system development. So, our subject matter has been lifting the agent metaphor up from the code level to the more abstract analysis level, freeing the model of language and architectural dependencies in the process. Now I want to stand the approach on its head and ask: Can the agent metaphor be applied to describing systems in the world instead of systems inside a machine?

SOMA was designed to combine object-orientation with rapid application development (RAD) and business process re-engineering (BPR). It is a complete, full life-cycle method and not just a design notation like the majority of object-oriented methods. Its other distinguishing features include:

- A tailorable object-oriented model of the software development process itself: the contract-driven model.
- An advanced but very practical requirements capture technique offering 'specification reuse' and considerably in advance of the standard use case technique.
- A suite of metrics.
- The rule extensions necessary to model agents.

These topics were covered in the body of the text. In addition, SOMA places new emphasis on intelligent agents in two areas:

- as an implementation technique;
- in the business process model.

It is to the latter topic that we now turn our attention.

6.4 The agent object model

The Agent Object Model, which is a business process model, provides a framework in which activities may occur. It initially provides an enumeration of the players involved in the activities, and these players are agents as discussed in Chapter 5. It provides a high-level view of the ambit of the system being designed, in a simple graphical way. These features introduce the reviewer of the system design as documented to the key features and interactions of the system.

What the agent model explicitly does not do is to introduce any concept of *sequence* into the arena. The further level of detail regarding sequence of activity is developed through our concept of 'task association sets' which are part of the Task Object Model discussed in the previous chapter.

As I have said, external agents are 'black boxes' outside our control and organization. Internal agents work within the context and have motives known to us. Either may adopt rôles as direct system users and become actors thereby. However, it is very unusual for an external agent to adopt a user rôle. If this does happen the external agent should be modelled as an actor and a suitable note made in the actor's description slot.

Internal, external and system agents communicate with each other by passing messages. A message is represented by a 'Post-It note' icon. A *message* is emitted under the stimulus of an *event*.

The Context Model (*SOMATiK*'s rather misleading name for the visual part of the Agent Object Model) is the only graphic that is drawn by the user in *SOMATiK*. All other diagrams are automatically generated by the software. This both saves time and more importantly guarantees the semantic consistency of all visualizations of the model. Icons are deposited and named by picking them off a toolbar, and linkages between elements are introduced by clicking and dragging off a drop-down menu.

The drop-down menu of options associated with an agent can be displayed by right clicking the agent icon. For all elements in the model, the first menu option is always *Properties,* which opens the dialogue associated with the agent for the completion of the agent's description. For agents, the other important options are:

- Trigger: this allows us to simulate the arrival of a triggering event, and then simulate the system response. These simulations were discussed in detail in Chapter 5.
- Link: this allows us to link the agent to some other agent, and implicitly generate the message that passes between them.
- Agent Class: this allows us to generate or access the Agent Class in the Business Object Model which is associated with this agent.

Only one occurrence of a given message is permitted in an agent model. If message X is passed from agent A to agent B, and subsequently it seems that message X should also pass between agent C and agent B, *SOMATiK* will not permit you to re-use the message. This restriction is quite deliberate and is important. The apparent need to re-use the message is telling us that there is a further level of discrimination to be uncovered in our agent modelling. There is some rôle which agents A and C share which is concerned with this message. Imagine a business which has employees called 'Purchasing Office', 'Accountant' and 'Salesperson'. If the accountant needs a new consignment of storage boxes, a purchase requisition must be sent to the Purchasing Office. Similarly, if the salesperson needs to order a new batch of sales brochures, a purchase requisition is raised. It would be an error to model this situation with just three actors labelled 'Purchasing', 'Accountant' and 'Salesperson'. Two of these agents would need to send the same 'Purchase Requisition' message to the purchaser – and this is not allowed. Instead, one should define the rôle 'Purchase Authority' which is shared by the accountant, the salesperson and indeed any other manager with a budgetary authority for expenditure. This approach of analyzing activities into rôles lies at the heart of effective business process engineering.

Messages have the following properties:

- a label and a description (including a description of any negotiation)

- a Source: the agent sending the message
- a Target: the agent receiving the message
- a Triggering Event: the stimulus for the message
- a Goal: a world state that is the goal of sending the message
- an associated Task: the behaviour to be induced on the target of the message
- an Information Content: a description of the data sent to the Target
- an expected outcome: a description of the possible outcomes of the message including the data returned to the Source

It was explained in Chapter 5 how this dialogue corresponds to the semiotic theory of Winograd and Flores.

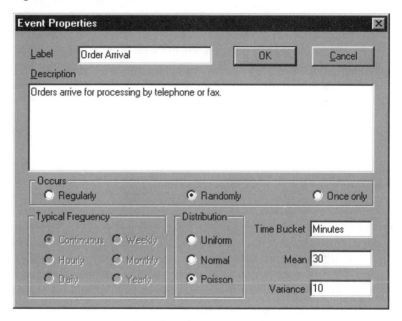

Figure 6.6 Event properties

An event is an external stimulus that causes a response by the system as a whole. An event impacts an agent, triggering the agent to send a message, this message being intended to induce a behaviour on the recipient of the message. This concept of message passing to induce a behaviour is of course one of the fundamental concepts of object orientation and means that, as has been stated already, SOMA is object-oriented from end to end.

There is no need to fill in all the details of an event. Only those events which are available or relevant should be completed. In the example shown in Figure 6.6 the 'Order Arrival' event is the trigger for an order processing activity. The dialogue box has slots for an event label and description, an occurrence pattern, which may be *Regular, Random* or *Once only*, and information on the frequency and distribution. In the example, orders arrive randomly, every 30 minutes on average. Since the arrivals are uncorrelated, we would expect the arrival intervals to form a Poisson distribution.

There is no particular limit to the size of an Agent Object Model, which can if really necessary be of a size that prints on many pages. But the general principle to observe is to keep it at a high level, and to keep it as simple as possible. Message interactions are most emphatically not data-flows. A message encapsulates the semiotic act of invoking a task on the recipient of the message; it does not attempt to explicate all the data flows which will arise as a result of the invocation of the behaviour represented by the task. These details should be deferred to the Task Object Model, where further and different tools are available.

Consider, for example, a system to support telephone sales of motor insurance policies. The customer phones a sales operative, who with the aid of an online computer system acquires all the details necessary to prepare a quotation. The amount of data to be transacted is quite large, and some elements of the data are conditional. After the basic details of the proposer – name, age, address etc. – and vehicle-type, engine size, age, value etc. – we come to conditional blocks of data which will affect the premium loading. Any recent motoring convictions? If so, process the convictions screen. Any recent accident history? If so, process the accident screen. Any medical conditions? If so, process the medical conditions screen. And so forth.

None of the detailed transaction data should appear in the agent model. This merely captures the contracts and commitments that are implicit (or sometimes explicit) in conversations.

The important thing to note is that we are capturing the essence of the *business process* that is being modelled. This business process could be changed so that the customers write their own proposals directly onto a form on the company web site.

Agents perform tasks. Tasks are therefore the *operations* of agent objects. We reify these operations into *bona fide* objects in the Task Object Model (TOM). The correct place to model the full complexity of the interaction, and the detailed data flows associated with it, is precisely in the TOM. The complexity of the task is modelled using task decomposition. The data flow is modelled using task association sets. Variants of essentially similar tasks are modelled using task classification. Exceptions to task scripts are modelled using usage (message passing) structures. All these facilities arise naturally from the treatment of tasks as *objects* in the proper sense, as explained in Chapter 5.

In conclusion we can state first that a rule-enhanced object-oriented method such as SOMA is highly suitable for modelling projected agent-based systems and that less semantically rich methods are likely to fail or introduce unnecessary complexity. Secondly, using the agent metaphor at the beginning of requirements engineering or business process re-engineering provides a theoretically sound way of deducing user requirements and their relationship to business objectives. We can reify these requirements as task objects with far more confidence that we have discovered them correctly than we would have with a more arbitrary and non-object-oriented technique such as use cases.

⊟ 6.5 Bibliographical notes

Part of this chapter is based on material from Farhoodi, Graham and Powell, *Intelligent Agents: An object-oriented approach* (in preparation) and articles that appeared in my column in *Object Magazine* in 1997. The last section draws on material from the *SOMATiK* user documentation.

An excellent introduction to the topic of multi-agent systems is given by Ferber (1995). At the time of writing an English translation of that work is expected shortly. An excellent and very easy to read account of how to build intelligent agents using Java is provided by Bigus and Bigus (1998). Source code for simple search, inference and learning algorithms is usefully included on an accompanying CD-ROM.

7

Architecture, reuse and requirements patterns

*No person who is not a great sculptor or painter **can** be an architect. If he is not a sculptor or painter, he can only be a **builder**.*

John Ruskin (Lectures on Architecture and Painting)

It is now almost universally recognized that architecture is a key issue in the development of any coherent approach to software engineering. A good architecture must enable easy, rapid development, rapid change, and high levels of confidence in the resultant products. It must also support the reuse of software components, specifications, code and architectural layers. The trouble is that no one has yet been able to give a totally satisfactory and general definition of what architecture is; we just know good architecture when we see it.

In the world of object technology the topic of design patterns for programming languages has received a great deal of attention recently. The same view can be extended to the more abstract level of system 'architecture' in general.

This chapter describes current and continuing work on architecture, patterns and component-oriented development and how this affects our approach to reuse. We will also delve into the issue of measuring object-oriented systems and explain the background to the product metrics that *SOMATiK* collects automatically.

7.1   The importance of architecture

It is widely acknowledged that software architecture is of prime importance. Unfortunately no one seems able to give a clear and unambiguous definition of what architecture is. Progress has been made, but still there is little more than informal consensus. As Shaw and Garlan (1996) have pointed out, the informal system structure diagrams used, almost universally, by developers have no consistent interpretation. The lines that join boxes can represent data-flow, subroutine invocation or almost anything – sometimes on the same diagram. Furthermore, current module interconnexion languages (MILs) are too close to the language level to describe different architectural styles. Such languages can only represent connexions that describe invocation and cannot describe links with meanings such as 'follows in time' easily. Garlan and Shaw set out to create a better defined language for describing system architecture. In doing so they considered several existing patterns for system organization: batch, pipes and filters, layered hierarchies and blackboards.

Although the current plethora of papers of patterns will indisputably produce something of value, I remain a little sceptical about the level of hype. For one thing many of the design patterns that we have seen seem to be there mainly to fix deficiencies in a programming language rather than to solve a genuine design problem. For example, there are several patterns that are designed to eliminate memory leaks or clean up unreachable memory – problems that cannot arise in languages like Java that support garbage collection or eschew pointers. From this point of view we could argue that Assembler programmers used an 'if-then-else' pattern until FORTRAN came along and made it unnecessary. This said, it does seem worthwhile to explore patterns at the architectural level where such criticisms are less likely to apply.

There is a need to describe the semantics of the connectors as well as the boxes on typical box and line diagrams. For me this is equivalent to saying that connexions should be represented as *bona fide* objects. Of course, we now need pointers linking the connectors to the 'boxes' that are not represented this way – to avoid an infinite regress – but clearly any sound architectural design language needs some such approach.

Shaw and Garlan argue, with some justice admittedly, that an object-oriented approach is not always appropriate to every problem and a case study of oscilloscope design supports this. They also contrast what they call 'implicit invocation' architecture (i.e. actor or blackboard systems where objects register interest in events) with object technology. They seem to be unwilling to admit that implicit invocation is readily modelled using object-oriented methods. To me, OO is a rather general knowledge representation technique not directly comparable with, say, a pipe-and-filter architecture that does not generalize to arbitrary modelling problems. They also opine that object-orientation is just one of many architectural styles and that it is inappropriate for many problems. However, their view of object-orientation is limited to the models of current object-oriented programming languages. In the same work they use object-oriented design for their architectural design tool AESOP – implicitly admitting that OO can describe other styles. Worse still, they criticize OO for not being able to represent stylistic constraints. This narrow view of OO excludes object-oriented methods where objects with embedded rulesets can represent such things as semantic integrity constraints and the like. On the other hand, they do present some sound arguments for the extension of the object-oriented metaphor. It is argued, for example, that architectural description languages imply a need for rôle modelling (and thus dynamic classification).

Selic *et al*. (1994) argue for the importance of an approach to architectural design and their ROOM method and the ObjecTime tool that supports it both provide for the specification of architectural layers and their APIs (ports). ObjecTime, like *SOMATiK*, emphasizes the importance of executable specifications. The difference between the two approaches is that ROOM starts later in the life cycle than SOMA: beginning with state-transition diagrams and object diagrams. This reflects its background and apotheosis in real-time telecommunications engineering where users (engineers) know their requirements and can reasonably begin modelling in this way. In other domains it is fair to say that an approach to requirements engineering is needed and that ROOM does not contain such an approach.

As we will see below, much of recent work on software design patterns can be lifted to the level of architecture, giving rise to architectural patterns such as blackboard and pipe-and-filter patterns. In parallel with this trend many modern software development organizations are planning their systems strategy around an ORB enabled, service-based architecture. In such an approach the aim is to enhance opportunities for component reuse and increase system interoperability. Figure 7.1 sketches such an architecture. Notice that the ORB acts as a general bus, carrying service request to various servers at different levels of abstraction. At the lower levels the organization hopes to buy nearly everything: naming services, databases, etc. At the top this organization will write most of its business-specific applications. The middle layers are more problematical; while it may be desirable to buy ready-made business objects, the fact is that there are few on the market and, anyway, the firm may not always reflect the way others do business. This issue is discussed further in Section 7.4. The best hope is that third parties will be able to supply horizontal components of use in all business sectors, such as GUI frameworks or database access tools. The vertical components will be far harder to agree upon. Thus we see the provenance of business objects (whether specifications or code) crossing the buy/make boundary. Notice the area labelled 'BOM', which designates the organization's business object model overlaps both the common facilities and custom-built applications areas. This signifies the extreme unlikelihood of external suppliers being able to offer genuinely useful vertical business object libraries in generic domains such as finance, telecommunications or manufacturing. Such libraries will appear, but they will only contain a fragment of the classes needed. In finance, for example, there has recently been an agreement – fostered by the OMG task force in that area – on a Currencies object. What use such a class will be – without classes for the hundreds of financial instruments that exist as well – defeats my understanding.

An alternative, more specific instantiation of this architecture is shown in Figure 7.2. In this set-up, common financial services such as curve generators (used for pricing) and calendars (that determine when markets are open) are represented as CORBA services. This is usually a C++ program with an IDL wrapper. Users rarely access these services directly or even uniformly. Traders pricing trades and sales staff bidding for business may access these services from Excel spreadsheets or custom built applications. Other users may access the same services from a Web browser.

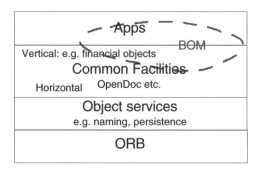

Figure 7.1 An object technology inspired architecture

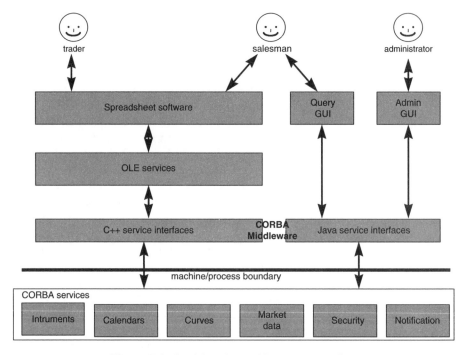

Figure 7.2 Applying the architecture to trading

Object request brokers are at the centre of most early adopters' strategies for object-oriented systems. Many of these companies are also moving closer to agent-based technology, for the reasons outlined in Chapter 2 and subsequently. It makes sense to ask if object request brokers can be useful in this. Common sense and wishful thinking dictate that CORBA products ought provide an infrastructure for agent-based systems including, especially, a standard agent communication language. Currently, this is very far from the case, primarily due to the semantic limitations of IDL, which has no conception of rulesets or even invariants. However, many ORB vendors that I have spoken to would like to add this kind of functionality to their products and, if enough do so, we may well see some standardization of their efforts in the future. For now, each organization that wants to implement agent-based systems must write its own agent communication language. Doing this on top of CORBA still makes a great deal of sense.

▱ 7.2 Problem frames and requirements patterns

One of the most important and topical ideas in object technology is that of a design pattern. Design patterns are groups of linked classes that solve a commonly recurring programming problem. They are represented by commonly recurring arrangements of classes and structural connexions between them. Perhaps the best known and useful examples of patterns occur as application frameworks associated with graphical user interface building or other well-defined development problems. In fact, some of the motivation for the patterns movement came from the apprehension of already existing frameworks that led people to wonder how general the approach was. Nowadays it is more usual to deliver frameworks in the form of flexible class libraries for use by programmers in languages that support the class concept, often C++ and Java. Examples of frameworks range from class libraries that are delivered with programming languages through the NeXTSTEP Interface Builder to the many GUI and client/server development systems now on the market such as Delphi, Visual Studio, Visual Age or Visual Basic.

Patterns are most useful because they provide a language for designers to communicate in. Rather than having to explain a complex idea from scratch, the designer can just mention a pattern by name and everyone will know, at least roughly, what is meant. This is how engineers in many other disciplines communicate their design ideas.

The earliest work on the idea of patterns seems to have been Coplien's (1992) book on programming idioms for C++. His idioms represented standard 'tricks of the trade' used by experienced C++ programmers. It was paralleled by a great deal of interest in the work of the architecture theorist Alexander (1977), who had suggested developing standard pattern books for building designs. Abstracting from work on idioms, Gamma *et al.* (1995) came up with a book of supposedly language independent design patterns. These authors were quickly and widely nicknamed: 'The Gang of Four' or GoF.

The GoF book includes 23 useful design patterns, including the following particularly interesting and useful ones:

- Facade. (Useful for implementing object wrappers.)
- Adapter.
- Proxy.
- Observer. (This helps an object to notify registrants that its state has changed and helps with the implementation of blackboard systems.)
- Visitor and State. (These two patterns help to implement dynamic classification.)
- Composite.
- Bridge. (Helps with decoupling interfaces from their implementations.)

Some of the GoF patterns are really only useful for fixing deficiencies in the C++ language. Examples of these include Decorator and Iterator. Recognizing this, Buschmann *et al.* (1996) (also known as the Gang of Five or GoV) divide their patterns up into architectural patterns, design patterns and language idioms. Architectural patterns include: Pipes and Filters, Blackboard systems, and the Model View Controller (MVC) pattern for user interface development. Typical GoV design patterns are called:

- Forwarder Receiver;
- Whole Part; and
- Proxy.

The reader is advised by the GoV to refer to all the GoF patterns as well. The whole-part pattern is exactly the implementation of the composition structures that form part of basic object modelling semantics. In that sense it is a trivial pattern. However, since most languages do not support the construct, it can be useful to see the standard way to implement it. It is a rare example of a design pattern that maps directly to an idiom in several languages: a multi-language idiom.

Coad *et al.* (1997) and Fowler (1997) introduce the idea of analysis patterns as opposed to design patterns. Coad's patterns do not differ greatly from design patterns but are fairly easy to understand. In fact, there is a slight feeling of triviality about some of them, but this need not be a withering criticism for the neophyte analyst. Fowler's patterns are closer to what one thinks of as genuine analysis patterns, *qua* analysis. Examples include:

- Party: how to store the name and address of someone or something you deal with.
- Organization structure: how to represent divisional structure.
- Posting Rules: how to represent basic bookkeeping rules.
- Quote: dealing with the different way financial instrument prices are represented.

There are many more, some specialized into domains such as Health Care or Accounting.

The problem with these patterns is the opposite of that with Coad's. Even the simplest ones – like Accountability – are really quite hard to understand compared to the difficulty of the underlying problem that they solve. My experience was that it took three attempts at reading the text before really understanding what was going on. At the end of this process I found that I knew the proposed solution already but would never have expressed it in the same terms. Nevertheless, Fowler's patterns like Coad's are still a useful reference for beginners, and he notes some interesting ideas in the text.

PROBLEM FRAMES

A more profound approach is due to Jackson (1995). He defines a problem frame as a structure consisting of *principal parts* and a *solution task*. The principal parts correspond to what I have called agents and task and business objects. The solution task is the work one has to do to meet some requirement concerning these parts or objects. He then abstracts from the objects to problem domains and the phenomena that are shared between them: in the sense of the elements that can be described in the languages of both domains. More importantly, each frame may have a set of rules that connect pairs of domains. I think that problem frames are a better requirements engineering technique than patterns because they suggest not a solution but a suitable *approach* to finding a solution. This idea is focused more on the problems of the requirements analyst trying to understand a problem and select an approach than the object-oriented designer who has already selected the architectural approach and implementation technology. It is the latter who has the most to gain from the use of patterns and pattern languages. However, there is a case for arguing that problem frames are patterns, though not design patterns. They are a more radical departure from design than Fowler's analysis patterns; but patterns still they may be called.

Typical problem frames include the following:

- Connexion: introduces a separate problem domain between the application and solution domains. Examples: a post office; CORBA.
- JSP: helps to describe a program in terms of its input and output streams. Example: a typical accounting or stock control system.
- Simple control: describes the situation where known control rules are applied to a controllable phenomenon. Examples: embedded real-time controllers; vending machines.
- Simple information systems: the real-world analogue of the JSP frame, the problem concerns users requesting and updating information about some domain. Example: database systems.
- Workpieces: describes the way operators' commands are linked to the manipulation of objects. Example: text editors.

Realistic problems usually involve several frames. Jackson argues that identifying the frame is a precursor to selecting an appropriate method. He characterizes, by way of example, the use case approach as such a method and points to some of its limitations – as I have in Appendix B – with the aim of showing that its use is restricted to problem frames where user I/O dominates. This is quite correct, but I feel that viewing object modelling as a form of knowledge representation frees me from this criticism. Although SOMA undoubtedly has frame dependent limitations, it can be specialized to deal with quite a variety of frames. The main reason for this is the semantic richness provided by rulesets and, for example, the inclusion of invariance conditions as well as pre- and post-conditions.

I would encourage readers to think about their own set of familiar problems and ask if there are other frames at this level of generality. My contribution and experience are beginning to suggest that there is a frame that abstracts our recurring order processing or trading problem, one for modelling agents (called Assistant) and one for general simulation problems. Describing these frames in Jackson's language of domains and shared phenomena is left as an exercise for the reader.

OTHER PATTERN TYPES

Even more recently there has been interest in developing patterns for organizational development (Coplien, 1995; O'Callaghan, 1997, 1997a, 1998) and requirements engineering (Maiden *et al.,* 1998). Coplien applies the idea of patterns to the software development process itself and observes several noteworthy regularities. A typical such **organizational pattern** is GATEKEEPER where a nominated individual is responsible for shielding a busy development team's members from unwanted interruptions, such as junk mail, circulating magazines and unwelcome visitors.

O'Callaghan argues that migrating to object technology is more than mere reverse engineering, because reverse engineering is usually (a) formal and (b) focused purely on the functional nature of the legacy systems in question. He argues that the most flexible solution is the construction of an object-oriented analysis of these systems followed by object wrappers; as discussed in Chapter 4. He proposes the use of patterns, such as Facade (Gamma *et al.,* 1995) and Layered Architecture (Buschmann *et al.,* 1996), to provide an abstract description of the services of the legacy system wrappers. Incidentally, he also demonstrates the relative expressiveness of the OML notation over UML when it comes to describing wrappers and layered architectures. More interestingly, he proposes a **requirements pattern language** for the legacy system migration process, based on the above mentioned use of Facade for wrapping identified subsystems, Composite and several of Coplien's organizational patterns. This pattern language is consistent with the patterns hinted at in OPEN process specification (Graham *et al.,* 1997).

Maiden *et al.* (1998) propose a pattern language for socio-technical system design to inform requirements validation thereof, based on the CREWS-SAVRE prototype discussed in Chapter 5. They specify three patterns as follows:

- Machine-Function: this represents a rule connecting the presence of a user action (a task script in our language) to a system requirement to support that action (an operation of a business object that implements the task). I feel that it is stretching language somewhat to call this rule a pattern.
- Collect-First-Objective-Last: this pattern tells us to force the user to complete the prime transaction after the subsidiary ones; e.g. ATMs should make you take the card before the cash. (For a discussion of the

psychological phenomenon of *completion* in user interface design, see Graham, 1995.)
■ Insecure-Secure-Transaction: this suggests that systems should monitor their security state and take appropriate action if the system becomes insecure.

The value of these patterns may be doubted because, like Coad's and Fowler's analysis patterns, they seem to state the obvious; and they fail to address the sort of task or system usage patterns represented by our task association sets or task decomposition trees. Also it could be argued that they are nothing but design principles; just as *completion* provides a well-known design principle in HCI. On the other hand their operationalization in the CREWS-SAVRE system indicates that they may have a specialized practical value in this and certain other contexts.

⊟ 7.3   Component-based development

Re-inventing the wheel is a bootless but all too common pastime. Top down development leads naturally to the formulation of requirements for specific modules or objects that are unlikely to be found in any off-the-shelf library. On the other hand, bottom up development using existing components or packages may make it necessary to alter the requirements or the business processes to fit in with the available functions of the components. The question is, therefore: how is an organization to stop its developers re-inventing everything and at the same time make the best use of in-house and purchased components?

Catalysis (D'Souza and Wills, 1997) is an object-oriented design method that specifically takes account of the requirements of component-based development. The components that it uses include not only off-the-shelf binaries but business objects and entire frameworks. The authors point out the design patterns can also be viewed as components. Catalysis emphasizes many of the same points that I have made in this book: layered architecture, methodical transformation of a sequence of models (with increasing detail) and the importance of interface design. Catalysis is weak on requirements capture, relying as it does on standard UML class models and use cases – albeit with additional structure. Its strength is in the incremental design of component based software. In particular, Catalysis introduces the idea of several different kinds of 'refinement' each of which must preserve class invariants: collaboration refinement, action refinement and model refinement. This approach supports better traceability through successive model iterations. It also depends heavily on the incorporation of class invariants representing certain kinds of business rule into objects. I show in Appendix A exactly why all object-oriented methods should do this. Research is currently underway at two academic institutions to integrate the best feature of Catalysis and SOMA.

WHEN TO SELECT COMPONENTS

Components should be identified early in the development life cycle. Choosing components as an implementation decision has several drawbacks:

- It fails to give due consideration to corporate architectural standards and existing corporate libraries.
- Developers often tend to use components that are easy to incorporate into code that they have already written. This can lead to similar functions in different parts of a system using different components, often with the consequence of inconsistency in the user interface.
- Choosing components in a hurry often leads to considerable extra coding to make up for the component's deficiencies or its unneeded extra functionality.
- If the choice of components is made late, they cannot be taken into account when designing the look and feel of the application at design time. This too can lead to inconsistency.
- The data requirements of components cannot be allowed for during design. As a result, many programs that we have seen contain extensive sections of data conversion code, which is merely there so that data in one form can be handled by a component that expects it in another.

The last point leads me to recommend that applications that have to inter-operate with other applications or with existing components should use a common data interchange language. Rather than write one-off conversion routines, convert all incoming data to a standard form, agreed as standard within the development organization. Write them out in the same form. The arguments for doing this echo the arguments for Agent Communication Languages discussed in Chapter 6. As applications become more distributed, we may expect to utilize many more of the features of agent-based architecture.

The life cycles of business objects offer a good starting point for identifying components early in the life cycle.

COMPONENT OR OBJECT?

We have heard much discussion recently on the difference between a component and an object; and I have done so mostly with gasps of disbelief. From my viewpoint a component is merely an object (specification, source code or binary) that is published for reuse: the interface defines exactly what it will do. Perhaps my surprise is a result of the fact that most other methods have no equivalent of my rulesets and cannot therefore fully express a component's specification. Nevertheless, users of methods such as BON, Catalysis or SOMA need have no such concerns. Components are just those objects that have been placed in the library under reuse management.

7.4 Business object libraries

At present there seem to be three competing conceptions of a business object. Perhaps the oldest is due to Oliver Sims (1994) who meant something representable by an icon that means something sensible to users. My conception of a business object developed independently at around the same time. I meant any *specification object* that is mentioned in business process and task descriptions. The third conception emerges from discussion within the OMG. Their Business Object Modelling interest group is promulgating the idea of a business object as a commonly used *software component* that occurs in the domain terminology. I have problems with this last definition insofar as it restricts business objects to the territory of commercial software vendors and excludes our ambitions of being able to model businesses, tasks and agents and of keeping our reusable objects totally machine and language independent. The OMG conception of a business object in its current form excludes intelligent agents from being business objects because IDL objects cannot easily express semantics equivalent to rulesets. I expect, however, that this will change at some point in the future.

There are several companies now claiming to offer libraries of business objects in vertical markets. These mostly consist of code libraries, the most well-known being the Infinity model for financial instruments. The Infinity offering uses a proprietary, but relational, data model known as Montage as the sub-structure upon which its C++ object model is built. This leads to performance problems, especially when complex derivative instruments are involved; because the database has to do many small joins to compose these complex composite objects. There is also a degree of incompleteness, with several instruments not being included in the model; users are expected to complete the model themselves. However, the product has been successfully used by several banks and is well suited to the smaller such institutions or to those not specializing in high volume derivatives markets. Infinity do not sell their abstract object model; they only offer the code. Other offerings, that do represent themselves as abstract object models of financial instruments are usually, in my experience, little more than re-badged data models.

Continuing with Finance as a typical domain for business object modelling, let us pause to consider what types of thing are suitable for modelling as business objects or not. The class of financial instruments seems to be a good candidate because every instrument has a clear, stable and unambiguous definition. However, there are well over 300 classes in even the crudest model of financial instruments. This means that building a stable classification structure is extremely difficult. Furthermore, many financial products are composites. This leads to two completely different ways in which instruments can be modelled. The simplistic way is to build a broad, deep classification structure, noting the composition structures of each instrument as it arises. I have built such models and found them useful, if unwieldy. This is the approach taken by Infinity. A possibly more elegant approach exploits a theorem of financial engineering that says that every instrument is a composite of fundamental commodities and options on them. This means that instead of relying solely on classification structure we can also exploit composition. At least one important and successful risk management system at the Chase Manhattan Bank uses this approach. However, these general classification problems are still very tricky and should not be tackled by the inexperienced modeller. Smaller classification structures, however, are good candidates for inclusion in your first library of reusable specifications.

Corporate actions are a very good example of ideal candidates for business objects. There are (arguably) exactly 42[1] of them and they can easily be classified. Figure 7.3 shows a fragment of this classification structure. It can be seen immediately that even this structure is reasonably complex. Imagine what a structure with 350 classes would look like!

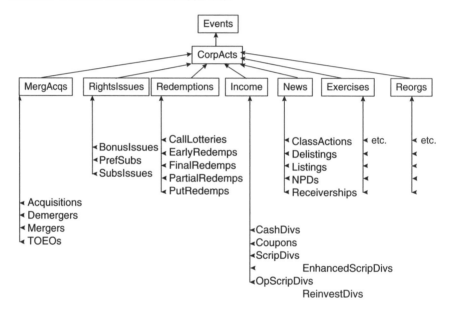

Figure 7.3 Classifying corporate actions

On the face of it, pricing algorithms appear not to be good candidates because they are pure function and, of course proper objects must have data too. Reasoning in this way, the product should know how to price itself. However, in Finance there are many, many ways to price the same product, all of the algorithms being subject to evolution as new discoveries are made in financial engineering. It is therefore crazy to pack all these algorithms into Products. Here is a definite case where

---

[1] Possibly answering a question posed by Douglas Adams.

algorithms should be objects; these of course are nothing more nor less than function libraries resurrected in object-oriented form. And whyever not!

Events, such as trades, payments, cash flows, etc., are more problematical. Trades go through complex life-cycles that could perhaps be represented by state machines. I am thinking of states such as: quoted, agreed, affirmed, confirmed, matched, settled, etc. The difficulty here is that different instruments have very different life-cycles: foreign exchange settles quite differently from equities. The question is whether we should attempt to design a business object Trades that covers all eventualities or have different ones for the different kinds of instrument. Our instinct as object designers tells us that a single Trades class should refer to a complex instrument hierarchy with each instrument responsible for knowing its peculiar life cycle. However, I have already mentioned that the instrument hierarchy is extremely complex, so that making it more so may be considered unattractive. In practice, this is a difficult decision that will be taken according to the circumstances and judgment of different organizations.

But what of our customers, regulators, and so on? These are the worst candidates for business objects that we can think of because there is no such thing as a customer. Look at your own company's computer systems. The likelihood is that every system has a different definition of what a customer is. This is not because all past generations of developer were brain dead. It is because each department relates **differently** to its customers. Looked at one way, customerhood is a *rôle* adopted by a legal entity. Equivalently we can say that customerdom is a *relation* between your organization and another. Thus your business object library should have what Martin Fowler would call a Parties class and a series of relations representing concepts like account customers, overseas customers, etc.

Business processes are often advanced as candidates for modelling as business objects. This is, I feel, both right and wrong. Having actual software objects to represent a process is only apposite for the simplest processes and can lead to horribly rigid workflow systems in my experience. However, the approach presented in this book does use objects (agents, messages and tasks) to model business processes, albeit indirectly. This gives more flexibility and expressive power. Beware therefore of people selling 'business process objects'.

There seem to be several current conceptions of what a business object model is. I regard one as a specification model of the domain concepts expressed in terms of objects. Of course, it is not (in this sense) a model of the business and its processes. Neither is it a pure system model (until refined by logical design).

Most commercial offerings labelled 'vertical business object model' are little more than re-badged data/process models, replete with false assumptions about business processes taken from the small number of other organizations that were used to finance the original development. Often they are tied to the semantics of a particular language such as C++. Usually they are associated with a relational database, leading to potentially massive performance problems.

Creating a business object model of your own may be thus a better solution. It will provide a tailor-made resource and gives you more control and power. Such a strategy permits you to optimize performance if necessary, by choosing appropriate database technology for example. Your approach can take advantage of new technology, such as Java, ODBMS or *SOMATiK*, as these innovations come along. However, it can be very expensive.

Business objects have been hyped. If you are considering buying a commercial business object model, then ask yourself if the model fits your business or if you will have to adapt to its foibles. Beware particularly of data models in disguise as object models. These are common. Beware too of models extracted from coded implementations, especially when the implementation is in some non-object-oriented language such as PowerBuilder or Visual Basic. Ask the supplier to give you the history of the product with this consideration in mind. Ask too, if the model is implemented, how the database is implemented and designed: is performance going to be adequate for the type and scale of application you have? Use binaries only when you trust them. Buy or build the right middleware; and be prepared to pay for it. An architecture based on sound middleware decisions is the only basis for profitable gains from re-use.

In conclusion, remember that models are powerful representations of knowledge, not just computer stuff! Object models can be used to represent many things: any kind of object knowledge that is. The semantics of the modelling language you use must therefore be powerful enough to express this knowledge; which means that it should include class invariants (ideally rulesets), usage links and other features necessary to model business processes. This is because it is never enough to just model the computer system. A good model should include users' conversations, contracts, goals and tasks. Take control over the specification yourself rather than relying entirely on external suppliers.

7.5 Metrics and process improvement

Accurate estimation of the resource and elapsed time requirements for delivery of a defined project is clearly a matter of the highest importance in effective management of the IT function. The drive is to move accurate estimation of the resources demanded by a project further back up the life cycle of the project. If we want to understand and improve the way we develop software we must measure ourselves and our products. In other words we must collect both product and process metrics. Conventional measures of software products include lines of source code, function points, defects found in testing and so on. Measures (the proper word for metrics) of the process include time taken.

Historically, the SLOC (Source Lines Of Code) approach has been widely used; but the volume of code is only known when the work has been completed; and prior to that, the estimate is based largely on experience of similar projects. Attention more recently has been focused on the *function point analysis* approach, which at least moves us back up to the point where a detailed functional specification has been developed. The problems here largely reside in the definition of what exactly constitutes a function point: experience shows that given a definition, competent analysts may come up with widely differing estimates of the function point content. In addition, there is a problem in applying function point analysis in a pure object oriented development environment, in that there are no functions in such a system that are separate from data structures and arguably therefore no function points in the accepted sense.

This section focuses attention on *task point analysis* – estimating on the basis of the business task points in a requirements definition: the number of atomic tasks that the users are helped to do by the system. This has many benefits. For one thing, the estimation is carried out at the requirements capture stage of the life cycle – early enough to assist in project justification and estimation. Also, business task points at the requirements definition stage do not presuppose any particular delivery vehicle or strategy. Before defining the SOMA metrics suite, including task points, we review the state of the art in the field of object-oriented metrics.

7.5.1 MOSES

The MOSES method (Henderson-Sellers and Edwards, 1994) collects metrics as part of its quality evaluation activity to permit code testing and reuse assessment. MOSES distinguishes three kinds of metric: internal (intra-) class metrics, inter-class external (i.e. interface) metrics and system metrics. Intra-class metrics are concerned with size and complexity, inter-class metrics with coupling and cohesion. Other metrics are concerned with cognitive complexity: how hard it is for programmers to understand. MOSES is one of the most complete methods published in respect of metrics yet it remains consciously tentative in its prescriptions. Its intra-object metrics are size, average operations per class and average method size (in SLOCs). Size is defined as

$$W_A * A + W_M * M$$

where A is the number of attributes and M is the number of operations or methods. W_A and W_M are empirically determined weights. W_A is expected to be close in value to 1 and W_M in the range 5–20. Complexity is measured by a variant of McCabe's cyclomatic complexity (McCabe, 1976).

The inter-object metrics are average system fan-out, depth of inheritance and the 'reuse ratio' of the number of superclasses to the total number of classes. Average system fan-out does not distinguish between the different structural relationships that objects may enter into. MOSES also permits the collection of the metrics suggested by Chidamber and Kemerer discussed below.

7.5.2 The MIT metrics

Two workers at MIT, Chidamber and Kemerer (1991), developed a suite of six collectable metrics as follows.

Weighted methods per class (WMC) is the sum of the static complexities of the methods of a class. If the complexities are taken to be unity this reduces to a simple count of methods. They do not state how the complexity is to be determined and presumably it could be a subjective estimate or a formal measure like cyclomatic complexity. This is an intra-object metric.

Depth of inheritance tree (DIT), an inter-object metric that should more properly be called depth of inheritance network, is the maximal length of a chain of specializations or the distance from the root of the tree when viewed as a class rather than system metric.

Number of children (NOC) is the fan-in in the classification structure: the number of subclasses. Of course this is a global system metric since classes do not know their children. It is not made clear whether this metric allows for dynamic classification schemes where NOC can change at run time.

Coupling between objects (CBO) is a count of the non-classification structure couplings. It fails to make a distinction between association, composition and usage; effectively treating them all as messaging. This is an inter-object metric.

Response for a class (RFC) is a measure of the structural coupling of the class and the most novel of the six. It counts the number of methods available to the class either directly within it or via one message to another class and could be regarded as closely related to the fan-out of the usage structure. According to Chidamber and Kemerer, RFC should be minimized although this militates against subcontracting.

Lack of cohesion in methods (LCOM) is also innovative. It measures the non-overlapping of sets of instance variables used by the methods of a class. An alternative, operational definition is: the percentage of methods that do not access an attribute, averaged over all attributes. The lowest, and most desirable, value of LCOM occurs when all the methods use all the instance variables and the highest when no instance variable is used by more than one method. This measures structural cohesion but not logical or semantic cohesion and there may be no correlation between the two. High LCOM may be an indicator of the need to split up a class but this should never be done automatically or without due reference to semantic cohesion.

These metrics have been quite widely adopted. For example, the McCabe Tools software product collects five out of six of them, adds more and provides an additional degree of structuring. That is, the McCabe Tool divides its 13 object-oriented metrics into four categories: quality, encapsulation, inheritance and polymorphism. The encapsulation metrics are LCOM together with measures of the features of the class that are public and protected (Pctpub) and the number of accesses to these features (Pubdata). Inheritance measures are the number of root classes (Rootcnt), fan-in, NOC and class level DIT. Polymorphism is measured by

WMC, RFC and the percentage of calls not made to overloaded modules (Pctcall). Quality is measured using the maximum cyclomatic and essential complexity of a class's methods and the number of classes that depend on descendants.

7.5.3 A critique of the MIT metrics

The six MIT metrics are also said to be founded on a sound theoretical basis in measurement theory and mathematics. The basis used is Wand's version of Bunge's mathematical ontology (Wand, 1989). Here, the work is less than convincing because this ontology itself suffers from some grave philosophical defects. It is atomistic: it conceives things as reducible to irreducible components. Further, it can probably not stand up to the Phenomenologist critique that an object's identity is independent of its properties (i.e. they could all change), although Whitmire (1997) overcomes this objection by stating that if we perceive two objects as identical, then we have not identified all the important properties; i.e. have not discovered the identities. Whether the demolition of the base affects the correctness of the superstructure is arguable. Having arrived at the proposed metrics by an incorrect route need not necessarily mean that they are flawed.

As remarked above, in some systems NOC may vary at run time due to dynamic classification. I would suggest that max, min, mean and mode values for NOC should be collected in such circumstances.

Coupling depends on interaction. One is tempted to suspect that the type of interaction matters. My solution is to collect separate metrics for all the structures of an object model: classification, composition, usage and association. This view can be applied to fan-out and fan-in and to RFC.

Cohesion based on LCOM is purely structural cohesion. It is logical or conceptual cohesion that matters most from the point of view of reuse. I am also concerned that only instance variables are referred to in these metrics. Class attributes should not be excluded from the definition since they contribute to complexity and cohesion.

Henderson-Sellers *et al.* (1996) found that there were some inconsistencies and errors in the MIT metrics. They reference various versions of the paper by Chidamber and Kemerer (1991, 1993, 1994) which offer radically differing definitions of the CBO and LCOM metrics. This paper remarks that although Chidamber and Kemerer evaluated their suite against the axioms proposed by Weyuker (1988), the latter are known to be inconsistent and have dubious validity. It is shown that the 1991 version of LCOM always gives zero – whatever the input – and that the later version does not discriminate between classes that intuitively have radically different structural cohesion. Furthermore, LCOM seems to increase with cohesion where it should decrease. The other metrics are subjected to a detailed critique as well but that need not concern us directly here. The 1996 paper's main contribution from our perspective is a new definition for LCOM that overcomes all these problems.

Consider a class with m methods $\{M_i\}$ and a attributes $\{A_j\}$. Let $a(M_i)$ represent the number of attributes that M_i accesses. Also, let $m(A_j)$ be the number of methods that access A_j. Define:

$$LCOM* = \frac{\left(\dfrac{1}{a}\displaystyle\sum_{j=1}^{a} m(A_j)\right) - m}{1 - m}$$

This definition provides a metric that decreases as cohesion increases, gives values in the unit interval and gives values that discriminate classes of intuitively different cohesion (for details see Henderson-Sellers, 1996). This is an improvement over the McCabe version described in the preceding section, which does not give values in the unit interval and therefore makes comparison harder. It turns out that it is possible to construct classes for which LCOM* takes values outside the unit interval. However, if one examines these examples it soon becomes apparent that they have been very badly designed from an OO standpoint. I therefore suggest that the magnitude of a negative value of LCOM* is a measure of the class's degree of 'non-object-orientation'.

The MIT suite was an important and seminal contribution and the flaws that Henderson-Sellers *et al.* point out can easily be corrected as I will show.

7.5.4 Connasence

An intriguing possibility is to attempt to unite coupling and cohesion as is done in Page-Jones' *connascence* metric (Page-Jones, 1992). This generalizes Constantine's classic notion that good design minimizes coupling and maximizes cohesion by defining connascence[2] and three kinds of encapsulation. Level 0 encapsulation represents the idea that a line of code encapsulates a certain abstraction. Level 1 is the encapsulation of procedures into modules and level 2 is the encapsulation provided in object-oriented programming. Two elements of a system are connascent if they share the same history and future or, more exactly, if changes to one may necessitate changes to the other. Good design should eliminate unnecessary connascence and minimize connascence across encapsulation boundaries and maximize it within them. For level 0 and level 1 encapsulation this reduces to the principle of coupling and cohesion. In general, inheritance compromises reuse. The connascence principle tells us that inheritance should be restricted to visible features or that there should be two separate hierarchies for inheriting the implementation and the interface. It would also discourage the use of friends in C++. Page-Jones classifies several kinds of connascence as name, type, value, position, algorithm, meaning and polymorphism. Polymorphism

---

[2] Literally, connascence means being 'born together'.

connascence is particularly interesting for object-oriented design and is closely related to the problems of non-monotonic logic. For example if FLY is an operation of BIRDS and PENGUINS is a subclass of BIRDS then FLY may sometimes fail and sometimes succeed. This causes maintenance problems should the system be changed. Rules, as in SOMA, may be used to avoid this problem as may the fuzzification of objects and inheritance. It is not yet clear how connascence could be measured in practice.

Another attempt to unify coupling and cohesion can be found in Cox and Novobilski (1991) where a hardware analogy is used to show how objects at different levels can coexist inside an application.

In SOMA, attribute values can be fuzzy sets and inheritance links can have a certainty factor attached. It is unclear whether this fuzziness of attribute values or classification increases or reduces complexity according to the metrics discussed so far. Intuitively one would expect fuzziness to reduce complexity since it does so in other areas of application; e.g. a fuzzy process controller needs fewer rules than a numerical one. The same question arises for multiple inheritance. It is likely that the use of multiple inheritance will reduce WMC but increase some of the inter-object metrics.

Another open question is whether cohesion metrics can be made to deal with the fact that a whole may be greater (more cohesive) than the sum of its parts.

Metrics are often related to reward structures. Those used to measure domain class developers may not be appropriate to application developers and vice versa.

7.5.5 Other approaches

Lorenz and Kidd (1994) seek to draw on their experience of managing object-oriented projects and recommend a list of metrics suitable for such projects together with useful heuristics for their use. Some of the metrics are obvious (such as number of methods per class) and some are novel (such as the number of support classes per key class and the number of scenario scripts). Support classes are those that support the solution without being essential to modelling the business. I would call them 'implementation classes'. Examples include Stacks, Windows, Buttons and so on. The scenario scripts used seem to suffer from the same weakness as use cases since there is no attempt to emphasize their 'stereotypical' character nor are they reduced to 'atomic' components. SOMA shows how this decomposition gives an important new metric analogous to the function point as we will see below.

The advice given is soundly based in experience. However, fundamentally this is just an arbitrary list of metrics with no theoretical cohesion and no compelling arguments for either including or excluding a particular metric. Little account is taken of other work done in this area (notably that of Henderson-Sellers and his students in Australia) and the book castigates the only work referenced (Chidamber and Kemerer, 1991) for being 'grounded in theory'. For me, this is adding insult to injury: a sound approach to metrics must be grounded in both theory **and** practice. Such a grounding would perhaps reduce the unmanageably long list of metrics given by Lorenz and soften the arbitrary character of some of these metrics. On the other hand Lorenz gives valuable heuristics and advice on thresholds which are not to be found elsewhere in the literature.

De Champeaux (1997) presents three sets of metrics for analysis, design and implementation, each linked to a fairly informal micro-process model. His idea of analysis is very different from my idea of requirements engineering; he sees it as a matter of re-writing an existing requirement document. He also emphasizes the central rôle of state-transition diagrams much more than I do. On the other hand, he also makes use of use cases and insists on defining a domain ontology or vocabulary in ways analogous to those of SOMA. The analysis process is defined by stating how the existence of each deliverable or artefact contributes to the production of other artefacts; notably, in the case of analysis, of class diagrams and sequence diagrams. The metrics for analysis are mostly based on counting such things as vocabulary items, use cases and classes appearing on the various diagrams. These are used to predict the effort associated with the production of analysis artefacts. The danger here, of course, is the creation of a 'deliverables fixation' of the type associated with structured methods; the focus should be on the end product rather than intermediate deliverables. But in bureaucratic organizations the approach would be popular. All of Chidamber's metrics except LCOM are included in de Champeaux's suite.

De Champeaux makes the absolutely crucial point that analysis objects should be viewed as independent, parallel processors with their own threads of control, whereas design must eliminate this implicit parallelism because implementation objects usually share a single thread per process. De Champeaux pays a lot of attention to eliminating high 'arity' associations. In SOMA we do not need this machinery because of our insistence on uni-directional mappings in place of bi-directional associations. The design process focuses on creating an executable model, mainly from the state transition diagrams. This is then organized into clusters for each distributed process, which are then serialized and optimized. Design metrics focus on quality and effort estimation. Finally, the implementation metrics introduced are all based on C++. However, both the design and implementation metrics are essentially extensions of the metrics introduced for analysis. The product metrics introduced have much in common with the SOMA business object metrics suite discussed in the next section.

In another interesting book on object-oriented metrics, Scott Whitmire (1997) also ties the issue of metrics to the development process. Whitmire's approach is undoubtedly the most theoretically based approach among those discussed so far. Most creditable is his attempt to provide a firm foundation for both his metrics and object modelling in general. He does this using category theory, a branch of applied algebra dealing with abstract mathematical structures, and measurement theory. Briefly, he views a class as a category whose *objects* are attribute domains and state spaces defined on them, and whose *arrows* are the set theoretic projections from the Cartesian product of these domains together with functions representing state transitions. In other words a class is a *diagram* of arrows. These categories then become the objects in a category of categories representing the designed class model. The arrows are functors and represent associations, including inheritance, aggregation and usage relationships. For non-trivial classes these diagrams become extremely complicated and therefore the resultant method is probably too complicated for the average development organization, but it does mark an important step forward in our understanding of both metrics and the foundations of object modelling. One minor problem with Whitmire's approach is that it is not clear that, in this model, classes can be objects; which would mean that the theory would have to be so extended to be compatible with SOMA. Multiple inheritance also is not catered for. Some category theorists might find the categories rather pathological because arrows that represent associations (except inheritance) do not compose. This is quite unlike the categories found in most of mathematics and suggests that a different formulation may be possible. Whitmire provides a recipe for developing metrics rather than merely suggesting things to measure in the manner of the other approaches discussed in this chapter. This again makes his approach rather complex for normal organizations. What is very different is that he proposes a way to measure the goodness of a design. Formal properties are stated for all the metrics developed and considerable attention is paid to getting the measurement scales right.

7.5.6 The SOMA metrics

The suite of metrics proposed within SOMA represents an attempt to synthesize and add to the MOSES, MIT and Lorenz work described above. It should also be noted that MOSES and SOMA converge on a single suite of metrics in the OPEN framework.

Measures such as WMC are not quite sufficient to capture the complexity of a SOMA object since the former does not allow for complexity due to rulesets. Our metric allows for this but does not measure the effect of assertions where they are used. This is open to discussion since clearly some assertions stand for rules and should be counted. On the other hand this is more difficult to automate and one could argue that attribute constraints should be counted too. I propose that the following metrics should be collected. In every case, collection can be made automatic by appropriate software such as *SOMATiK* at the requirements and analysis levels and other proprietary software (e.g. McCabe Tools) at the code level.

For the Business Object Model the metrics are:

BM1) The weighted complexity WC_C of each class C, defined as:

$$WC_C = W_A*A + W_M*L_M*M + W_R*N_R*R$$

where
- A = number of attributes and associations
- M = number of operations/methods
- R = number of rulesets

- N_R = number of rules per ruleset * average number of antecedent clauses per rule
- L_M is the proportional excess of SLOCs per method over an agreed, language dependent standard (this definition ensures that equation is dimensionally correct)
- W_A, W_M and W_R are empirically discovered weights.

BM2) The fan-outs and fan-ins for all four structures together with their averages.

BM3) The structure depths for the two acyclic structures: Dclass and Dcomp. This generalizes DIT.

BM4) The numbers of abstract and concrete classes.

BM5) The numbers of interface, domain and application objects incorporated into a project.

It should be noted that there is enough information collected here to reconstruct all the MIT metrics except LCOM.

For the Task Object Model the metrics are:

TM1) The weighted complexity WC_T of each task T, defined as:

$$WC_T = W_I * I + W_A * A + W_E * E + W_R * N_R * R$$

where

- I = number of objects (in the grammatical sense) per task. Usually this corresponds to the number of noun phrases
- A = number of associated tasks (if any)
- E = number of exceptions or side scripts
- R = number of rulesets
- N_R = number of rules per ruleset * average number of antecedent clauses per rule
- W_I, W_A, W_E and W_R are empirically discovered weights, which may be zero if empirical study shows that a factor such as E has no effect.

TM2) The fan-outs and fan-ins for all four structures in the task object model together with their averages; e.g. number of exceptions (side-scripts) per task (usage fan-out).

TM3) The structure depths for the two acyclic structures: Dsub and Dcomp.

TM4) The numbers of abstract and concrete tasks.

TM5) The numbers of interface, domain and application tasks incorporated into a project.

TM6) The numbers of external agents, messages and internal agents in the Agent Object Model.

TM7)   The number of atomic tasks; i.e. those with no component tasks: the leaf nodes of the task tree.

This last metric, called the number of **task points**, is the most important and most novel SOMA metric.   It offers a potential replacement for function points as a measure of overall complexity with the added benefit of automated collection. Furthermore, it can be collected earlier in the life cycle; i.e. at requirements capture.

SLOC measures are poor estimating tools because they are highly language, environment and programmer dependent and estimation is most needed before any language decisions have been made.   Function point counts, which address these points, suffer because of the labour intensive process required to collect them and their poor mapping onto object-oriented systems, event driven systems, real-time systems, computationally intensive systems, GUIs and the like.   What is required is a code independent measure that can be collected at the requirements capture stage and onwards and which correlates well with the business benefits to be delivered. Fortunately, the SOMA Task Object Model suggests just such a measure and this measure has the additional benefit of being able to be counted automatically.   The measure is the number of task points.

Task points represent atomic tasks that the system will help the user carry out. This includes autonomous tasks carried out within the system *en route* to the accomplishment of externally visible tasks.   A task is **atomic** with respect to a problem if further decomposition would introduce terms inappropriate to the domain.   For example, the register deal task might be decomposed into sub tasks such as send confirmations, check positions and so on.   We could go on decomposing until a level is reached where further decomposition would introduce sentences such as press key with finger.   The nouns are no longer in the trading domain, though they may well be in the domain of user interface design.   This is a clear rule, though it relies on the fuzzy evaluation of whether a term is a term of a domain or not. In practice, it is nearly always obvious when to stop decomposing. The atomic tasks are the leaf nodes (terminals) of the task tree (network) and the count can be automated by counting the tasks with no component tasks.

It is assumed that each task is expressed in a Subject, Verb, Direct Object, Preposition, Indirect Object (SVDPI) sentence.   The approach also assumes some skill and consistency on the part of developers in identifying when atomic task level is reached.   It is recommended that one person, the class librarian is ideal, examine all task models with this in mind; at least at the beginning. Eventually, the cultural norm should be established and consistent.

Task points have two major significant advantages over function points: they can be collected automatically and earlier in the life cycle. Furthermore, they are a metric specifically and deliberately developed as part of an object-oriented approach to system building.

METRICS IN SOMATiK

The SOMA metrics (with the exception of WC_T) are collected automatically by SOMATiK along with statistics related to them, such as max, min, median and variance. To access these facilities for an individual class, click the Metrics button on its class card. To access all metrics, select **Metrics Reporter** from the **Run** menu.

Other metrics, which can only be collected at the physical design and coding stage, are not collected by *SOMATiK*. These are as follows:

- *LCOM** (the modified version of LCOM defined in Section 7.5.3 above);
- the cyclomatic complexity of methods.

ESTIMATING MODELS

It is proposed that effort estimation will be based on the same model as almost every other estimating technique; i.e.

$$E = a + pT^k$$

where E is effort in staff hours, T is the task point count, p is the inverse of productivity in task points per staff hour (to be determined empirically) and k and a are constants; a may be thought of as start-up and constant overhead costs. Productivity will itself be a function of the level of reuse and may depend of the ratio of domain to application objects in the BOM and on the complexity of the BOM based on weighted class complexity, fan measures and so on. Much empirical work remains to be done in this area.

7.5.7 Process improvement

Collecting metrics is central to process improvement, simply because you cannot know that you have improved upon your process objectively unless you have a measure of the goodness of both process and product. Process improvements that produce inferior products are all too common, as discussed by Morgan (1997). You must therefore measure defects, time to failure, satisfaction ratings and other product metrics, in addition to the SOMA metrics defined above. You need to measure, in addition, productivity: time spent on a project, time taken, resources used, etc. Soft factors should also be included in the metrics programme: educational background of developers, working environment and even personality traits. Then you can begin to see if there are ways to improve, and measure the amount of improvement. Visible success is a great way to motivate developers and gain credibility with business sponsors.

It is currently fashionable to cast process improvement programmes within a so-called 'process maturity model' such as the one promulgated by Humphrey (1989) and the Software Engineering Institute: the SEI Capability Maturity Model. The latter is given false credibility because parts of the US government will not buy from an organization not accredited as 'mature' at some level against this model. It divides organizations into five arbitrary categories labelled: Initial, Repeatable, Defined, Managed and Optimizing. These are in increasing order of brownie points. The absurdity of the labels is evident: how an undefined process can be repeatable beats me! But there is worse to come. It turns out that the cost of reaching the highest level is quite astronomical – and you have to pay a fee to be accredited as such. As far as I know only one organization in the world is at that level. Capers Jones (1994) puts it nicely: 'The kind of uncertainty in mapping the complexities of the real world into the constraints of the artificial taxonomy tends to create "priesthoods" of consulting specialists who assist in dealing with arcane topics'. For these reasons, I am totally against immature and arbitrary process maturity models. However, there is nothing to stop an organization that must conform for commercial reasons from using SOMA to achieve accreditation; and it may even help because of the rigorous nature of the approach and its well-defined process model and metrics.

7.6 Getting started

This book has laid out a prescriptive, object-oriented requirements engineering approach before its reader. Our closing topic is what that reader needs to do in order to reap the benefits of such an approach.

The first step, apart from understanding the material I have presented, is to establish the OO development method within the organization within which you work. Consultants may be used to initiate this but an in-house manager for the project is highly recommended. That manager can then liaise with the various outside organizations that might be involved. S/he should be the 'methods champion' within the organization and must start with a clear notion of what a business object is. The chosen method should have sufficiently rich semantics to capture business rules within objects, have a clear process and have a metrics suite. Clearly SOMA has these characteristics, but I am not ruling out the existence of other methods that have them too. The MOSES variant of OPEN could be an example.

Have chosen the method a manual should be produced and distributed to all development staff. Knowledge transfer becomes the critical issue now and it is essential that developers and users receive appropriate training. When this has been established the organization can contemplate establishing a reuse programme along the lines covered in Chapter 2. We now consider what else needs to be done.

The organization must either recruit developers already skilled in object-oriented development or re-train existing developers. I have found that a mixture of the two approaches is beneficial for several reasons:

- Developers with relational training often find it hard to adapt to object-oriented thinking, even when they appear to relish it. Surprisingly, some converted COBOL programmers seem to take to the new approach better.

- Synergy between the two groups is beneficial. The PhD computer recruits can learn much about the business and the legacy environment from the old hands, just as they can explain to the latter the idioms of the new languages.

Sound education and training are vital for all members of staff, new and old. The approach and especially, I find, the basic principles of object technology must be well understood. People with experience of OMT or UML have usually picked up many of the bad habits associated with the defects outlined in Appendices A and B. They need to be re-educated – just as much as the folk emigrating from Mainframeland. Make sure that everyone (users too) understands the approach taken to modelling. It is not just about business objects. It includes models of the agents (internal and external) involved with the business, their objectives and priorities, the business processes (conversations) that they engage in and the tasks that they carry out. Remember that the latter are reusable objects too. The business objects can be discovered from a study of these tasks and, for seamlessness, we must include implementation links between business objects and tasks. Implementation objects may include several library components, but packages of these should correspond to business objects, at least approximately.

Good people are expensive. Acquire the right tools for them. There is little point in refusing a costly developer an extra workstation or software licence if his productivity can be improved thereby; even if the improvement is only a few percentage points. The sort of tools to consider include languages, middleware, databases and modelling and reuse tools. *SOMATiK* is a modelling tool. It has an add-on Repository Manager that is designed to support the reuse practices set out in this book. Other reuse tools may be required to help you manage source code, which can be cross referenced within the *SOMATiK* Repository Manager.

Finally, attend to quality and process improvement. Set up a metrics and process improvement programme and get involved with benchmarking against other software development organizations. Set up quality circles and institute a programme of formal inspections.

7.7 Bibliographical notes

Shaw and Garlan (1996) is one of the first books to look at the issue of software architecture in an abstract way. It is worth consulting. Selic *et al.* (1994) contains so many excellent architectural insights that it is definitely recommended further reading, especially for those interested in real-time embedded systems, although it has little to say about requirements engineering *per se*.

The first book to explore the issue of patterns in software was Coplien (1992), but this treated only C++ idioms. People interested in the field ascribe considerable influence to the work of the architect Alexander (1977, 1979), although patterns seem to have been applied more widely to software than to buildings. Emerging largely from work on frameworks, the book by Gamma *et al.* (1995) was immediately influential in the C++ world. Pree (1995) added interesting notions concerning metapatterns. Buschmann *et al.* (1996) introduced the classification of patterns as architectural, design or language (idiomatic) patterns. Their book is the first treatment to attempt to present patterns in a language independent fashion and provides a clearer rationale than the other works.

Larman (1998) uses a variant of UML to exploit patterns for software development. His book is interesting for the gloss it provides on UML and use cases, which reveals several defects in those techniques and suggests minor remedies – though nothing so thoroughgoing as those presented in this book. It still, however, would make interesting further reading.

Coad *et al.* (1997) and Fowler (1996) presented analysis patterns for the first time. The PLOPD series of conference proceedings (Coplien and Schmidt, 1995; Vlissides *et al.,* 1996) is the major source of reference material on all sorts of patterns including particularly interesting (for me) work on organizational (i.e. development and business process) patterns by Coplien.

Jackson (1995) introduced problem frames and contains much else of interest. Any one interested in requirements engineering should put it on their reading list.

Lewis (1995) provides a critical survey of the idea of frameworks and some of its more important commercial instantiations. It consists mainly of chapters written by authors with considerable expertise in the field such as Paul Calder, Erich Gamma, Wolfgang Pree and John Vlissides: all authors of patterns and frameworks in their own right. Coverage includes MacApp, Microsoft Foundation Classes (MFC), ET++, InterViews, and Taligent's Commonpoint. The editor provides four introductory chapters that constitute an excellent tutorial introduction and survey and there are two case studies. This book will be of value to anyone evaluating frameworks or class libraries. The reviews manage to point out strengths and weaknesses of each approach that even a thorough trial evaluation would often miss. On the other hand the bias of the authors sometimes shows through. For example, the withering critique of MFC by Pree resonated strongly with actual experience of using it but one could be left with a slight sense of hubris in that Pree obviously prefers the approach taken in the less well known ET++.

Henderson-Sellers (1996) and Whitmire (1997) are the best coherent works on object-oriented metrics, the later being particularly interesting in attempting to explicate solid mathematical foundations. de Champeaux (1997) is full of interesting and novel ideas and shows how to incorporate detailed design metrics within an overall development process. Not only will the contributions on metrics and design process be influential, his discussion of methodology is interesting in its own right.

For an understanding of category theory, consult MacLane (1971).

Part II

Appendices

A

Associations, integrity and rules

Integrity without knowledge is weak and useless, and knowledge without integrity is dangerous and dreadful.

Dr Johnson (Rasselas)

We showed in Chapter 4 that bi-directional associations violate the principle of encapsulation and are therefore **totally incompatible** with object-orientation. The object-oriented principle of encapsulation implies that bi-directional associations must be abandoned in object-oriented modelling, in favour of either uni-directional pointers or converted to *bona fide* classes.

In my formalism as we have seen, objects encapsulate rulesets, along with the usual attributes and methods. In this appendix we examine the notion of associations and their 'inverses' in some depth and point out some inconsistencies in current terminology within the database community that go back as far as Abrial's work. With the new foundation I then construct, I show how referential integrity rules can be embedded in classes rather than attached to external associations, as is the current normal practice. Finally, I argue that classes with rulesets are capable of modelling any semantic integrity constraint. This has, I believe, implications for the design of object-oriented CASE tools as well as for database design. Because of this argument it can be seen that to maintain the principle of encapsulation, objects **must** have rulesets; they are not an optional extra. I prove that the absence of bi-directional associations **requires** the presence of encapsulated rulesets in order to represent the integrity of relationships. The material is a little technical compared to the remainder of the text and has therefore been reserved for an appendix. However, the results are of great importance and lie at the roots of SOMA.

Most of the material in this appendix is based on a paper by Graham, Bischof and Henderson-Sellers (1997).

⊟ A.1 Associations and encapsulation in object-oriented methods

Most of the popular first-generation methods for object-oriented analysis (e.g. Coad and Yourdon, 1991; Rumbaugh *et al.,* 1991; Shlaer and Mellor, 1988) and several of the less widely used ones offered a construct that placed a link between object types depicting static connexions other than generalization and composition. This construct is generally called an association. Some authors use the term 'relationship' as its synonym; whilst yet others use 'relationship' as a higher level abstraction which groups together association, usage, aggregation, collection, various flavours of inheritance, etc. Such associations describe one aspect of the connectivity between object types. This approach is familiar to most developers who have used entity relationship techniques and is semantically identical since these associations refer only to the data structures of the objects and not to their behaviour (except in those rare instances where associations are used to denote messaging; e.g. object-oriented SSADM (Robinson and Berrisford, 1994)).

A study of the literature of semantic data modelling reveals that there are two fundamental ways to connect data structures or entity types: constructors and pointers. Delobel *et al.* (1992) explain that in the first approach, emphasis is placed on building structures using constructors such as the tuple or the set. In the second, the stress is on linking types using attributes. In the 1980s the former approach was dominant, largely because of the popularity and widespread use of relational databases. In entity-relationship models there are two logical types: entity-relationships and relationship-relationships. Both are represented by sets of tuples and no links between them are stored; the run-time system of the DBMS must search for the linkages. Attempts to enrich the relational model led quickly to systems with more than two relationship types. This unsatisfactory situation soon led to suggestions to replace these arbitrary type systems with a single notion of classes reminiscent of object-oriented programming. (See Graham, 1994, p143 for a brief history of these developments.) The pointer based approach is far more natural to an OO thinker but one suspects that the popularity of methods such as OMT or UML is due largely to the fact that developers with a relational background find their approach familiar and anodyne. The danger here is that object-oriented principles will be ignored and highly relational models produced instead of truly object-oriented ones.

A.1.1 Associations as types

I think that associations should point in one direction only because to do otherwise would violate the principle of encapsulation. Several object-oriented methodologists have argued against my position, saying that you can always add link attributes to an association and create from it an association object type. However, this new object type must retain links to its progenitors. Therefore, if we accept this as a solution, these new relationships must in turn give rise to new association object types. At some point we must stop this process and will still have to represent the residual associations connecting our, now more numerous, set of classes. This is not to deny the utility of association object types. Some associations are so important that they are themselves concepts; i.e. object types. An often quoted example is the marriage relationship between people, discussed below.

Of course, in any particular case, one can find a natural place to stop this process. It is usual to create types out of associations only when the association has interesting properties in its own right. This still leaves us with associations between the newly constructed types and the types that were previously linked by the original associations. Thus, in *all* practical cases, we will have failed to convert *all* associations to types although we will typically have removed all the many-to-many associations through this process. It is worth noting that while relational databases forbid the use of many-to-many relationships, they are not precluded by modern object-oriented databases. Thus the habit of always removing them, common among traditionally educated database designers, is no longer necessarily a good one.

A.1.2 Associations versus mappings

I will now begin to show how all the problems alluded to above are overcome by abolishing bi-directional associations in favour of uni-directional associations or **mappings**, which can be thought of as pointers embedded in object types, coupled with rulesets to preserve referential and semantic integrity. This last point is crucial. Without encapsulating class invariants in objects there can be no way of storing referential integrity rules apart from as a part of some external and generally bi-directional association, and thus violating encapsulation.

In SOMA, a class may encapsulate public rulesets that concern the other public features of the class. They provide second order information about the class. For example, a single rule within a ruleset could represent a database trigger that causes a method to execute when an attribute changes value or it could represent necessary sequencing among methods. More unusually rules can represent the control régimes under which the class operates. For example, the rules could state whether default values should take precedence over multiple inheritance conflict resolution or vice versa. Rulesets for resolving multiple inheritance conflicts on numerical attributes can include mathematical formulae. For example, we could use such a formula to average the values of two conflicting, inherited attributes. Rulesets are unordered sets of production rules and are always subject to a defined inference régime. This means that classes can infer facts that are not stated explicitly.

Some existing object-oriented methods already regard associations as mappings. MOSES (Henderson-Sellers and Edwards, 1994) advocates uni-directional associations or mappings as does SOMA where they are simply called 'associations' or 'association attributes'. In the latter method, certain associations are designated 'pure attributes' when they point at primitive types. This is what permits *SOMATiK* to generate uncluttered association diagrams automatically. In fact, undirected connexions ('associations') are often all that need to be presented on such diagrams but the underlying model, which describes completely what is likely to be implemented, must contain the richer uni-directional 'pointers'. Several other methodologists have noted that associations can be represented as mappings though they still work with associations directly and fail to explain how integrity is to be represented when mappings are used.

With uni-directional associations (mappings) we can still construct object types from them if needed. If aMan is married to aWoman, then both aMan and aWoman should know this. From the point of view of these two individuals this is often sufficient. However, to a registrar of births, deaths and marriages, the Marriage object type itself is important and has attributes like date, time, and place and may even exhibit behaviour, such as computing the correct substance to give as an anniversary gift. In which case it is indeed an object type. But it is NOT synonymous with the mapping of aMan to aWoman. Its nature is more substantive. Now the marriage object type must be responsible for knowing the identities of the partners involved and the partners must store uni-directional associations (mappings) to the marriage instance. This does not break encapsulation since Man then maps to Marriage and Woman maps to Marriage. It is not a (second class or even first class) *relationship type* but a true *object type*.

Odell (Martin and Odell 1995) suggests that associations are really pairs of 'mappings' corresponding to the *rôles* of an association (Bachman, 1977). A mapping is a one way connexion. It is part of the object (the client object) and therefore does not break encapsulation. An association *à la* UML, Coad, Rumbaugh or Shlaer/Mellor is external and does break encapsulation. We will examine Odell's argument and present a slightly firmer foundation in much the same spirit.

⊟ A.2 Integrity constraints

The obvious problem with replacing bi-directional associations with mappings is that there is now no obvious container in which to store referential integrity constraints. I must therefore now show how this is accomplished using mappings. Fortunately, SOMA rulesets provide a neat solution.

In order to regard 'associations' as pairs of rôles or mappings we must be prepared to store the relationships, if there are any, between these pairs of mappings. An example where this is important arises when there are integrity rules. Take marriage again but forget the registration object. aMan is married to aWoman and aWoman is married to aMan. If aMan unmarries (divorces) aWoman it is necessary (in most countries at any rate) that aWoman unmarries aMan too. But aMan has no knowledge of what aWoman knows. Therefore aMan and aWoman must store rulesets that encapsulate this 'business rule' or at least trigger a call to some external rule base. The absence of rulesets in methods such as UML prevents them from this expedient — though they could hard code some methods to the same effect. Of course, such rulesets are not always necessary. For example, aMan and aWoman could remember each other's telephone number and aWoman could forget aMan's number with no effect on the adjoint relationship.

A.2.1 Inverses

Basing himself on the terminology prevalent in work on databases and, especially, functional databases (Gray, 1984), Odell suggests that pairs of related mappings pointing in opposite directions are inverses (in the sense of set theory). This is actually incorrect but close enough to the truth to make it worthwhile reiterating his set-theoretic foundations more rigorously. I suspect that related pairs of uni-directional associations (or, more accurately, mappings as we will call them from now on) are adjoint functors in the sense of category theory, which means that they give rise to inverses in a comma category (McLarty, 1992). This idea will not be explored further herein as the assertion about adjoints does not affect my arguments, although I have assumed it to be true by using the term *adjoint* rather than *inverse* above.

In mathematics, a relation is a set of ordered n-tuples and a mapping is a single valued relation. Consider two object types A and B. Forget that they are types and regard them simply as sets. Strictly speaking, a mapping takes elements of A to elements of B. However, such an interpretation does not capture the notion of association that we require, because it cannot represent one-to-many relationships such as the 'has children' association where A and B are both the set of all people. Odell, following a suggestion of Abrial and in conformity with the literature of functional data models, asserts that mappings are from the set to the power set and that an association consists of two 'inverse' mappings (Martin and Odell, 1995). This definition does not stand up to close scrutiny. To see this, consider the bi-directional publications association of Figure A.1.

Figure A.1 gives the layout:

0..m   1..n

| PAPERS |━━━━━━━| PEOPLE |

Figure A.1 A bi-directional association

This can be broken into two mappings:

$$f: \text{Papers} \longrightarrow \mathcal{P}(\text{People}) \qquad (f' = \text{writtenBy});$$

$$g': \text{People} \longrightarrow \mathcal{P}(\text{Papers}) \qquad (g' = \text{wrote}).$$

where $\mathcal{P}(A)$ represents the power set of A: the set of all subsets of A. Actually, we could work with power types but only the set theory is relevant to the present argument. These functions cannot even be composed, much less satisfy the definition of being inverse to each other:

$$f'.g'=1 \qquad\qquad (g' \text{ is a right inverse of } f')$$

$$g'.f'=1 \qquad\qquad (g' \text{ is a left inverse of } f')$$

The correct formulation is to say that the mappings should go between the power sets, so that:

$$f: \mathcal{P}(\text{Papers}) \longrightarrow \mathcal{P}(\text{People})$$

$$g: \mathcal{P}(\text{People}) \longrightarrow \mathcal{P}(\text{Papers})$$

These mappings are completely determined by their values at singleton subsets since, for all subset S and T, $f(S \cup T) = f(S) \cup f(T)$. In this sense, these mappings may always be reconstructed from mappings whose domain is the set rather than the power set by setting, for example, $f(\{p\}) = f'(p) \; \forall \; p$.

Observe that, for any A, $\mathcal{P}(A)$ is a complete lattice with the preorder relation defined by set inclusion: $\supseteq$ (read 'contains'). In fact, the power lattice is a category with these inclusions as arrows. This is the basis of my claim that the two mappings are adjoints rather than inverses.

Taking any two arbitrary mappings in opposite senses between a pair of power types is not sufficient for a true association. Intuitively there must be some relationship between the pair. This definition enables one to represent many-to-many relationships properly and to compose the two mappings as originally claimed. However, in general, we still do not have to have an inverse pair as claimed by Odell. What we must at least have, is that these mappings should be left and right **semi-inverses** (where the = in the definition of inverse is replaced by $\supseteq$):

$$\text{Rule 1: } f.g(\{p\}) \supseteq \{p\}$$

($f.g(\{p\})$ is the set of all the people that wrote (or co-wrote) papers written by p; this contains $\{p\}$.)

$$\text{Rule 2: } g.f(\{q\}) \supseteq \{q\}$$

($g.f(\{q\})$ is the set of all papers written by people who wrote q; this contains $\{q\}$.)

Intuitively, these two rules represent the minimal referential integrity constraint on a pair of mappings for them to constitute an association. In fact, we *define* an **association** as a pair of opposed mappings on the power types such that rules 1 and 2 above are satisfied. An association need not be strong enough to enforce referential integrity and I will show in Section A.2.3 how these conditions must be strengthened to achieve this.

A.2.2 Integrity and encapsulation

The above two conditions can be expressed by rulesets (or, more specifically, class invariants) encapsulated in the classes as follows.

Each object type corresponds to a set of classes that implement it. We choose one class as a representative. The mapping f is an instance attribute of the class Papers which would normally be written in SOMA as writtenBy(People,1,n). This pointer to the People class indicates that a paper may be written by one to many people (authors). Then, in this example, g is an instance attribute of People which would normally be written as wrote(Papers,0,n).

Since the associations are attributes that form part of the interface, an instance q of the class Papers can determine the set of instances of People that wrote the paper. Call that set of identifiers AuthorsOf(q). For each member of AuthorsOf(q), People can check its Wrote attribute and return the set of papers written by this author. Call this set WrittenBy(AuthorsOf(q)). Rule 2, above, just states that q is a member of this set, for all q in Papers. The rule is encapsulated by Papers. Dually, Rule 1 is encapsulated by People. The reader should work through the dual processing steps.

Inserting the obvious cardinalities we could write the attributes and Rule 2 in a more familiar style:

- For all papers there must be someone, possibly many people, who wrote the paper.
- For all papers q, q is a member of the set of papers written by people who wrote q.

For those readers more familiar with Smalltalk-like programming languages than with databases, the above can be thought of as being implemented by message sends rather than mappings.

It should also be noted that, since f and g are in the public interfaces of their respective classes, there is no violation of encapsulation when the rules are encapsulated. The existence of a mapping implies that the class stores the identity of the associated class and this, of course, gives access to its interface. Encapsulation would be violated if a class referred to an instance of another class, because this would be an assumption about the instantiation of the other class. Therefore, it is assumed that reference to instances happens via the class extension (which is part of the public interface of the class).

Using this approach, no integrity information is lost and encapsulation is totally maintained. The approach to rules taken in other methods such as OMT (Blaha and Premerlani,1998; Rumbaugh *et al.*, 1991), UML (Rational, 1997) or Martin and Odell (1995) wherein rules are extraneous to objects does not have this advantage. Encapsulating rulesets not only makes classes more reusable but increases the effectiveness of rules since they are propagated readily via the classification structure (by inheritance). In SOMA, rulesets have an inferencing capability that makes them more general and powerful than class invariants. However, in the example given, exactly the same effect could be achieved with class invariants as in the MOSES (Henderson-Sellers and Edwards, 1994) or BON (Waldén and Nerson, 1995) methods.

The suggestion above does not allow us to search for the association member that caused the integrity violation (as the rule is applied *a postiori*), although this is a necessity for any DBMS. To be able to provide a solution for this, the assumption that the other class can process its g function in the reverse direction (starting from the result) is not a violation of encapsulation. Starting from this, the first step would be to retrieve the set of authors of aPaper, wrote(aPaper), by sending a message to the People class. To ensure integrity it is then sufficient to compare the image of the returned set wrote(aPaper) under writtenBy with the Papers class's instance aPaper. This argument is made clearer in the next section.

A.2.3 Rules for referential integrity

Another way of looking at Rule 1 is to say that q is contained in the *union* of the individual sets of papers written by each author who wrote q (who are represented in the writtenBy association of the Papers class). These sets are found in the People class by checking the wrote association for each author who wrote paper q. This, in itself, is insufficient to ensure referential integrity.

For example, imagine the case when a paper q establishes that it is in writtenBy({Hugh}). Author Hugh would then have to establish that paper q is in the image of its wrote association. In case author Hugh could not establish this association for any reason, Rule 1 in the Papers class would compare the union of the sets of papers written by the Authors who wrote q as provided by the People class. If paper q had also been co-written by other authors, the resulting set would contain q, even though author Hugh's wrote association does not contain paper q and integrity would be violated. Thus, the rule given does not allow us to search for the association member that caused the integrity violation, although this is a necessity for any DBMS.

The solution is to build the *intersection* (rather than the union) of all the applications of the mapping. If the intersection (of the sets of papers written by each author) does not contain paper q, you know that an integrity violation has occurred. Thus, People and Papers must contain rules that state:

$$\text{Rule 3: } \{p\} \subseteq \bigcap_{q_a \in g(\{p\})} f(\{q_a\})$$

$$\text{Rule 4: } \{q\} \subseteq \bigcap_{p_a \in f(\{q\})} g(\{p_a\})$$

An association with these rules encapsulated in its classes ensures referential integrity and gives a precise meaning to the intuitive notion of 'inverse' mappings, although:

PROPOSITION 1: Rules 3 and 4 are weaker conditions than saying that f and g are true inverses.

PROOF:

Assume that g is left inverse to f so that: $gf(Q) = Q$. Choose any q and let $pa \in f(\{q\})$. Then $g(\{pa\}) \subseteq gf(\{q\}) = \{q\}$. Therefore either $g(\{pa\})$ is empty or equal to $\{q\}$. Being empty would violate our assumptions. Therefore Rule 4 holds (actually with the inclusion replaced by a stronger equality).

That the converse is not true may be seen by considering a group of three authors, Hugh, Ivan and Jane, who all co-authored the two papers q and r. Here $\{q\}$ is a proper subset of $\{q,r\} = g(f(\{q\})) \cap g(f(\{r\}))$. Figure A.2 illustrates this counter-example.

QED

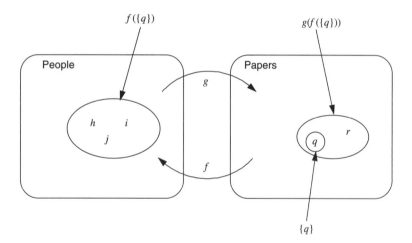

Figure A.2 The counterexample of Proposition 1

To get true inverses we must assert equality in the two rules but this seems counter intuitive. Define a **strong association** to be a pair of mappings satisfying Rules 3 and 4. Also define such a pair as **strong semi-inverses**.

SEMANTIC
INTEGRITY

For many years we have known how to represent referential integrity constraints in network, relational and object-oriented databases. However, a general method of representing semantic integrity constraints – that is, the most general constraints on how entities or objects are related – has eluded the collective understanding of the database community. Some progress has been made with deductive databases, so that it is known how to represent such constraints as 'all children who like sweets also like dogs'. But this has not been generalized to all constraints or to other types of database, notably object-oriented ones. The most common method for representing semantic integrity constraints is to use database triggers, but it is known that this does not generalize to all possible semantic constraints. In this text, I treat this problem as a modelling or knowledge representation problem and propose a general solution that can be readily implemented within object-oriented databases and, with a little thought, in others.

In the foregoing, I showed that class invariants in objects were both necessary and sufficient to model the referential integrity of objects using uni-directional mappings. However, I actually presented the arguments using SOMA rulesets. It is a well known result that rulesets (production rules) operating under a non-procedural régime, such as backward chaining, are Turing complete. That is to say that all computable results are reachable in this way or, equivalently, that all statements about the semantics of a certain subject matter (the object) can be represented. On this basis I claim that objects which encapsulate rulesets offer a very convenient way to represent the most general semantic integrity constraints in an object-oriented style.

It remains a specific problem to implement these general models in any given DBMS, but the modelling solution is general and compact. Procedural language bindings and/or database triggers may be adapted to implement the model but it seems impossible to give any general guidelines. The problem with a procedural implementation is that much traceability from the abstract model will be lost. Also, as we shall see below, while the model may retain full encapsulation and support reuse of the specification thereby, the implementation need not do so. Nevertheless, I will now show how some of my ideas, notably those relating to inverses and referential integrity, are already realized in a typical current object-oriented database management system.

⊟ A.3 Associations in object databases

The ODMG-93 standard for object-oriented databases (Cattell, 1994) uses the term 'relationship' as a synonym for association. We will stick to the term association here. The standard object model as suggested by ODMG supports one-to-one, one-to-many and many-to-many associations. They are defined as *traversal paths* for each direction of traversal between objects and are declared in the public interface definitions of the objects (e.g. wrote/writtenBy for the Papers/People example given above). An *inverse* clause in both of the traversal path declarations indicates that the traversal paths both apply to the same association. The *inverse* clause ensures that associations maintain referential integrity, which is done by the ODBMS automatically. If the *inverse* clause is omitted, traversal is not possible in the reverse direction.

In ODMG-93, associations are considered types that do not have object identities (OIDs) and that are uniquely identified by the participating instances. The many-to-many association type is composed of two sets of one-to-many associations. These one-to-many associations in turn are defined by sets of one-to-one associations (pointers). There is only a traversal function defined for one direction of traversal of a one-to-many association; i.e. from the single object to the set of related objects. However, the traversal function defined on each of the components' one-to-one associations allows one to go from any element of the set back to the single related instance.

To illustrate how the ODMG-93 standards relate to my suggestions, I offer the example of ObjectStore, since the inverse association construct of ObjectStore is compliant with the ODMG-93 Standard. I follow the presentation in the ObjectStore manual (ODI, 1992).

ObjectStore is an object-oriented database programming language and management system that has been sold commercially by Object Design Inc. since 1990. ObjectStore's data model keeps closely to the data model of C++. ObjectStore can be used in three different ways:

■ using C programs calling C library functions;
■ using C++ programs calling the C++ library functions, with or without generic classes;
■ using its C++ extension, the DML, which provides generic classes (based on the C++ templates), query facilities and exception handlers in addition to C++ constructs.

The latter will be the approach considered here with respect to the association integrity maintenance mechanism provided by ObjectStore.

We will need to know the way ObjectStore defines some of its collection classes. A collection is an object used to group other objects together as ordered or unordered collections that may or may not allow duplicates:

- os_Set: unordered/ no duplicates
- os_Bag: unordered/ duplicates
- os_List: ordered/ duplicates

The collection classes contain member functions to insert, remove and retrieve elements.

In ObjectStore's own C++ extension, associations are represented as data members in the public interface of a class. These links can represent one-to-one, one-to-many, and many-to-many associations. They are implemented as binary associations with pointer-valued or 'collection-of-pointer'-valued data members. The use of a collection type in the **inverse_member** declaration indicates the cardinality of the association.

The ObjectStore approach may be regarded as the implementation equivalent of strong associations as defined above and corresponds to my notion of mappings as strong semi-inverses from power type to power type, although the term INVERSE is still used.

ObjectStore offers a construct and mechanism to enforce integrity constraints automatically. The data members can be declared inverses of each other (OODM-Language keyword: **inverse_member**), so that an update to one data member automatically triggers a corresponding update to its 'inverse'.

The integrity constraints underlying the **inverse_member** declaration are quoted here in a slightly modified version to enhance readability:

> If a and b are inverse data members (representing an association), then, for any two instances x and y of the two classes, x is a value of a (which is a data member in the public interface of instance y) if and only if y is a value of b (which is a data member in the public interface of instance x).

In a many-to-many association, the value of a data member is a collection type grouping the pointers together. Thus, strictly speaking, every data member is single-valued. Since ObjectStore provides collection classes that allow duplicates (os_List, os_Bag), a more general version of the integrity constraint enforced has to be presented to cover these cases:

> If *a* and *b* are inverse data members (representing an association), then, for any two instances *x* and *y* of the two classes, and for any integer n, *x* occurs n times as a value of *a* (which is a data member in the public interface of instance *y*) if and only if *y* occurs n times as a value of *b* (which is a data member in the public interface of instance *x*).

Table A.1 Example for many-to-many associations:

Class S		Class T	
Instance	inverse association *a*	Instance	inverse association *b*
y	a.(x, x, z, r)	x	b.(y, y, s, t)
s	a.(x)	z	b.(y)
t	a.(x)	r	b.(y)

The **inverse_member** declaration implicitly contains the rule that the integrity constraint quoted above has to be enforced. This is in conformity with my suggestion to impose integrity constraints by encapsulating rules in the class declarations corresponding to the associations represented as pointers with strong semi-inverse rules.

```
class people
{public:
  people *spouse inverse_member spouse;      // 1-1
  os_Set<companies*> employers inverse_member employees;//n-m
};

class companies
{public:
  os_Set<people*> employees inverse_member employers; // n-m
};
```

Figure A.3 Using the ObjectStore inverse_member keyword

In Figure A.3, the data members employers (instances of class companies) and employees (instances of class people) are grouped together in collection classes (class os_Set) referring to each other via the **inverse-member** keyword. If an approach other than using ObjectStore's C++ extension (the DML) is chosen, the example above can be expressed in C++ as well. The association concept as such is not supported in C++, but is simulated by the support of automatically generated C++ methods (system predefined macros) that implement it. I will not explain this further here.

Integrity constraints are enforced in the following cases:

- establishing a value for an association (if x is established as a value of a for y, y is established as a value of b for x);
- de-establishing a value for an association (if x is de-established as a value of a for y, y is de-established as a value of b for x);
- deletion of an instance (if x is deleted, it is de-established as a value of a for y).

Internally, the enforcement of integrity constraints is implemented by a relationship class – embedded in the class – containing the association that encapsulates the pointer (collection-of-pointers) of the data member. If the ObjectStore DML **inverse_member** feature (which is a macro) is not used, the relationship and collection classes in the class library can be used. The implementation of the relationship class entirely hides the inverse maintenance tasks from the code that manipulates the instances of the class containing the association.

An association data member in ObjectStore refers to its 'inverse' in the public interface of the other class. Thus, encapsulation is not compromised.

Integrity is automatically maintained by the ObjectStore DBMS. The **inverse_member** declaration ensures that integrity constraints (which could be regarded as rules or class invariants implicitly contained in the inverse association) are enforced. This seems to be a good exemplar of a solution to the problem of associations that we have discussed: representing associations as mappings that are implemented as pointers and coupled with rules to impose integrity constraints. The same thing can be done in other object-oriented databases such as O2 (Delobel *et al.,* 1992), although there some code must be written to accomplish this. In either case, encapsulation is not maintained by the implementation, which depends on the global features of the DML rather than on rules encapsulated in the database classes themselves.

Other object-oriented databases such as O2, Jasmine and Versant product model integrity rules in a similar way. In Versant, for example, this is done using its BiLinkVstr keyword in place of ObjectStore's inverse_member, as illustrated in Figure A.4.

Reuse, considered one of the major advantages of object-orientation, is not threatened either, because – as soon as only one of the classes containing an inverse-member declaration is reused – the DBMS will ensure at compile time that the corresponding class is imported as well. Thus, association information cannot be lost. My contribution is to offer a general language for modelling such problems that is independent of such implementation niceties.

```
BiLink_to_BiLink<x,r>::add();            // one-to-one
BiLink_to_BiLinkVstr<x,r>::add();        // many-to-one
BiLinkVstr_to_BiLink<x,r>::add();        // one-to-many
BiLinkVstr_to_BiLinkVstr<x,r>::add()     // many-to-many
```

Figure A.4 Constructing integrity rules in Versant

A.4 Summary

I showed in Chapter 4 that object-oriented methods that permit bi-directional associations compromise encapsulation and thereby reuse. I showed here how uni-directional mappings can replace associations entirely, with no loss of expressive power and complete conformance with the principle of encapsulation. The way the set-theoretic foundation of mappings – that was inherited from work on semantic data modelling – is normally presented, was shown to be defective. A corrected version was presented, where mappings are between power types. I also showed how encapsulating rulesets or class invariants in object types can be used to record the referential integrity constraints normally thought of as belonging to associations – outside of the classes. In doing this I questioned the common misuse of the term 'inverse' and suggested a more precise terminology with a firmer mathematical basis.

I believe firmly that methods that support bi-directional associations, such as UML, need urgent modification in this area if they are not to be used as covert relational modelling techniques by their users. The danger is that such bad practices will inevitably lead to the creation of a new generation of un-maintainable, un-reusable, 'object-oriented' legacy systems.

Object-oriented principles are not compromised by our solution:

- Encapsulation is not violated as only the public interface of the corresponding class is referenced, but no assumptions about internal handling are made.
- Integrity can be maintained by adding a rule that states that the two sets have to be compared. Should there be any mismatch, integrity could be re-established (this is in line with the inverse clause declaration of ODMG-93).
- By adding rules to the classes reuse is not thwarted, as knowledge about the integrity constraints is contained in the class itself. (If an ODMG-93 class is reused, association knowledge cannot be lost, since – at compile time – an exception would be raised stating that another class has to be imported as well.)

Finally I suggested that my framework provides a completely general and implementation independent way of modelling semantic integrity constraints of all types.

My conclusions about the best way to model associations may be of significance for database designers incorporating automatic integrity checking tools into their systems. It will undoubtedly influence the design of software tools that support object-oriented analysis and design. At present, the only tool known to me that implements this philosophy is *SOMATiK* but I suspect that other tools are likely to emerge as the issue of reuse becomes better understood through industrial practice.

B

Use cases and tasks

One of the best ways of avoiding necessary and even urgent tasks
is to seem to be busily employed on things that are already done.

J.K. Galbraith (The Affluent Society)

Use cases were introduced as a technique for object-oriented requirements capture by Jacobson *et al.* (1992) and have been almost universally recognized as a brilliant and useful idea by the object-oriented methods community. Most methodologists have either integrated use cases into their methods, intend to do so or acquiesce at the thought of users of their methods doing so themselves. Use cases offered possibly the first technique within object-oriented development that did not assume that a written requirements specification existed at the start of object-oriented analysis.

Task scripts were first introduced within the SOMA method and have three main intellectual ancestors: Jacobson's use cases, hierarchical task analysis as found in the HCI (human computer interaction) literature and the *scripts* found in the conceptual dependency theory of Schank and Abelson (1977). Rubin and Goldberg (1992) use the term *script* in their work on OBA and one suspects that this usage is derived in a similar way, though this was not stated explicitly; nor were their conclusions the same as ours.

Jacobson *et al.* (1992) define a **use case** as 'a behaviourally related sequence of transactions in a dialogue with the system' and 'a sequence of transactions in a system whose task is to yield a result of measurable value' (Jacobson *et al.*, 1995). The vagueness of these and other definitions in those two books indicates a number of problems with the theory and application of use cases that we discuss in this appendix in order not to interrupt the argument of the main text. This appendix sets out to define and clarify the exact nature of use cases and their relationship with our task scripts and task objects. I show how the task object modelling approach overcomes all deficiencies of use cases while introducing no new difficulties of its own.

⊟ B.1 Problems with use cases

At first sight, the use case approach appears to have a much more functional flavour than the object-oriented practitioner would be comfortable with. Blaha and Premerlani (1998), leading thinkers behind OMT, go so far as to include a treatment of use cases within the dataflow-based Functional Model of OMT. This has led some critics to claim that use cases are not really object-oriented at all. However, when use cases emerged it was clear that object-oriented analysis and design methods lacked an approach to requirements capture. Furthermore, most of these methods were entirely data-driven and this led to difficulties in communicating with users who were more comfortable with functionally oriented descriptions than with data-centred ones. So, while use cases and the Objectory method within which they were situated were rather 'functional' there was at least a small step forward beyond the methods that assumed the pre-existence of the requirements statement. The challenge was to integrate this advance and its functional viewpoint within a genuinely object-oriented, responsibility-driven approach rather than cobbling it together with a data-driven one.

MULTIPLE DEFINITIONS Far more seriously, the lack of a precise and universally accepted definition has led to a proliferation of approaches all calling themselves 'use case' based. It seems that every company has their own version of the theory. At a goldfish bowl session at Object Technology 96, held in Oxford, England, participants were asked if they used use cases. Of the 14 who said they did, each was asked to give a definition of a use case. The result was 14 different definitions; even though three of the respondents worked for the same company (in different divisions). Cockburn (1997) has obtained similar results in the USA. At a workshop on use cases at OOPSLA'97 Graham asked the other participants if they would deduce that this meant that a precisely defined notion of use cases (such as task scripts) should use a different name to make the issues clearer. The consensus that emerged from the discussion was, yes, we should really rename the idea but, no, the industry had bought the idea of use cases and so we had to live with the label – however ill defined. I disagree with this pessimism and continue to talk about task scripts, while recognizing our deep debt to Jacobson. Precision matters in Science and Engineering.

TOO MANY USE CASES Our experience with use cases dates back to about 1991, when I attempted to use them to capture the requirements for part of a banking application: deal capture. I quickly discovered that this relatively simple application was generating hundreds of use cases; far too many to be manageable! With task scripts there were ten: an order of magnitude improvement! This defect is potentially very serious, though in some domains (designing equipment such as vending machines or switch gear for example) it may not happen. In MIS domains I have often found that there are hundreds or even thousands of use cases precisely because there are many exceptional paths through a business process. The exceptions are not 'errors' as they would be in a computer program; they are important − often business critical − variants on the use case. Nor are they concrete scenarios, because they themselves are implemented in a multiplicity of concrete executable scenarios corresponding to actual use. From a practical point of view there was no longer any doubt which technique we would use in future, but the theoretical question of why this explosion in number took place remained. We now understand that there are several reasons that lead to this problem of multiplying too rapidly[1].

First of all we want to be able to treat use cases as *bona fide* objects so that we can reuse them. This turns out to be problematical because of the granularity of the typical use case, the fact that a use case can span several linked but independent tasks and because of the poor exception handling semantics in the theory.

Severe problems arise if we try to treat use cases as objects: a treatment that Jacobson hints at in several places. The structural links between use cases, *uses* and *extends* arrows, point in the wrong direction from the point of view of encapsulation. Therefore we are not able to treat use cases as *bona fide* objects. Therefore they are not really reusable. Since tasks are pure objects, we do not need to invent *uses* and *extends* links but can use existing and properly defined object-oriented linkage concepts such as composition and usage to cover the same semantics and, additionally, we get the notions of inheritance and task associations for free. Usage links give us a much better way of handling exceptions than is available with standard use cases, which suffer from the poor semantics of *extends*.

USES AND EXTENDS

One use case 'uses' another if the latter is 'part of its own description' (Jacobson *et al.,* 1995). Thus, the Objectory 'uses' relationship certainly corresponds to task decomposition using the APO (a-part-of) relation in SOMA. The difference here is one of interpretation. Objectory does not emphasize the discovery of use case components of this kind by top-down decomposition. Also the very term 'uses' could easily confuse people used to associating this word with some sort of client/server (usage) relationship.

A use case 'extends' another if it may be 'inserted into' the latter (Jacobson *et al.,* 1992). Thus, 'extends' in Objectory would correspond to 'is a side-script of' in SOMA, though the arrows are drawn in the opposite sense in the latter to preserve encapsulation; an extension of a task should not know that it is part of something bigger.

To use an example from Jacobson *et al.* (1992), consider the design of a vending machine, which accepts used containers for recycling. Returning item is the use case that describes a customer inserting a used container into the machine.

---

[1] This violation of Ockham's razor first emerged from several users' comments during a birds-of-a-feather session at Object Expo Europe in 1993. It is confirmed by anecdotal evidence from several projects known to us (but that may not be reported in detail for commercial reasons) and the observations of other practitioners.

The **Item is stuck** use case extends **Returning item** and describes what happens when the container jams in the chute. However, it does so in a foreseeable course of events, whereas the restaurant script only uses the **BananaSkin** script (discussed in Chapter 5) in the most exceptional circumstances, which may not be foreseen. One of the consequences of this in terms of implementation is that **EnterRestaurant** may have to perform a search for an appropriate script such as **BananaSkin** rather than store a reference to it statically. Once again, for reasons of encapsulation and the promotion of reuse, it is important that side-scripts do not know which scripts they 'extend', which is why it is important to model this relationship as a message send to the side-script, possibly involving a search.

The reader may be tempted to confuse our side-script notion with Jacobson's 'uses' or 'extends' relations. A careful reading of both the works of Jacobson cited reveals that this is not exactly the case though there is a considerable overlap. Our intention is to use a very pure concept of object modelling to model tasks. In this way the developer only has to learn only one set of terminology and concepts to model both tasks and business objects.

ATOMICITY As project managers we would like to believe that the number of use cases in a requirements analysis gives some indication of the business benefit or the final system or even of the amount of effort involved in building it. This would help with product pricing and project estimation. However, use cases are notoriously hard to measure, since a use case can be any length.

The lack of a notion of *atomicity* means that no metrics can be reasonably defined for use case models – unless we change their definition as many companies have indeed done: numbering the sentences of a use case for example. The task script notion includes a notion of atomicity that permits developers to measure task complexity by simply counting the atomic scripts. Recall that an atomic task script should ideally be a single sentence and be such that if further decomposed it would be necessary to introduce terminology from outside the domain ontology; i.e. words not in the vocabulary of users.

ESSENTIAL OR GENERIC USE CASES Another reason for the tendency to find too many use cases is the lack of any notion of essentiality or genericity.

There appears to be an overlap between the notion of task scripts and Constantine's *essential* use cases. However, the motivation is different and the embedding of the theory of task scripts within the approach to business process modelling described in Chapter 5 justifies its separate presentation.

Essential use cases abstract away from the detail of a use case in a different dimension from task scripts. As an example, the use case that deals with extracting cash from an ATM (Automatic Teller Machine) refers to inserting a card, entering a PIN and so on. The corresponding essential use case merely refers to withdrawing cash. This corresponds to what I have referred to as the *atomicity* of tasks. The atomic level depends on the purpose of the description and excludes terms foreign to the domain at that level of purpose. Constantine (1995) defines an essential use case as:

> 'an abstract use case describing the common structure of use cases representing a single intent or purpose of users in some rôle (Jacobson's "actors"), simplified and generalized to represent the essential core of something such users want or need to accomplish independent of implementation in a specific user interface or interface technology. An essential use case is expressed in user application domain terms and assumes idealized technology or is technology independent'.

This definition combines what I have called 'generification' and 'atomicity'. I think it is better to separate these concerns. As I show in the next section, a task script represents a generic use case. Thus, I would suggest that a task script that is atomic – or contains (has parts) nothing more specific than atomic tasks – should be called an essential task script. It then appears that an essential task script is the same as what Constantine calls an essential use case.

GOALS AND TRIGGERS   As several commentators have pointed out (e.g. Cockburn, 1997) it is problematic that use cases may be presented without business goals. This hampers traceability efforts and impedes the understanding of users. I would add that the absence of the notion of triggering events is also a deficiency. Recall from Chapter 5 that task objects have their scripts triggered by events in the agent model and that messages in that model have explicit goals. I think that this is a better solution than attaching the goals directly to use cases as suggested by Cockburn and by Rawsthorne *inter alia*. Clearly the goal or contract is in the mind of some agent rather than being something possessed by the task itself.

ASSOCIATION SETS OF TASKS   A use case covers a sequence of several possibly interchangeable tasks. For example consider a system that automatically prices orders and provides automatic quotations or diverts them, under certain criteria, to a salesman for manual pricing or quotation. It would be normal to have four use cases at the highest level of abstraction: autoprice quote, autoprice order, manual order and manual quote. This is not a parsimonious approach because the process of applying diversion rules that decide whether to re-route orders or quotes to the sales desk may be different for quotes and orders while the notification process is the same (or *vice versa*). For this reason it is better to have independent task scripts for the different components of the use case. These can then be assembled to model complete business processes. This promotes greater re-usability of task objects. We have already seen in Chapter 5 the rôle of SOMA sequence diagrams in illustrating the way user tasks are composed into end-to-end processes. I should remind the reader that SOMA sequence diagrams focus on users' task. UML sequence diagrams on the other hand focus on the operations of classes and are therefore intrinsically unsuitable for this purpose.

The upshot of this is that, while in most cases task scripts are merely generic use cases, it may be the case that a use case corresponds to a sequence or network of tasks linked by an association set; i.e. in a, possibly concurrent, sequence diagram.

RESTRICTION TO INTERFACE While they have been utilized successfully on many projects, use cases have been criticized for only dealing with the external, interface aspects of systems. This refers of course to all interfaces and not just the human computer interface.

The defect, if such it is, is deliberate. The intention was to focus designers' attention on what the system did for its users, rather than how it did it. While this is a laudable aim, and is quite the correct approach to take when building a telecommunications switch or a process controller, in many MIS applications – especially those replacing paper flow systems – the development team, consisting of users and developers, has expectations about how the system (not necessarily the computer system but the business system) will operate internally. These expectations are often the basis of insights into business processes and opportunities for re-engineering them. Thus, a variant on use cases that permits internal modelling can be desirable in such circumstances.

USE CASES AND SCENARIOS There has been some further confusion over the exact meaning of use cases among users of Jacobson's Objectory and OOSE methods and, therefore, of UML. For example, the problems referred to above are compounded by confusion over whether a use case is the same as a scenario. At OOPSLA 1994 a panel was posed the question of the relationship between scenarios and use cases. Jacobson and Booch agreed that a scenario was 'an instance of a use case' but the point was not elaborated further[2].

The use case approach asks developers to begin by discovering behaviourally related sequences of transactions in a dialogue with a system whose task is to yield a result of measurable value to actors who use the system. These descriptions are then mined for concepts and actions that will be implemented as classes and methods in a future system. Several other approaches recommend the study of scenarios of system use. In most cases a scenario is more detailed and specific than a use case and may mention individuals by name. Thus, 'The user enters the number' is a use case whereas 'John enters his wife's number' is a scenario – at least that is the understanding that will suffice for the purposes of this book.

CONTROLLER OBJECTS These problems with use cases are not the end of our critique of OOSE and, by implication, Objectory and UML. OOSE recommends that its use cases should be linked to three kinds of implementation object: entity objects [sic], interface objects and controller objects. The introduction of controller objects later in the analysis process can seriously violate the principle of encapsulation, leading to severe maintenance problems downstream. This is because controllers often act as main routines (especially when a data-driven approach is adopted) and have to know a great deal about the other objects that they control. Thus, when one of these objects changes the controller may have to be modified. This style of implementation, where the controller objects access several entity objects (i.e. datastores), was shown

---

[2] See Addendum to the OOPSLA 1994 conference proceedings.

to be inferior to a responsibility-driven design in the study of Sharble and Cohen (1992) discussed in Chapter 1, Section 1.5.1. A far better approach is the use of rule-based agents as discussed in Chapters 5 and 6.

As if all these criticisms were not enough, there is even a problem with the phrase USE CASE itself being, I suspect, a literal translation of a Swedish construction. It makes for very unwieldy and unprosodic expressions in English, such as 'using uses links between the use cases we use is used to show ...'.

What can be done to fix all these problems? What is needed is an approach with a sound, theoretical basis and a precise definition. We need a notion of *genericity* and a notion of *atomicity* for use cases or their equivalent. Use cases have no clear link to a business process model and are offered as such a model in their own right, which I feel does not make good sense. Finally, we need an approach that is properly object-oriented in supporting encapsulation and inheritance. The task modelling approach of SOMA, presented in Chapter 5 fulfils all these criteria.

I suspect that the different ways of thinking about the problems of requirements engineering partly reflect differences in the domains within which Objectory and SOMA grew up, and especially differences among the typical users that are encountered in these domains. Telecommunication engineers are usually quite happy with detailed specification and will be comfortable with, for example, state machine notations. Bankers do not often respond well to such approaches. A further practical consequence is a vast reduction in the sheer size of the model. Booch, who has accumulated experience of the technique, remarked that: 'Most systems are characterized by 10 [high level] use cases, an order of magnitude more primary use cases and an[other] order of magnitude more secondary use cases' (Grotehen, 1995). The chief reason for this explosion seems to be the lack of generic exception handling and the nature of the 'uses' and 'extends' notion as discussed above.

⊟ B.2 Task scripts as generic use cases

Now we are in a position to define the differences and relationships between the concepts of task scripts, use cases and scenarios. To overcome the lack of essentiality referred to above, what is required is a generification[3] of the idea of use cases that prevents this explosion in their number. Task scripts are just such a generic concept that, additionally, allows developers to model the internals of the business process and its implementation.

---

[3] The OED describes this word as more precise than GENERALIZATION: 'the abstraction which carries up species into genera'. It is used here in the sense of 'making a generic representative'.

As remarked earlier, a scenario is often seen as an instance of a use case: it describes an actual occurrence of the use case. Intuitively, too, a use case could be thought of as an instance of a linked set of task scripts: it describes a typical path through the business model. Unfortunately, this terminology does not bear closer scrutiny because a scenario is an instance of the class of scenarios and the class of *all* scenarios will not correspond to a sensible use case. The idea, however, is sound and can be rephrased by saying that task scripts *generify* use cases in the sense that a set of task scripts is a generic use case or an equivalence class of use cases. They do not *generalize* use cases; they make them generic. Similarly, a use case is a generic scenario. Thus we have three levels of abstraction or genericity: scenarios, use cases and task scripts as shown in Figure B.1.

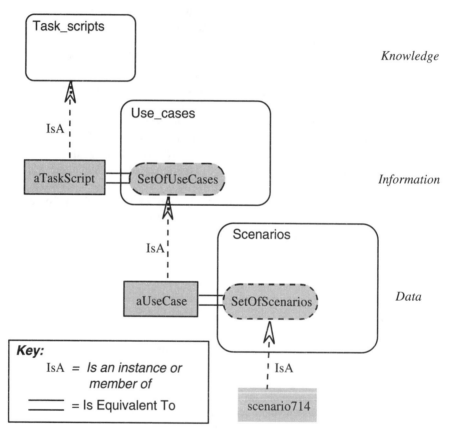

Figure B.1 Scripts, use cases and scenarios

Examining Figure B.1, we may now define a **use case** as *an equivalence class of scenarios* and a **task script** as *an equivalence class of use case segments*. Task scripts *generify* use cases in the sense that a task script is a **generic** or **essential** use case segment. Similarly, a use case is a generic scenario. A use case is equivalent to the set of scenarios that can implement it and a task script sequence is equivalent to the set of use cases that can implement it. The equivalence relations are easily defined informally but may often be fuzzy relations in the sense of Zadeh (1971). For example, the relation could equate all scenarios where some individual enters the phone number of some other individual, or all 'eating out' use cases. For an example of the fuzzy case, we could instantiate the EnterRestaurant script with the use case for entering a fast food establishment although, so far as I can see, most of the latter bear a very fuzzy relationship to any normal concept of a restaurant. In fact, we know that the term restaurant is misapplied *precisely* because of our sense of unease when we try to invoke our standard restaurant script in McDonalds or Wendy.

Figure B.1 shows a particular scenario as an instance of a subclass of the class of Scenarios. That subclass consists of all the scenarios that are equivalent to scenario714 under the nominated equivalence relation[4]. This subclass is identified with a particular use case which, in turn, is viewed a belonging to a subclass of the class Use_cases defined by an equivalence relation. This latter subclass is (identified with) a task script.

So, a use case is equivalent to the set of scenarios that can implement it and a task script sequence is equivalent to the set of use cases that can implement it. A use case represents the intension of its set of scenarios, whose extension will rarely be described exhaustively. Similarly, a task script represents the intension of its set of use cases. The advantage of moving to the task script level is principally that we abstract away from specific exceptions that tend to increase the total number of use cases to an unacceptable extent.

The three levels of abstraction correspond (informally) to the three traditional levels of information systems modelling: data, information and knowledge. The levels are nothing to do with the difference between abstract and concrete use cases as Jacobson has suggested[5]. That distinction only tells us how we classify or generalize scenarios and use cases. We can do the same thing with task scripts and define an abstract task as one having no instances. What is needed is not generalization but generification.

As we saw earlier, the advantage of moving to the task script level is principally that we abstract away from specific exceptions that tend to increase the total number of use cases to an unacceptable extent

The arrangement of instances, classes and subclasses shown in Figure B.1 is actually a very common one in object modelling and suggests what is now widely referred to as a *pattern*, although it is a pattern related to knowledge elicitation

---

[4] Note that SOMA uses IsA for the instance/class relationship and AKO for the subclass/superclass relationship in accordance with the standard practice in work on artificial intelligence but at variance with that of semantic data modelling.

[5] Private communication.

rather than to design or systems analysis where most currently known patterns have been discovered. We call this pattern the Syllogism pattern.

B.3 The syllogism pattern for use case generation

Diversion

As we saw in Chapters 2 and 5, in workshops, users walk through the dynamics of the system they have defined, rôle-playing the class cards that represent the Business Object Model to ensure that every task script can be executed by the combined class cards working together in parallel. The walkthrough tests that the Business Object Model actually supports all the users' tasks. It is instructive to analyze exactly what goes on during such a simulation from the point of view of the pattern given in Figure B.2. The event trace that the walkthrough produces represents a use case but this use case is generated from the task script and the process is initiated by the workshop facilitator giving a very concrete scenario. For example, for the order capture task, the facilitator might – in acting the rôle of the order clerk – say: 'Elvis, my pal down at ZapMart has just phoned in a order asking for 200 chocolate covered widgets for delivery next Tuesday'.

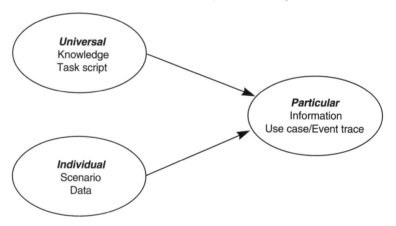

Figure B.2 The syllogism pattern

The movement here is from the individual to the particular via the general: start with the (individual) scenario and then use the (universal) task script to generate a corresponding (particular) use case. This is a particular case of a syllogism, although the reader should be aware that we are using the term in the very general sense used by Hegel in his *Science of Logic* (Miller, 1969) rather than in the common manner that refers only to Aristotle's syllogism of deduction: Gaius is a man, all men are mortal, therefore Gaius is mortal. Hegel's syllogisms dealt with the various relationships between categories, notably between Particular,

Individual and Universal. The deductive syllogism can be represented by the triplet: I-P-U[6]. In the syllogism pattern of Figure B.2 we are dealing with the same I-P-U triplet but using it to generate the particular (use case – event trace) out of the universal (task script) together with the individual (scenario). Clearly, this is not the same as ordinary deductive logic but it is a syllogism in this Hegelian sense and it is, from a more practical viewpoint, a formula for a certain process of knowledge elicitation or requirements capture. Nor should this pattern be thought of as or confused with a 'design pattern' in the sense of Gamma *et al.* (1995); it is more akin to a pattern of thought that recurs in many analysis contexts but one that may have little relation to program design. Thus, I make no attempt to present it in the so-called Alexandrian[7] form.

⊟ B.4 Summary and conclusions

This appendix set out a view on the relationship between the concepts of task scripts, use cases and scenarios. This serves to clarify much of the terminological confusion that exists currently. I believe that our approach to object-oriented requirements engineering and business process re-engineering has a number of advantages over the widely used use case technique. I pointed out some problems with the use case approach. I offered a *generification* of the use case idea: the task script. Task scripts have real, practical advantages over use cases in terms of preventing the unnecessary multiplication of use cases and permitting analysts to penetrate the system boundary more effectively with their understanding. This is significant in MIS domains. Use cases are not abandoned but they cease to be either the starting point for requirements capture or the units of business process reuse. Task scripts can be represented as objects and fill these rôles very well.

Whether you accept that task scripts are a genuine generification of use cases or regard them as two names for the same thing, one thing is clear: the whole approach to knowledge discovery and business modelling is quite different in the two approaches.

Practical experience has borne out the advantages of our approach on over 100 projects undertaken since 1993. This experience confirms that the method of requirements engineering based on task script elicitation within a business process model and described in this book is intensely practical. I conclude that it should be of wide applicability and could be used as a precursor to the use of almost any

---

[6] Hegel describes this syllogism as follows: 'Individuality unites with universality through particularity'. The first term is a statement of a subsistent universal, the second relates an individual (instance) to a particular (class) leading to the proposition in the third term.

[7] The architect Christopher Alexander is responsible for inspiring among software engineers a standard way of presenting patterns (Alexander, 1977).

method of object-oriented analysis, not just SOMA, and I recommend it to practitioners for their further evaluation.

Our experience, and that of others, on various projects has been that the approach described here is very effective, especially in building an understanding of projects that is shared by both users and developers. The subject matter of these projects was varied, including trade settlement, battle scenario planning, compliance, client data management, client position reporting, credit card clearing, stock lending and borrowing, merchant banking, accounting, order processing, visitor management, service management, telephone system management, project administration, derivatives processing and settlement, repo trading, electronic stock exchange trading, corporate actions, network management and security, CASE tool development, workflow and document image management. Of course, I am not claiming that the approach was uniformly successful on all projects and it is probably impossible to isolate the effect of the approach from all the other factors that affect the success of projects. However, most of the project managers that I have interviewed have responded that the approach to requirements gathering had been effective, beneficial and had helped to lay the basis for a good relationship with users throughout their projects.

In conclusion, use cases were a brilliant idea and no one before Jacobson had addressed requirements for object-oriented projects. They matched the needs of people building telecommunications switches well ... but they weren't perfect. For example, some commercial MIS proved too tough. Task scripts were developed to provide software developers with a choice.

Some of the material in this appendix first appeared in Graham (1996).

REFERENCES

Abbott, R.J. (1983) Program design by informal english descriptions, *Communications of the ACM* **26**(11), 882–894

Alexander, C. (1977) *A Pattern Language*, New York: Oxford University Press

Alexander, C. (1979) *The Timeless Way of Building*, New York: Oxford University Press

Austin, J.L. (1962) *How to Do Things with Words*, Cambridge MA: Harvard University Press

Bachman, C. (1977) The rôle concept in data models. In *Proceedings of the 3rd International Conference on Very Large Databases*, IEEE, New York, 464–476

Berard, E.V. (1993) *Essays on Object-Oriented Software Engineering – Volume 1*, Englewood Cliffs NJ: Prentice Hall

Bezant (1997) *SOMATiK: A Tutorial*, Wallingford, England: Bezant Ltd.

Bigus, J.P. and Bigus, J. (1998) *Constructing Intelligent Agents with JAVA*, New York: Wiley

Blaha, M. and Premerlani, W. (1998) *Object-Oriented Modelling and Design for Database Applications*, Upper Saddle River NJ: Prentice Hall

Booch, G. (1982) Object-Oriented Design, *Ada Letters* **1**(3), 64–76

Booch, G. (1991) *Object Oriented Design with Applications*, Benjamin/Cummings

Booch, G. (1994) *Object Oriented Design with Applications*, 2nd Edition, CA: Benjamin/Cummings

Browne, D. (1994) *STructured User-interface Design for Interaction Optimisation*, Hemel Hempstead, England: Prentice Hall

Buschmann, F., Meunier, R., Rohnert, H., Sommerlad, P. and Stal, M. (1996) *Pattern-oriented Software Architecture: A System of Patterns*, Chichester, England: Wiley

Carrington, D., Duke, D., Duke, R., King, P., Rose, G. and Smith, G. (1990) Object-Z: An object-oriented extension to Z. In *Formal Description Techniques II*, Amsterdam: North-Holland

Carroll, J.M. (1995) *Scenario-Based Design*, Chichester, England: Wiley

Cattell, R. (Ed) (1994) *The Object Database Standard: ODMG-93,* San Mateo, CA: Morgan Kaufmann Publishers

Champeaux, D. de (1997) *Object-Oriented Development Process and Metrics*, Upper Saddle River NJ: Prentice Hall

Checkland, P. (1981) *Systems Thinking, Systems Practice*, Chichester, England: Wiley

Checkland, P. and Scholes, J. (1991) *Soft Systems Methodology in Action*, Chichester, England: Wiley

Chidamber, S.R. and Kemerer, C.F. (1991) Towards a metrics suite for object-oriented design, in Paepcke, A. (Ed) (1991) *OOPSLA'91 ACM Conference on Object-Oriented Programming Systems, Languages and Applications*, Reading MA: Addison-Wesley

Chidamber, S.R. and Kemerer, C.F. (1993) A metrics suite for object-oriented design, CISR Working Paper 249, MIT Sloan School of Management, Cambridge MA

Chidamber, S.R. and Kemerer, C.F. (1994) A metrics suite for object-oriented design, *IEEE Trans. Software Engineering* **20**, 476–493

Coad, P. and Yourdon, E. (1989) *Object-Oriented Analysis*, 1st Edition, Englewood Cliffs NJ: Yourdon Press/Prentice Hall

Coad, P. and Yourdon, E. (1991) *Object-Oriented Analysis*, 2nd Edition, Englewood Cliffs NJ: Yourdon Press/Prentice Hall

Coad, P., North, D. and Mayfield, M. (1997) *Object Models: Strategies, Patterns and Applications*, Upper Saddle River NJ:Prentice Hall

Cockburn, A. (1997) Using goal-based use cases, *J. Object-Oriented Programming* **10**(5)

Coleman, D., Arnold, P., Bodoff, S., Dollin, C., Gilchrist, H., Hayes, F. and Jeremaes, P. (1994) *Object-Oriented Development: The Fusion Method*, Englewood Cliffs NJ: Prentice Hall

Constantine, L.L. (1995) Essential modeling: use cases for user interfaces, *Interactions* (ACM), **2**(2)

Cook, S. and Daniels, J. (1994) *Designing Object Systems*, Hemel Hempstead, England: Prentice Hall

Coplien, J.O. (1992) *Advanced C++: Programming Styles and Idioms*, Reading MA: Addison-Wesley

Coplien, J.O. (1995) A generative development-process pattern language. In Coplien and Schmidt, 1995

Coplien, J.O. and Schmidt, D. (Eds) (1995) *Pattern Languages of Program Design*, Reading NJ:Addison-Wesley

Cox, B.J. and Novobilski, A. (1991) *Object-Oriented Programming – An Evolutionary Approach*, 2nd Ed., Reading MA: Addison-Wesley

Cox, E. (1994) *The Fuzzy Systems Handbook* , New York NY: Academic Press

Davenport, T.H. (1993) *Process Innovation: Reengineering work through Information Technology*, Harvard: Business School Press

Davenport, T.H. and Short, J.E. (1990) The new industrial engineering: information technology and business process redesign, *Sloan Management Review*, Summer 1990, 11–27

Delobel, C., Lecluse, C. and Richard, P. (1992*) Databases: From Relational to Object-Oriented Systems*, International Thompson Publishing

Dorfman, M. and Thayer, R.H. (1990) *Standards, Guidelines and Examples on System and Software Requirements Engineering*, Los Alamitos, CA: IEEE Computer Society Press

D'Souza, D. (1997) Framework and Component Based Design, Tutorial Notes, Object Expo Europe '97

D'Souza, D. and Wills, A.C. (1997) *Component-Based Development using Catalysis*, Draft manuscript

Duke, R., King, P., Rose, G. and Smith, G. (1991) *The Object-Z Specification, Version 1*, Software Verification Research Centre, University of Queensland Technical Report 91–1

Eason, K.D. (1989) Tools for participation: How managers and users can influence design. In Knight, K. (Ed) *Participation in Systems Development*, London: Kogan Page

Ehn, P. (1988) *Work-oriented Design of Computer Artifacts*, Arbetslivscentrum, Stockholm

Ehn. P. and Kyng, M. (1991) Cardboard computers: mocking up hands-on-the future. In Greenbaum, J. and Kyng, M. (Eds) *Design at Work: Co-operative Design of Computer Systems*, Hillsdale NJ: Lawrence Erlbaum

Ehn, P., Mollervd, B. and Sjogren, D. (1990) Playing in reality: a paradigm case, *Scand. J. Inf. Systems* **2**, 101–120

Farhoodi, F. (1994) CADDIE: an advanced tool for organizational design and process modelling. In *Software Assistance for Business Re-Engineering*, Chichester: Wiley

Ferber, J. (1995) *Les Systèms Multi-Agents: Vers une intelligence collective*, Paris: InterEditions

Firesmith, D., Henderson-Sellers, B. and Graham, I.M. (1997) *OPEN Modeling Language Reference Manual*, NY: SIGS Books, Cambridge University Press

Flores, F. (1997) The leaders of the future. In Denning, P.J. and Metcalfe, R.M. (Eds) *Beyond Calculation: The next 50 years of computing*, New York: Copernicus

Fowler, M. (1996) *Analysis Patterns*, Harlow, England: Addison-Wesley

Fowler, M. (1997) *UML Explained*, Harlow, England: Addison-Wesley

Gabriel, R.P (1996) *Patterns of Software*, Oxford: University Press

Gamma, E., Helm, R. Johnson, R. and Vlissedes, J. (1995) *Design Patterns: Elements of Reusable Object-Oriented Software*, Reading NJ:Addison-Wesley

Gause, D. and Weinberg, G. (1989) *Exploring Requirements*, New York NY: Dorset House

Goldberg, A. and Rubin, K. (1995) *Succeeding with Objects*, Reading NJ:Addison-Wesley

Goodall, A. (1994) The year of the agent, *AI Watch* **3**(8), 1–10

Graham, I.M. (1991) *Object-Oriented Methods,* 1st Edition, Wokingham, England: Addison-Wesley

Graham, I.M. (1994) *Object-Oriented Methods,* 2nd Edition, Wokingham, England: Addison-Wesley

Graham, I.M. (1995) *Migrating to Object Technology*, Wokingham, England: Addison-Wesley

Graham, I.M. (1996) Task scripts, use cases and scenarios in object-oriented analysis, *Object-Oriented Systems* **3**(3), 1996, 123–142

Graham, I.M. and Jones, P.L.K. (1988) *Expert Systems: Knowledge, Uncertainty and Decision*, London: Chapman & Hall

Graham, I.M. and O'Callaghan, A. (1997) Migration Strategies, Tutorial Notes: Object World London.

Graham, I.M., Bischof, J. and Henderson-Sellers, B. (1997) Associations considered a bad thing, *J. Object-Oriented Programming*, **9**(9)

Graham, I.M., Henderson-Sellers, B. and Yanoussi, H. (1997a) *The OPEN Process Specification*, Harlow, England: Addison-Wesley

Gray, P. (1984) *Logic, Algebra and Databases*, Chichester: Ellis Horwood

Grotehen, T. (1995) Notes on a meeting with Grady Booch 1995.07.27 (unpublished communication)

Guilfoyle, C. and Warner, E. (1994) *Intelligent Agents: The New Revolution in Software*, Ovum Ltd.

Halé, J. (1996) *From Concepts to Capabilities: Understanding and Exploiting Change as a Competitive Advantage*, Chichester UK: Wiley

Hammer, M. (1990) Reengineering work: don't automate, obliterate, *Harvard Business Review*, July-August 1990, 104–112

Hammer, M. and Champy, J. (1993) *Re-engineering the Corporation: A manifesto for the business revolution*, New York: Harper Collins

Harmon, P. and Taylor, D.A. (1993) *Objects in Action*, Reading NJ: Addison-Wesley

Hart, A. (1989) *Knowledge Acquisition for Expert Systems*, 2nd Edition, London: Kogan Page

Henderson-Sellers, B. (1996) *Object-Oriented Metrics: Measures of Complexity*, Sydney: Prentice Hall

Henderson-Sellers, B. (1998) OPEN relationships – associations, mappings, dependencies and uses, *Journal of Object-Oriented Programming* **10**(9), 49–57

Henderson-Sellers, B. and Edwards, J. (1994) *BOOK TWO of Object-Oriented Knowledge: The Working Object*, Sydney, Aus: Prentice Hall

Henderson-Sellers, B. and Pant, Y.R. (1993) Adopting the reuse mindset throughout the lifecycle, *Object Magazine* **3**(4), 73–75

Henderson-Sellers, B., Constantine, L.L. and Graham, I.M. (1996) Coupling and cohesion: towards a valid metrics suite for object-oriented analysis and design, *Object-Oriented Systems* **3**(3), 143–158

Humphrey, W.S. (1989) *Managing the Software Process*, Reading MA: Addison-Wesley

Jackson, M.A. (1983) *System Development*, Chichester, England: Prentice Hall

Jackson, M.A. (1995) *Software Requirements and Specifications*, Harlow, England: Addison-Wesley

Jacobson, I., Christerson, M. Jonsson, P. and Overgaard, G. (1992) *Object-Oriented Software Engineering: A Use Case Driven Approach*, Wokingham, England: Addison-Wesley

Jacobson, I., Ericsson, M. and Jacobson, A. (1995) *The Object Advantage: Business Process Re-engineering with Object Technology,* Wokingham UK: Addison-Wesley

Jones, C. (1994) *Assessment and Control of Software Risks*, Englewood Cliffs NJ: Yourdon Press

Jones, P.L.K. (1999) *Practical Rapid Development*, Harlow UK: Addison-Wesley

Kelly, G.A. (1955) *The Psychology of Personal Constructs*, New York: W.W. Norton

Kendall, E.A., Malkoun, M.T. and Chong, J. (1997) The application of object-oriented analysis to agent-based systems, *J. of Object-Oriented Programming*, **9**(9), 56–65

Kristen, G. (1995) *Object-Orientation: The KISS Method*, Wokingham UK: Addison-Wesley

Larman, C. (1998) *Applying UML and Patterns*, Upper Saddle River NJ: Prentice Hall

Lewis, E. (Ed) (1995) *Object-Oriented Application Frameworks*, Greenwich, CT: Manning

Lorenz, M. (1993) *Object-Oriented Software Development: A Practical Guide*, Englewood Cliffs NJ: Prentice Hall

Lorenz, M. and Kidd, J. (1994) *Object-Oriented Software Metrics*, Englewood Cliffs NJ: Prentice Hall

Macaulay, L.A. (1996) *Requirements Engineering*, London: Springer

MacLane, S. (1971) *Categories for the Working Mathematician*, New York: Springer

MacLean, R., Stepney, S., Smith, S., Tordoff, N., Gradwell, D. and Hoverd, T. (1994*) Analysing Systems: Determining Requirements for Object-Oriented Development*, Hemel Hempstead, England: Prentice Hall

Maiden, N.A.M. and Rugg, G. (1996) ACRE: selecting methods for requirements acquisition*, IEE Software Engineering Journal*, May, 183–192

Maiden, N.A.M. and Sutcliffe, A.G. (1994) Requirements critiquing using domain abstractions, *Proc. of IEEE Conference on Requirements Engineering*, IEEE Computer Society Press, 184–193

Maiden, N.A.M., Minocha, S., Manning, K. and Ryan, M. (1997) *SAVRE: Systematic Scenario Generation and Use*, Centre for HCI Design, City University, London

Maiden, N.A.M., Cisse, M., Perez, H. and Manuel, D. (1998) *CREWS Validation Frames: Patterns for Validating Systems Requirements*, Centre for Human Computer Interface Design, City University, London

Malan, R., Letsinger, R. and Coleman, D. (1996) *Object-Oriented Development at Work*, Upper Saddle River NJ: Prentice Hall

Martin, J. and Odell, J. (1992) *Object-Oriented Analysis and Design*, Englewood Cliffs NJ: Prentice Hall

Martin, J. and Odell, J.J. (1995) *Object-Oriented Methods: A Foundation*, Englewood Cliffs NJ:Prentice Hall

Martin, J. and Odell, J.J. (1998) *Object-Oriented Methods: A Foundation (UML Edition)*, Englewood Cliffs NJ: Prentice Hall

McCabe, T.J. (1976) A complexity measure, *IEEE Trans. on Software Engineering*, **2**(4), 308–320

McLarty, C. (1992) *Elementary Categories, Elementary Toposes*, Oxford University Press

Menzies, T., Edwards, J.M. and Ng, K. (1992) The case of the mysterious missing reusable libraries, in Meyer, B. and Potter, J. (Eds) (1992) *TOOLS 9*, Sydney: Prentice Hall

Meyer, B. (1988) *Object-Oriented Software Construction*, Englewood Cliffs NJ: Prentice Hall

Meyer, B. (1994) *Reusable Software: The Base Object-Oriented Component Libraries*, Hemel Hempstead, England: Prentice Hall

Meyer, B. and Nerson, J-M. (Eds) (1993) *Object-Oriented Applications*, Englewood Cliffs NJ: Prentice Hall

Miller, A.V. (1969) *Hegel's Science of Logic* (translation), London: George, Allen and Unwin

Morgan, G. (1997) *Images of Organization*, Thousands Oaks, CA: Sage

Mumford, E. (1986) *Designing Systems for Business Success: The ETHICS Method*, Manchester: Business School

O'Callaghan, A. (1997) Object-oriented reverse engineering*, Application Development Adviser* **1**(1), 35–39

O'Callaghan, A. (1997a) Realizing the reality, *Application Development Adviser* **1**(2), 30–33

O'Callaghan, A. (1998) A plethora of patterns, *Application Development Adviser* **1**(3), 32–33

Odell, J.J. (1994) Six different kinds of composition, *J. of Object-Oriented Programming* **5**(8), 10–15

ODI (1992) *ObjectStore Release 2.0 User Guide and Reference Manual*, Object Design Inc., 1 New England Executive Park, Burlington MA

Ousterhout, J.K. (1994) *Tcl and the Tk Toolkit*, Reading MA: Addison-Wesley

Page-Jones, M. (1992) Comparing Techniques by means of Encapsulation and Connascence, *Comms. ACM* **35**(9), 147–151

Parson, J. and Wand, Y. (1995) Using objects for systems analysis, *Communications of the ACM*, **40**(12), 104–110

Pohl, K. (1993) The three dimensions of requirements engineering. In Rolland, C., Bodart, F. and Cauvet, C. (Eds) *Proc. CAISE'93*, Paris: Springer, 175–292

Pohl, K., Jarke, M. and Weidenhaupt, K. (1997) The use of scenarios during systems development – the current state of practice, submitted to *ICRE*

Pree, W. (1995) *Design Patterns for Object-Oriented Software Development*, Reading MA: Addison-Wesley

Rational (1997) *UML Notation Guide*, Internet: www.rational.com

Reason, J.T. (1990) *Human Error*, Cambridge: University Press

Reenskaug, T., Wold P. and Lehne A. (1996) *Working with Objects: The OOram Software Engineering Method*, Englewood Cliffs NJ: Prentice Hall

Riecken, D. (1994) Special Issue on Intelligent Agents, *Comms ACM*, July

Robinson, K. and Berrisford, G. (1994) *Object-Oriented SSADM*, Englewood Cliffs NJ: Prentice Hall

Rubin, K. and Goldberg, A. (1992) Object Behaviour Analysis, *Comms. of the ACM* **35**(9), Sept 1992, 48–62

Rumbaugh, J., Blaha, M., Premerlani, W. *et al.* (1991) *Object-Oriented Modelling and Design*, Englewood Cliffs NJ: Prentice Hall

Rush, G. (1985) The fast way to define system requirements, *Computerworld*, October 7th

Russell, S. and Norvig, P. (1995) *Artificial Intelligence: A Modern Approach*, Englewood Cliffs NJ: Prentice Hall

Schank, R.C. and Abelson, R.P. (1977) *Scripts, Plans, Goals and Understanding,* Boston MA: Lawrence Erlbaum Associates

Searle, J.R. (1969) *Speech Acts*, Cambridge: University Press

Selic, B., Gullekson, G. and Ward, P.T. (1994) *Real-time Object-Oriented Modelling*, New York: Wiley

Senge, P.M. (1990) *The Fifth Discipline: The Art And Practice Of The Learning Organization*, New York: Doubleday

Sharble, R.S. and Cohen, S. (1994) The object-oriented brewery: a comparison of two OO development methods, *ACM Sigsoft* **18**(2)

Shaw, M. and Garlan, D. (1996) *Software Architecture: Perspectives on an Emerging Discipline*, Englewood Cliffs NJ: Prentice Hall.

Shlaer, S. and Mellor, S.J. (1988) *Object-Oriented Systems Analysis – Modelling the World in Data*, Englewood Cliffs NJ: Yourdon Press

Short, J.E. and Venkatramen, N. (1992) Beyond business process redesign: redefining Baxter's business network, *Sloan Management Review*, Fall, 7–17

Sims, O. (1994) *Business Objects: Delivering Cooperative Objects for Client-Server*, London: McGraw-Hill

Stapleton, J. (1997) *Dynamic Systems Development Method: The Method in Practice*, Harlow, England: Addison-Wesley

Suchman, L.A. (1987) *Plans and Situated Actions: The Problem of Human Machine Communication*, Cambridge, England: University Press

Swatman, P.A. and Swatman, P.M.C. (1992) Formal specification: an analytic tool for (management) information systems, *J. of Information Systems*, **2**(2), 121–160

Taylor, D. (1992) *Object-Oriented Information Systems: Planning and Implementation*, New York: Wiley

Taylor, D.A. (1995) *Business Engineering with Object Technology*, New York: John Wiley & Sons

Taylor, D. (1997) *Object-Oriented Technology: A Manager's Guide,* 2nd *Edition*, Reading MA: Addison-Wesley

Texel, P.T. and Williams, C.B. (1997*) Use Cases Combined with Booch/OMT/UML: Process and Products*, Upper Saddle River NJ: Prentice Hall

Vlissides, J., Kerth, N. and Coplien, J.O. (Eds) (1996) *Pattern Languages of Program Design 2*, Reading NJ:Addison-Wesley

Wand, Y. (1989) A Proposal for a Formal Model of Objects. In Kim, W. and Lochovsky, F.H. (Eds) (1989) *Object-oriented Concepts, Databases and Applications*, Reading MA: Addison-Wesley

Waldén, K. and Nerson, J-M. (1995) *Seamless Object-Oriented Software Architecture*, NY: Prentice Hall

Webster, J. (1996) *Shaping Women's Work: Gender, Employment and Information Technology*, London: Longman Sociology

Weyuker, E. (1988) Evaluating software complexity measures, *IEEE Trans. on Software Engineering* **14**(9), 1357–1365

Whitmire, S.A. (1997) *Object-Oriented Design Measurement*, New York: Wiley

Wieringa, R.J. (1996) *Requirements Engineering*, Chichester, England: Wiley

Winograd, T. and Flores, F. (1986) *Understanding Computers and Cognition*, Reading MA: Addison-Wesley

Wirfs-Brock, R. and McKean, A. (1996) *Responsibility-Driven Design*, unpublished tutorial notes

Wirfs-Brock, R., Wilkerson, B. and Wiener, L. (1990) *Designing Object-Oriented Software*, Englewood Cliffs NJ: Prentice Hall

Yuan, G. (1995) A depth-first process model for object-oriented development with improved OOA/OOD notations, *Report on Object-Oriented Analysis and Design* **2**(1), 23–37

Zadeh, L.A. (1971) Similarity relations and fuzzy orderings, *Information Sciences* **3** 177–200

NAME INDEX

A

Abbott, R.J., 82
Abelson, R.C., 141, 243
Abrial, J.R., 227, 231
Alexander, C., 201, 222, 253
Austin, J.L., 133

B

Bachman, C., 230
Beck, K., 27
Berard, E., 12
Berrisford, G., 228
Blaha, M., 26, 244
Booch, E.G., 6, 18, 25, 26, 28,
    29, 248, 249
Browne, D., 87
Bunge, M., 213
Buschmann, F., 202, 204, 223

C

Calder, P., 223
Carrington, D., 33
Carroll, J.M., 58
Cattell, R., 237
Checkland, P., 37, 179
Chidamber, S., 211-13, 215,
    216
Coad, P., 6, 26, 99, 202, 205,
    223, 228, 230
Cockburn, A., 244, 247, 138
Cohen, 249
Cohen, S., 24
Coleman, D., 27
Constantine, L.L., 213, 214,
    246, 247
Cook, S., 8, 27, 33, 85, 86
Coplien, J.O., 201, 204, 222,
    223
Cox, B., 215
Cunningham, W., 27

D

D'Souza, D., 33, 89, 205
Daniels, J., 27, 33, 85, 86
Davenport, T.H., 179
de Champeaux, D., 86, 216, 223
Delobel, C., 228, 240
Dorfman, M., 32
Duke, D., 33

E

Eason, K.D., 35
Edwards, J., 26, 28, 54, 211,
    229, 234
Ehn, P., 35
Fagan, 56
Farhoodi, F., 189, 195
Ferber, J., 195
Firesmith, D., 28, 88, 90, 96,
    121
Flores, F., 35, 132, 133, 135,
    167-68, 176
Fowler, 88, 90, 202, 203, 205,
    209, 223

G

Gamma, E., 91, 201, 204, 222,
    223, 253
Garlan, D., 197, 198, 222
Gause, D., 83
Genesereth, M.R., 180
Goldberg, A.,27, 243
Goodall, A., 181
Graham, I.M., 3, 5, 19, 28-29,
    44, 49-51, 58, 81, 83, 90,
    117, 122-23, 126, 195, 204,
    213, 228, 244, 254
Gray, P.M.D., 231
Grotehen, T., 249
Guilfoyle, C., 180

H

Halé, J., 179
Hammer, M., 179
Harmon, P., 22
Hart, 81
Hegel, G.F., 252, 253
Henderson-Sellers, B., 28, 45,
    52, 54, 103, 211, 213-15,
    223, 229, 234
Humphrey, W., 220

J

Jackson, M.., 32, 34, 58, 84, 85,
    86, 134, 203, 204, 223
Jacobson
Jacobson, I., 27-28, 42, 128,
    134, 139, 141, 165, 176,
    184, 188-89, 243-48, 251,
    254
Jones, C., 221
Jones, P.L.K., 81, 83, 117, 123,
    126, 176

K

Kay, A., 5
Kelly, G.A., 80
Kemerer, C., 211, 212, 213, 215
Kendall, E.A., 180, 182
Ketchpel, S., 180
Kidd, J., 215
Kristen, G., 134

L

Larman, C., 223
Lewis, E., 223
Lorenz, M., 215, 217

M

Macaulay, L.A., 32, 57, 83
McCabe, T.J., 211, 212, 214, 217
McKean, 94
MacLane, S., 223
McLarty, C., 231
MacLean, R., 36, 58
Maiden, N.A.M.,35, 58, 155, 204
Malan, R., 27
Martin, J., 23, 26, 117, 230, 233
Mellor, S.J., 6, 23, 24, 26, 228, 230
Menzies, T., 52
Meyer, B., 14, 22, 98
Miller, A.V., 252
Morgan, G., 56, 220
Mumford, E., 34

N

Nerson, J-M., 22, 27, 188, 234
Norvig, P., 180
Novobilski, A., 215

O

O'Callaghan, A., 121, 204
Odell, J., 23, 26, 102, 117, 230, 231, 232, 233
Ousterhout, J.K., 181

P

Page-Jones, M., 214

Pant, Y.R., 52
Pohl, K., 32, 155
Powell, J., 195
Pree, W., 223
Premerlani, W., 26, 244

R

Rawsthorne, D., 138, 247
Reason, J.T., 155
Reenskaug, T., 91
Riecken, D., 180
Robinson, K., 228
Rubin, K., 27, 243
Rugg, G., 58
Rumbaugh, J., 23, 26, 28, 228, 230, 233
Rush, G., 39
Russell, S., 180

S

Schank, R.P., 141, 243
Schmidt, D., 223
Scholes, J., 37
Searle, J.R., 133
Selic, B., 199, 222
Senge, P., 37, 56
Sharble, R.S., 24, 249
Shaw, M., 197, 198, 222
Shlaer, S., 6, 23, 24, 26, 228, 230
Short, J.E., 136, 179
Sims, O., 207
Stapleton, J., 40, 41, 42, 58
Suchmann, L., 35
Sutcliffe, A.G., 155
Swatman, P.A., 33

T

Taylor, D., 4, 22, 29., 179
Texel, P.P., 102
Thayer, R.H., 32
Thomas, P.M., iv

V

Venkatramen, N., 136
Vlissides, J., 223

W

Waldén, K., 27, 188, 234
Wand, Y., 213
Warner, E., 180
Webster, J., 35
Weinberg, G., 83
Weyuker, E., 213
Whitmire, S., 213, 216, 223
Wieringa, R.J., 33, 57
Williams, C.B., 102
Williams, M., iv
Wills, A.C., 33, 205
Winograd, T., 35, 135, 168, 176
Wirfs-Brock, R., 24, 27, 94, 103, 126, 188

Y

Yanoussi, H., 28
Yourdon, E., 7, 23, 26, 228

Z

Zadeh, L.A., 251

SUBJECT INDEX

3-tier architectures, 178, 184
80/20 rule, 79

A

abstract classes, 218
abstract data types, 9, 23
Accountability pattern, 202
ACLs: *see* agent communication
    languages
Action Technologies Inc., 168
Action Technologies
    Workbench, 168
activation (activity) diagrams,
    148
    see also event traces
active objects, 189
active rôle of the subject, 37
activities, **45**, 46
    bounded and unbounded, **46**
actors, **142**
ad hoc enquiries, 16, 17
Ada, 6, 16, 18, 22, 26
Adapter pattern, 202
adjoints, 231-32
AESOP, 198
agent communication languages
    (ACLs), 177, 180-83, 189,
    201, 206
agent co-ordination, 188
agent design, 182
Agent Object Model (AOM), 87,
    134, 149, 191, 218
    completeness and
    consistency of, 137
agent-based systems, 200, 206
agents as objects, 133, 184
agents *v.* business objects, 142
agents, 6, 32, 36-8, 83, 86-8,
    103, 113, **132**, 134, 139,
    142, 150, 177, 180, 204,
    218, 249
    architecture of, 183

basic software, 181
    modelling of, 187
aggregation, 102
AI (artificial intelligence), 5-6,
    22, 35,43, 251
aircraft undercarriage design, 33
AKO (A Kind Of), 96, 251
Alexandrian form for patterns,
    253
alternative cost-centre model,
    53-4
ambassadors, 52, 55
analysis patterns, 85, 202-203,
    205, 223
animation scripts, 160
animation, 150, 156, 159, 163
Anthropology, 34
anthropomorphism, 10-11, 27
AOM: *see* Agent Object Model
APL, 17
APO (A Part Of), 245
applets, 15
application frameworks, 201
application objects, **94**, 218
apprenticeship, 57
architects, **55**
architectural layers, 199
architectural patterns, 186, 199,
    202
architectural standards, 48, 206
architecture, 5, 7-9, 20-21, 197
artificial intelligence: *see* AI,
assertions, 14, 33, 89, 93, 111-
    13, 115
Assistant problem frame, 204
association object types, 229
association sets, 164-65, 168,
    170, 172-74, 176
    nesting of, 172
    representing conversations
    with, 165
association set composition
    trees, 173

association structure diagrams,
    99
associations, 89, 92, 95-6, 99,
    100, 102-3, 105, 227-28,
    230, **232**
assumptions, 131
atomic task scripts, 246
atomic tasks, 141, 145, 147,
    149, 150, 153, **219**, 249
atomicity, 246
attributes, 9, 11, 23, 89-90, 92-
    4, 99, 102, 105, 112-13,
    122, 228
    attribute assertions, 112
    attribute facets, 94
    attributes and associations,
    92
    attributes as primitive
    associations, 99
automatic diagram generation,
    xii, 105, 230

B

backward chaining, 113-14,
    116, 190, 236
Baxter Healthcare, 136
beliefs, 182
benchmarking, 222
Bezant, xiii
bi-directional associations, 23,
    36, 99, 216, 227, 229-30,
    240-41
BiLinkVstr (Versant), 240
blackboard systems, 85, 185-86,
    189, 198-99, 202
black-box inheritance, 96
Boeing, 24
BOM: *see* Business Object
    Model
BON, 27, 111, 188, 206, 234
Booch method, 49, 88
brainstorming, 58
branching, 164, 166

Bridge pattern, 202
broadcasting messages, 85, 186, 189
browsing models, 108
bug fixing, 49
business areas, 130-32
business change, 4-6
business object libraries, 207
Business Object Model (BOM), 38, 48, 85, 87, 105), 140, 142, 148, 149, 199, 252
Business Object Model metrics, 217
business objectives: *see* objectives
business objects, 83, 86-8, 94, 102, 199, 205, 207, 210
business process modelling, 103, 121, 187, 190
business process re-engineering, 22-3, 34, 36-7, 71, 127, 131, 136, 143, 179, 191
business processes, **132**, 149, 209
business rules, 115-16

C

C, 188
C++, xiv, 6, 13-15, 17, 20-22, 25-6, 88, 102, 106, 108-10, 118, 156, 199, 201, 202, 207, 214, 223, 237, 239
CAD, 17
candidate participant matrix, 64
Capability Maturity Model, 220
card sorting, 58, 82
cardinality constraints, 92
CASE tools, x, 90, 117, 227
Catalysis, 33, 44, 205, 206
category theory, 216, 223, 231
CATWOE, 37
CBO, 212-13
change controllers, **56**
change management, 39
change requests, 4
changing requirements, 13, 60
Chase Manhattan Bank, 208
checklists, 69
CICS, 33
CIRTs, **90**
class attributes, 95, 213
class cards, 27, 147, 68-9, 72, 91, 94, 99, 105, 108, 116-17

class categories, 189
class invariants, 14, 27, 36, 89, 93, 111, **112**, 113, 188, 190, 201, 205, 210, 229, 233-34, 236, 240
class libraries, 15, 223
classes and instances, naming of, 89
classes, 5-6, 9, 11-15, 89, 90
classification structures, 96, 109, 207
classification, 13, 15, **96**, 138
client/server computing, 6, 16, 22
CLOS (Common Lisp Object System), 5, 187
clusters, 121, 189
COBOL, 4, 6, 13-15, 17-18
code generation, 25, 87, 150
cognitive dissonance, 143, 179, 190
cohesion, 213-14
collaboration graphs, 103
collaborative problem solving, 186
Collect-First-Objective-Last pattern, 204
COM, 21
command and control, 180
Commonpoint, 223
communication between agents, 132
completion, 204
complexity, 29, 219
component architecture, 5
component tasks, 139
components, 37, 42-4, 48, 53, 89, 91, 98, 102, 105, 109-10, 120, 197, 199, 205, 206, 222
Composite pattern, 204, 202
composition structures, 202, 207
composition (APO), 96, 99, 102-3, 105, 108-09, 120, 138, 228
Computer Supported Co-operative Working (CSCW), 180
conceptual dependency theory, 243
concrete classes, 218
concurrency, 7, 20, 89, 93, 161, 164, 172

concurrent sequence diagrams, 247
conditions of satisfaction, 134-35
conflicting requirements, 33
connascence, 214
Connexion problem frame, 203
consistency and completeness of models, 148
constant-creation model, 52
constraints, 36, 92, 95, 101, 111 in UML, 100
constructivism, 86
constructors *v.* pointers, 228
consultants, use of, 57, 221
context, 32
continuum of representation, 25
Contract Net, 185
contract-driven life cycle model, 41, **45**, 58
contracts, 32, 33, 36, 41, 44-5, 49, 132, 134-35, 189, 247
control régimes, 113, 229
control rules, 114
controller objects, 24, 184, 189, 248
convergence of OO methods, 28
conversations, 35, 133-34, **135**, 136-38, 150, 167 request canonical form for, 135 conversations for action, 135
conveyancing, 136
co-operating agents, 189
CORBA (Common Object Request Broker Architecture), 5, 20-21, 183, 199, 200, 203
corporate actions, 208
cost benefit analysis, 35, 57
coupling, 214
CRC cards: *see* class cards
CREWS, 35, 155-56, 204
CSCW: see Computer Supported Co-operative Working
customer facing, 51, 129
customer value propositions (CVPs), 128
customers, 128, 209
Cybernetics, 37
cyclomatic complexity, 211, 220

D

DAI: *see* distributed artificial intelligence
data conversion, 206
data dictionaries, 190
data filtering, 180
data flow diagrams (DFDs) , 25, 40, 132
data flow, 23, 133, 244
data interchange languages, 206
data retrieval agents, 182
data structures, 8
database access tools, 199
database design, 227
database management systems (DBMS), 7, 228, 234
database triggers, 112, 181, 229, 236
data-driven methods, 24, 26, 244
dates, 10
DBMS: *see* database management systems
DCOM, 21
deadlock, 16
Decorator, 202
deductive databases, 236
defaults, 113
defects, 210, 220, 222-23
degradation of work, 35
degree of non-object-orientation for a class, 214
delegation, 189
deliverables, 40, 41, 130
Delphi, 13, 15-16, 44, 157, 201
demons, 113
depth of inheritance tree (DIT), 212
derivatives trading, 17, 207
derived dependencies, 109
design patterns, 197-99, 201-203, 205
designations and descriptions in a model, 84
developers, 54, 62, 69
development process, 3-4, 26-8, 31, 40-41, 44-46, 216, 221
development skills, 54
DFD: *see* data flow diagrams
differential equations, 85
differentiating processes, 129
Discouraged tasks, 49

discrete event simulation, 5
discrete time simulation, 160
distributed artificial intelligence (DAI), 179, 181
distributed objects, 181
distributed problem solving, 185
distributed systems, 5-6, 143
DIT, 212, 218
documentation, 8
domain analysts, **55**
domain objects, **94**, 218
domain ontology, 141, 190, 216, 246
DSDM, ix, 40-44, 46, 55-58
dynamic binding, 12
dynamic classification and instantiation, 90, 189, 199, 202, 213

E

education and training, 222
educational technology, 35
effort, 220
eggs, 8
Eiffel, 6, 13, 14, 16, 22, 27, 93, 111-12, 150, 188
elements in Kelly grids, 80
elicitation by triads, 81
e-mail agents, 179
encapsulation, 4, 7-8, 10-13, 15, 18-19, 23-5, 43-4, 88-9, 92, 99, 105, 214, 227-30, 233-34, 236, 239-41, 245-46, 248-49
entity objects, 248
entity-relationship modelling, 23, 24, 26, 132, 228
entity-relationship models, 6, 33, 36, 40
entity-relationships, 228
enumeration constraints, 112
ergonomics, 32
ESPRIT, 155
essential task scripts, 247
essential use cases, 246-47
estimation, 210-11, 216, 219, 220
ET++, 223
ETHICS, 34, 35
ethnomethodology, 32, 34, 35
European Space Agency, 181
Evaluation activity, 49
evaluators, 56

event notification, 17
event traces, 148-49, 152-154, 159
event-based simulation, 156, 160
events, 193
evolutionary development, 31
Excel, 16, 21, 200
exception tasks: *see* side-scripts
exceptions, 139, 155, 245
exclusion arcs, 36
exclusions, 131
executable specifications, 86-7, 117, 149, 156
expert systems, 113
expressiveness of modelling languages, 88
extends links, 139, 245
extensibility, 12, 14, 25, 43, 55
external agents, 132, 141, 191
external goals, 128

F

Facade pattern, 201, 204
facets, 92, 93, 95, 99, 105, 112, 116
facilitators, 55, 56, 61-3, 67, 69, **72**, 73-80, 83, 130
fan-in, 212-13, 218
fan-out, 211-13, 218
features, 11-14, 88-9
financial engineering, 208
financial instruments, 207
first normal form, 23
Fitness for purpose, 40
flexibility, 4-5, 16
Flores nets, 36
focus groups, 57
focused interviews, 79-80
FOOM, 33
FOPC (first order predicate calculus), 112, 190
Forbidden tasks, 49
formal correctness, 14
formal methods, 14, 32-4, 155
FORTRAN, 4, 17
forward chaining, 190
Forwarder Receiver pattern, 202
frameworks, 205, 223
friends, 214
function calls, 12
function libraries, 4
function points, 210-11, 219

functional data models, 231
functional decomposition, 33, 132
functional specification, 32, 44
functionally oriented methods, 244
functions, 8
FUNs (functional units), 188-89
Fusion, 27
future workshops, 57
fuzzy inheritance, 123
fuzzy logic, 190, 215
fuzzy models, 38
fuzzy objects, 122-23
fuzzy rulesets, 115, 123

G

gaining consensus, 63
gaming, 180
Gang of Five, 202
Gang of Four, 201
Gatekeeper pattern, 204
gender, 35
General Magic, 181
generalization, **96**, 228
generic tasks, 249
generic use cases, 247, 249
    task scripts as, 141
genetic algorithms, 183
GIOP, 21
goals of messages, **134**
goals, 113, **134**, 138, 150
goals, 247
Gradygrams, 18, 120
graphical user interfaces, 6, 22, 25, 15, 201
group dynamics, 73, 77, 131
guaranteeing that the
    specification meets the
    requirement, 33
GUI frameworks, 199
GUIs: *see* graphical user
    interfaces

H

hairies and conscripts model, 50-51, 54-5
hand-over, **135**
HCI: *see* human computer
    interaction
help desks, 129
heterogeneous agents, 182

Hewlett Packard, 28
hierarchical databases, 16
hierarchical task analysis, 141
house of quality, 35
human computer interaction, 35, 43, 141, 243
human factors, 32
hypertext, 27

I

IBM, 6, 14, 16
ID3, 183
identity, 10-12, 88, 213, 237
idioms, 201, 202, 222
IDL (Interface Definition
    Language), 20, 21, 199,
    201, 207
IDMS, 16
IE: *see* Information Engineering
IEEE, 32
IIOP, 5, 20-21
Illustra, 17
impedance mismatch, 17, 143
implementation inheritance, 96, 110
Implementation Object Model
    (IOM), 88
implementation planning, 48
implementation shock, 46
implementation, 8-9, 13-15, 17, 24, 88, 99
Implemented By classes/links, 120, 154, 160
implicit invocation, 185, 189, 198
impressionism, 86
IMS, 16
incremental development and
    delivery, 31, 38, 40, 43, 46
inference régimes, 93, 112, 116, 190, 229
inference, 89, 183, 188, 234
Infinity, 207
Information Engineering (IE), 23, 26, 34
information hiding, 92
inheritance, 4-7, 12-16, 23-26, 43, 44, 89, 96-7, 101, 105, 111, 214, 234, 245
Insecure-Secure-Transaction
    pattern, 205
insourcing, 136
inspections, 34, 56, 222

instance attributes, 95
instances, 10-12, 89, 91
integrity constraints, 112, 198, 227, 229, 239-241
intelligent agents, 177, 179-83, 186, 188, 190-91 207
    deliberative, 181-82, 190
    hybrid, 181-82
    reactive, 181, 190
Intellisense, 177, 180
interacting goals, 188
interface design, 205
interface objects, **94**, 218, 248
interfaces, 6, 8-11, 13-15, 18-20, 22-24, -90, 99, 111, 120
internal agents, 141, 191
internal goals, 128
Internet, 5, 20, 177, 179, 182
interoperability, 4
InterViews, 223
interviews, 58-60, 65, 79, 80
invariance conditions, 93, **112**, 204
inverse_member (ObjectStore), 238-40
inverses of associations, 227, 231-32, 235-37
IsA, 96, 251
Iterator pattern, 202

J

JAD, 31
Jasmine, 240
Java Virtual Machine, 15
Java, 5-6, 13-16, 21-2, 157, 187, 198, 201, 210
JNI, 21
joins, 17
joint application development, 31
JSD (Jackson System
    Development), 23, 32-3, 57, 134
JSP (Jackson Structure
    Programming), 85
JSP problem frame, 203
just in time compilers, 15

K

Kelly grids, 35, 58, 80-81
    focusing of, 80
KISS, 134, 85

knowledge elicitation, 32-3, 58, 251
knowledge engineering, 35
knowledge representation, 40, 85, 182
knowledge reuse, 177
knowledge sharing, 188
KQML/KIF, 181

L

laddering, 80, 81
language independence, 88
Layered Architecture, 204, 205
LCOM (Lack of cohesion in methods) , 212-14, 216, 218, 220
lead user, **55**
learning, 179, 181-83, 190
legacy systems, 5, 17-20, 22, 142, 204, 241
Leonardo, xiv
levels of duty in the contract-driven process model, 49
libraries, 199, 206
linking models, 86
linking tasks to classes, 153
Lisp, 5
logic boxes, 89
logical design, 24, 25
logical rôles, 128
long transactions, 16
Lotus Notes, 34, 168

M

Machine-Function pattern, 204
main build time-box, 48
maintainability, 12, 45
maintenance costs, 4, 7-8, 10, 13, 17-18, 23, 25, 45
maintenance, 248
management control, 45
managing expectations, 39
Mandatory tasks, 49
many-to-many associations, 229, 232
mappings, **229**, 230
measurement scales, 217
measurement theory, 213, 216
measures for objectives, 130
melting ice, 14
mentors, 52, 56-7

message passing, 9, 10, 12, 18, 19
messages representing conversations, 133
messages, 89, 133-34, 137, 145, 150, 158, 246
    techniques for analyzing, 134
metaclasses, 12
metapatterns, 223
methods, 7, 9, 10-11, 18-19, 26, 89
metrics, 28, 45, 138, 141, 149, 197, 210-13, 215-18, 220-23, 246
    automatic collection of, 217, 219
    soft factors in, 220
    thresholds for, 215
Microsoft Foundation Classes (MFC), 223
Microsoft, 6, 15, 21
middleware, 3, 13, 20-21, 210, 222
migration, 19, 29
milestones, 41, 54-5
Miranda, 12
mission grids, 128, 131-32, 137
missions and mission statements, 37, 130-31, 150
MIT, 179, 211
ML, 12, 23, 26
mobile agents, 143, 178
mobile computing, 183
model refinement, 48
model transformations, 86-7
Model View Controller (MVC), 202
models of reuse, 52
models, **84**
    analytic, 84
    domain, 85
    essential, 85
    iconic, 84
    simulation, 84
    specification, 85
module interconnexion languages (MILs), 198
Montage, 207
MOSES, 25, 28, 211, 217, 221, 229, 234
motivating teams, 46
MS Access, 16
MS Office, 15, 177

MS Studio, 44
multi-agent systems, 177, 195
multidimensional browsing, 111
multidimensional diagrams, xii, 106
multiple inheritance conflicts, 115
multiple inheritance, 14-15, 97-8, 113, 217
    problems with, 98
multi-threading, 161

N

NATURE, 155
negotiation, **135**, 180
network agents, 180
network bandwidth, 178
network databases, 16
network traffic, 183
networks of commitments, 132
neural nets, 183
NewWave, 181
NeXTSTEP, 201
NOC, 212, 213
non-functional requirements, 36, 43
non-monotonic logic, 214
notation, 88-91, 97, 101
notes in UML, 90
null values, 95

O

O2, 17, 240
OBA, 27, 243
object assertions, 112
Object Expert, 176
Object Expo, 245
Object Magazine, 195
Object Management Group (OMG), 20, 199, 207
object modelling, 23, 36-7, 42, 45, 47
object models, 86
    scope and size of, 128
Object Pascal, 15
object request brokers (ORBs), 7, 13, 19, 20-21, 181, 183-84, 199-201
object technology, 96, 244
    reasons for adoption, 4, 5
    principles of, 7, 10
object types, 228-31, 240

object wrappers, 18-19
Object Z, 33
Object/Relational DBMSs, 17
ObjecTime, 199
Objective-C, 6, 14-15
objectives, 130-31, 137, 149-50
    number of, 130
objectives, 34, 36, 39, 46, 48-9
Objectivity, 17
object-oriented analysis, 6, 7,
    10, 13, 22, 24-28, 228
Object-oriented COBOL, 16
object-oriented databases, 5-7,
    13, 16-17, 19-20, 229, 236-
    37, 240
object-oriented design, 6, 22,
    24, 26, 29
object-oriented development, 32,
    36, 41-4, 57
object-oriented programming
    languages, 13
object-oriented software
    engineering, 10, 22
object-oriented SSADM, 228
Objectory, 27, 155, 188, 244-
    45, 248-49
objects, 3-14, 17, 18, 22, 24, 29,
    88, 89
    size of, 19
ObjectStore, 6, 17, 237-40
observational studies, 35, 58
observers, 61
Ockham's razor, 245
ODMG-93, 237, 241
offer/request, **134**
OLE (Object Linking and
    Embedding), 15, 21
OMG: *see* Object Management
    Group
OML (OPEN Modelling
    Language) , xii, 28, 88, 90-
    91, 96-97, 101-103, 120-21,
    173, 204
OMT, 16, 23, 26, 28, 88, 99,
    116, 188, 222, 228, 233,
    244
ontology, 213
OOPSLA'94, 248
OOPSLA'97, 244
OOSE, 42, 248
OPEN (OO Process
    Environment and Notation),
    xi, 3, 24, 28, 31, 40-41, 44,

47, 58, 90, 188, 204, 217,
    221
open issues, 63, 71, 77-8, 131
open questions, 80
OpenSTEP, 14
operation scripts, 104-105, 119,
    152, 157-58, 162
operational assertions, 112
operations of tasks, 138
operations, 5, 8-9, 11-12, 14,
    18, 23, 26, 87, 89-90, 92-3,
    98, 104-105, 112-13, 115,
    118, 122, 139
opportunistic chaining, **116**
opposites, 80-81
Optional tasks, 49
Oracle, 17
ORBs: *see* object request
    brokers
ORCA, 36, 58, 128, 134
Organization structure pattern,
    202
organizational structures, 36,
    55, 179, 189, 204, 223
orthogonality of structures, 109
OS/400, 19
outsourcing, 129
overriding, 92, 99
Ovum, 179-81
ownership, 39, 95

P

packages, 20, 120-21, 189, 205
parallel time boxes, 48-9
parallelism, 216
ParcPlace, 27
Participatory design, 35
Party pattern, 202
pattern books, 201
pattern languages, 203-204
patterns, 85-6, 91, 100, 115,
    198, 203, 252
    as a medium of
    communication, 201
    for knowledge elicitation,
    251
p-code, 15
PDP-11, 17
performance, 16-17, 209
PERL, 181
persistence, 17
persistent objects, 142
personal constructs, 80

physical design, 24-5
pipes and filters, 198-99, 202
PL/1, 17
plans, 182
PLOPD, 223
POET, 17
pointers, 227, 229-30
polymorphism, 7, 12-15, 100,
    212, 214
ports, in ROOM, 199
post-conditions, 36, 47, 49, 57,
    112
Posting Rules pattern, 202
power types, 231-32, 240
PowerBuilder, 16
pragmatics, 133-34
pre- and post-conditions, 14, 36,
    45, 49, 93, 95, 112-13, 117-
    19
pre-conditions, **112**
preference grids, 130
pricing algorithms, 208
priorities of objectives, 39, 42,
    46, 48, 130
private methods, 9
private operations, 112
private rulesets, 92, 158
probability distributions for
    tasks, 161
probes, **79**
problem frames, 34, 85, 203,
    223
process and product life-cycles,
    41
process improvement, 220, 222
process maturity models, 220
process models, 31, 35, 37, 39-
    40
process monitoring, 180
process synchronization, 161
product and process life cycles,
    45
production rules, 182-83, 188,
    236
productivity, 4, 5, 220
programme and resource
    planning, 46, 56
programmes, **46**
project initiation, 46-7, 56-7
project leaders, **54**
project management, 131
project managers, **54**, 61, 63-4
project planning, 39
project resource profiles, 51

project rôles and
   responsibilities, 54
project sponsor, **54**
Prolog, 183, 188
proofs of correctness, 33
protocol analysis, 58
protocols, 14-15
prototypes, 3, 15, 38, 43-5, 87,
   178
prototyping, 31, 42-3, 45, 48,
   53, 58
provable correctness, 149, 154
Proxy pattern, 202
pseudo-code, 12, 25
Ptech, 26
pure attributes, **99**, 230
purposive and behavioural
   entities, 36

Q

qualifiers, 116
quality circles, 222
quality function deployment, 35,
   57
quality, 4, 5, 54, 216
questionnaires, 35
Quote pattern, 202

R

RAD (Rapid Application
   Development) , 4, 31, 39,
   42, 46, 49, 51, 53, 55-6,
   178, 191
range constraints, 95, 112
Rational Inc., 28
Rational *Rose*, 88, 106, 117,
   169
   bridging to *SOMATiK*, 109
RDD: *see* Responsibility-Driven
   Design
real-time embedded systems,
   222
reasoning about organization,
   181
Recommended tasks, 49
recursion in conversations, 135
recursive aggregation, 105
referential integrity, 227, 229-
   30, 232, 234-37, 240
refinement of models in
   Catalysis, 205
regular grammars, 23

re-inventing the wheel, 205
relational databases, 6, 17, 20,
   26-7, 228
relationship-relationships, 228
remote procedure calls (RPCs),
   184
repertory grids: *see* Kelly grids
replication, 6
repositories
repositories, 48, 52-3, 72, 190
repository management, 52
requirements analysis, 32
requirements elicitation, 10, 32
requirements engineering, xiii,
   31-2, 58
requirements engineers, 32, 38,
   55-6, 61, 73-4
requirements pattern languages,
   204
requirements specifications, 59,
   243
resilience, 6
responsibilities, 9, 27, **89**
   for being, **89**
   for doing, **89**
   for knowing, **89**
Responsibility Driven Design
   (RDD), 24, 27, 41, 103, 188
responsibility-driven methods,
   244
restaurants, 140, 246
reusability of tasks, 138
reusability, 43, 48, 54, 55, 110
reusable components, 43
reusable specifications, 208
reuse libraries, 34, 51-3
reuse management, 41, 49-51,
   206
reuse ratio, 211
reuse teams, 50-51, 55
reuse tools, 222
reuse, 4, 14, 19, 24-5, 28, 48,
   70-71, 222, 240, 246
REVEAL, xiv, 123
reverse engineering, 204
rich pictures, 36-8, 128
rigour, x, 36-7, 39
RMI, 21
rôle playing, 153
rôles of an association, 230
rôles, 90, 91, 189, 209
ROOM, 199
root definition, 37-38

root tasks, 149-50
RPCs: *see* remote procedure
   calls
RPG, 18
rules, 182
rulesets, 44, 89-90, 92-3, 100,
   105, 111-18, 122-23, 125-
   26, 139, 143, 188, 190, 198,
   201, 204, 206, 207, 227,
   229-31, 233, 236, 240
rulesets,
   external, 112
   fuzzy, 122
   internal, 112

S

safety-critical systems, 33
SAVRE, 155, 204
scenarios, 155, 245, 248-51,
   253
schema evolution, 16
scribes: *see* requirements
   engineers
script theory, 35, 141
scripting language, 152, 156,
   161
scripts, 19, 27, 243, 247
seamlessness, ix, 14, 24-5, 27,
   43, 83, 87, 137, 149, 153,
   222
security, 12
semantic data modelling, 228,
   251
semantic integrity, 227, 236
semantic networks, 96
semantics, 133-34
semaphores, 162
semi-inverses, 232
semiotic acts, **132**, **134**
Semiotics, 133-34
sequence diagrams, 36, 89, 164-
   68, 170-72, 176, 216, 247
   concurrent, 247
   misuse of, 169
service-based architecture, 199
shared goals, 128
shared understanding, 5, 32, 39,
   42, 47, 57
Shlaer/Mellor method, 99
side-scripts, 138-41, 246
signatories, 63
signatures, 89, 111
signing repository items, **53**

sign-off sheet, 63, 78
sign-off, 63, 70, 72-3, 82
Simple Control problem frame, 203
Simple Information Systems problem frame, 203
Simula, 5, 14
simulation, 159, 163
SLOCs (Source Lines Of Code), 210, 211, 218-19
Smalltalk, 5, 13-14, 16, 22, 27, 157
social context, 35, 133
social responsibility, 35
socio-technical system design, 35, 204
soft systems, 32, 36-8, 128
software development life cycle, 83
SOMA (Semantic Object Modelling Approach) , xi, 24-5, 27-9, 31, 33, 35-8, 40-2, 44-7, 49, 53-4, 56-8, 88, 188, 190, 217, 221, 227, 229, 243
    origins of, 3
SOMA metrics, 211
SOMA Modelling Language, 83, 89
SOMATiK, xi, xiii, 25, 28, 82, 88, 91-2, 94, 99, 104-105, 107-10, 116-20, 138, 143-44, 146-50, 152, 154, 156-59, 161, 163, 176, 192, 220
    bridging to *Rose*, 109
space shuttle, 179
specialization *v.* interface inheritance, 89
specialization, **96**
speech acts, 133, 135
spiral models, 40, 44
sponsors, 38, 47, 53-7, 61, 63-4, 73, 76, 131
SQL, 184
SSADM, 34, 36
stages, 38, 45
stakeholders, 128, 132
Star workstation, 5
state attributes, 91, 117
state machines, 27, 86
state models, 26, 209
State pattern, 202

state-transition diagrams (STDs), 6, 23, 26, 33, 112, 117, 199, 216
STDs: *see* state-transition diagrams
stereotypes, 90, 93-4, 139
stereotypical tasks, 134, 139
stored procedures, 181
strong agents, 182
strong associations, **235**
strong hybrid intelligent agents, 182
strong semi-inverses, **235**, 239
structure charts, 25
structure depths, 218
structure diagrams, 99, 105, 107, 110
structured and focused interviews, 79
structured methods, 22-3, 79
structures (in object models), 96, 138, 164, 218
STUDIO, 87
subsystems, 189
suitability filter, 57
superclasses, 89, 91, 96, 109, 115
supertasks, 139
SVDPI sentences, 141, 147, 219
Sybase, 16
Syllogism pattern, 251, 253
symbolic representation, 182
Syntropy, 27, 33, 36, 111
system architecture, 7

T

Taligent, 223
task analysis, 34, 35, 80, 243
task association sets, **164**, 191, 247
task associations, 134, 146, **164**, 245
task cards, 146, 148
task decomposition, 141, 165
Task Object Model (TOM)), 37, 87, 139-40, 149, 191
Task Object Model metrics, 218
task objects, 134, 247
task points, 138, 211, 219-20
task rulesets, 134
task scripts, **139**, 140, 150, 243-44, 246-47, 249-51, 253

task-centred design, 35
tasks (in a project), **45**
tasks complexity, 145
tasks *v.* techniques, 49
tasks, 83, 134, **135**, 139
Tcl, 181
TCP/IP, 21
teachback, 80
technical co-ordinator, 55
Tektronix, 27
Telecommunications, 249
Telescript, 181
temporal logic, 156
ten minute rule, 77
test scripts, 154
testing, 40-2, 44, 48, 55, 57, 130, 148
textual analysis, 82, 147, 153
thin clients, 6
third normal form, 23
threads of control, 216
time to market, 4
time-based simulation, 160
time-box managers, **54**
time-box planning, 48
time-boxes, 39, 41, 45-6, 48-51, 53-4, 73
TOM: *see* Task Object Model
top down *v.* bottom up development, 205
top-down decomposition, 4, 245
traceability, x, 4, 25, 153, 205
trades (financial), 209
transaction monitors, 21
transformation of models, x, 205
transitions between activities, 57
traversal paths, 237
triggering events, 247
triggers and triggering events, **134**, 135, 141-42
triggers, 113
two-library model, 52
type constraints, 112
types of composition, 102
types, 89, 90

U

UAT, 42
UML, xii, 16, 25, 28, 36, 88, 90-91, 94, 96, 97, 99, 100, 102-103, 105-106, 117, 120-21, 134, 138, 141, 164,

168-70, 204, 205, 222-23,
  228, 230-31, 233, 241, 247
uncertainty, 190
UniSQL, 17
Universal Server, 17
Unix, 14
usage links, 99, 103, 106, 210,
  245
usage structures, 104, 109
use cases, as objects, 245
use cases, ix, 27, 132, 134, 138-
  39, 141, 149, 155, 165, 194,
  203, **243**, 244-51, 253-54
  not dealing with with single
    tasks, 247
  generic, 247
  lack of atomicity, 246
  lack of essentiality or
    genericity, 246
  multiple definitions of, 244
  proliferation of, 244
  restriction to system
    interface, 248
user I/O, 203
user interface agents, 180
user interface design, 204
user interfaces, 178
user involvement, 35, 39-40, 55
user review, 48
user-centred design, 35
users, **55**, 62, 64, 132
uses links, 245

V

validating user requirements,
  155
validation against task scripts,
  154
variable logics in SOMA, 112,
  190
VAX, 17, 19
VBA (Visual Basic for
  Applications), 15
VDM, 32
veracity, 182
Versant, 6, 17, 240
version control, 6, 16
vertical components, 199
visionaries, 55, 57
Visitor pattern, 202
Visual Age, 14, 16, 44, 201
Visual Basic (VB) , xiv, 15,
  157, 201
Visual Studio, 201
visualization, 111
Von Neumann architecture, 7
voting on priorities, 130

W

walkthroughs, 147, 149, 154
waterfall models, 44, 57
weak agents, 182
Web browsers, 5, 21, 200
weighted complexity of a class,
  217
weighted methods per class
  (WMC), 212

Weltanschauung, 37-8
white-box inheritance, 96
Whole Part, 202
WMC, 212, 215, 217
workflow, 34-5, 209
workpieces problem frame, 203
workshop reports, 68
workshop rôles, 61
workshops, 39, 47-8, 53-8, 131
  benefits of, 6
  checklists for running, 69,
  duration and timing of, 75,
  ground rules for running, 76,
  location of, 65,
  logistics, 66,
  recording of, 74
  refreshments at, 66,
  room layout for, 67,
World-Wide Web, 6
wrappers, 120, 189, 204
written requirements
  specifications, 33

X

Xerox PARC, 5

Y

Year 2000 problem, 10

Z

Z, 32, 154